ISBN: 9781407660790

Published by:
HardPress Publishing
8345 NW 66TH ST #2561
MIAMI FL 33166-2626

Email: info@hardpress.net
Web: http://www.hardpress.net

175

2977

THE INTERNATIONAL SCIENTIFIC SERIES
VOLUME LXVII

.

THE

INTERNATIONAL SCIENTIFIC SERIES.

Each book complete in One Volume, 12mo, and bound in Cloth.

New York: D. APPLETON & CO., 1, 3, & 5 Bond Street.

17. MONEY AND THE MECHANISM OF EXCHANGE. By W. STANLEY JEVONS, M. A., F. R. S. $1.75.

18. THE NATURE OF LIGHT, with a General Account of Physical Optics. By Dr. EUGENE LOMMEL. With 188 Illustrations and a Table of Spectra in Chromo-lithography. $2.00.

19. ANIMAL PARASITES AND MESSMATES. By Monsieur VAN BENEDEN. With 83 Illustrations. $1.50.

20. FERMENTATION. By Professor SCHÜTZENBERGER. With 28 Illustrations. $1.50.

21. THE FIVE SENSES OF MAN. By Professor BERNSTEIN. With 91 Illustrations. $1.75.

22. THE THEORY OF SOUND IN ITS RELATION TO MUSIC. By Professor PIETRO BLASERNA. With numerous Illustrations. $1.50.

23. STUDIES IN SPECTRUM ANALYSIS. By J. NORMAN LOCKYER, F. R. S. With 6 Photographic Illustrations of Spectra, and numerous Engravings on Wood. $2.50.

24. A HISTORY OF THE GROWTH OF THE STEAM-ENGINE. By Professor R. H. THURSTON. With 163 Illustrations. $2.50.

25. EDUCATION AS A SCIENCE. By ALEXANDER BAIN, LL. D. $1.75.

26. STUDENTS' TEXT-BOOK OF COLOR; Or, Modern Chromatics. With Applications to Art and Industry. By Professor OGDEN N. ROOD, Columbia College. New edition. With 130 Illustrations. $2.00.

27. THE HUMAN SPECIES. By Professor A. DE QUATREFAGES, Membre de l'Institut. $2.00.

28. THE CRAYFISH: An Introduction to the Study of Zoölogy. By T. H. HUXLEY, F. R. S. With 82 Illustrations. $1.75.

29. THE ATOMIC THEORY. By Professor A. WURTZ. Translated by E. Cleminshaw, F. C. S. $1.50.

30. ANIMAL LIFE AS AFFECTED BY THE NATURAL CONDITIONS OF EXISTENCE. By KARL SEMPER. With 2 Maps and 106 Woodcuts. $2.00.

31. SIGHT: An Exposition of the Principles of Monocular and Binocular Vision. By JOSEPH LE CONTE, LL. D. With 132 Illustrations. $1.50.

32. GENERAL PHYSIOLOGY OF MUSCLES AND NERVES. By Professor J. ROSENTHAL. With 75 Illustrations. $1.50.

33. ILLUSIONS: A Psychological Study. By JAMES SULLY. $1.50.

34. THE SUN. By C. A. YOUNG, Professor of Astronomy in the College of New Jersey. With numerous Illustrations. $2.00.

New York: D. APPLETON & CO., 1, 3, & 5 Bond Street.

35. VOLCANOES: What they Are and what they Teach. By John W. Judd, F. R. S., Professor of Geology in the Royal School of Mines. With 96 Illustrations. $2.00.

36. SUICIDE: An Essay in Comparative Moral Statistics. By Henry Morselli, M.D., Professor of Psychological Medicine, Royal University, Turin. $1.75.

37. THE FORMATION OF VEGETABLE MOULD, THROUGH THE ACTION OF WORMS. With Observations on their Habits. By Charles Darwin, LL. D., F. R. S. With Illustrations. $1.50.

38. THE CONCEPTS AND THEORIES OF MODERN PHYSICS. By J. B. Stallo. $1.75.

39. THE BRAIN AND ITS FUNCTIONS. By J. Luys. $1.50.

40. MYTH AND SCIENCE. By Tito Vignoli. $1.50.

41. DISEASES OF MEMORY: An Essay in the Positive Psychology. By Th. Ribot, author of "Heredity." $1.50.

42. ANTS, BEES. AND WASPS. A Record of Observations of the Habits of the Social Hymenoptera. By Sir John Lubbock, Bart., F. R. S., D. C. L., LL. D., etc. $2.00.

43. SCIENCE OF POLITICS. By Sheldon Amos. $1.75.

44. ANIMAL INTELLIGENCE. By George J. Romanes. $1.75.

45. MAN BEFORE METALS. By N. Joly, Correspondent of the Institute. With 148 Illustrations. $1.75.

46. THE ORGANS OF SPEECH AND THEIR APPLICATION IN THE FORMATION OF ARTICULATE SOUNDS. By G. H. von Meyer, Professor in Ordinary of Anatomy at the University of Zürich. With 47 Woodcuts. $1.75.

47. FALLACIES: A View of Logic from the Practical Side. By Alfred Sidgwick, B. A., Oxon. $1.75.

48. ORIGIN OF CULTIVATED PLANTS. By Alphonse de Candolle. $2.00.

49. JELLY-FISH, STAR-FISH, AND SEA-URCHINS. Being a Research on Primitive Nervous Systems. By George J. Romanes. $1.75.

50. THE COMMON SENSE OF THE EXACT SCIENCES. By the late William Kingdon Clifford. $1.50.

51. PHYSICAL EXPRESSION: Its Modes and Principles. By Francis Warner, M. D., Assistant Physician. and Lecturer on Botany to the London Hospital, etc. With 51 Illustrations. $1.75.

52. ANTHROPOID APES. By Robert Hartmann, Professor in the University of Berlin. With 63 Illustrations. $1.75.

New York : D. APPLETON & CO., 1, 3, & 5 Bond Street.

53. THE MAMMALIA IN THEIR RELATION TO PRIMEVAL TIMES. By OSCAR SCHMIDT. $1.50.

54. COMPARATIVE LITERATURE. By HUTCHESON MACAULAY POSNETT, M. A., LL. D., F. L. S., Barrister-at-Law ; Professor of Classics and English Literature, University College, Auckland, New Zealand ; author of " The Historical Method," etc. $1.75.

55. EARTHQUAKES AND OTHER EARTH MOVEMENTS. By JOHN MILNE, Professor of Mining and Geology in the Imperial College of Engineering, Tokio, Japan. With 38 Figures. $1.75.

56. MICROBES, FERMENTS, AND MOULDS. By E. L. TROUESSART. With 107 Illustrations. $1.50.

57. THE GEOGRAPHICAL AND GEOLOGICAL DISTRIBUTION OF ANI-MALS. By ANGELO HEILPRIN. $2.00.

58. WEATHER. A Popular Exposition of the Nature of Weather Changes from Day to Day. With Diagrams. By Hon. RALPH ABERCROMBY. $1.75.

59. ANIMAL MAGNETISM. By ALFRED BINET and CHARLES FÉRÉ, Assistant Physician at the Salpêtrière. $1.50.

60. INTERNATIONAL LAW, with Materials for a Code of International Law. By LEONE LEVI, Professor of Common Law, King's College. $1.50.

61. THE GEOLOGICAL HISTORY OF PLANTS. With Illustrations. By Sir J. WILLIAM DAWSON, LL. D., F. R. S. $1.75.

62. ANTHROPOLOGY. An Introduction to the Study of Man and Civilization. By EDWARD B. TYLOR, D. C. L., F. R. S. Illustrated. $2.00.

63. THE ORIGIN OF FLORAL STRUCTURES, THROUGH INSECT AND OTHER AGENCIES. By the Rev. GEORGE HENSLOW, M. A., F. L. S., F. G. S. With 88 Illustrations. $1.75.

64. ON THE SENSES, INSTINCTS, AND INTELLIGENCE OF ANIMALS, WITH SPECIAL REFERENCE TO INSECTS. By Sir JOHN LUBBOCK. With over 100 Illustrations. $1.75.

65. THE PRIMITIVE FAMILY IN ITS ORIGIN AND DEVELOPMENT. By Dr. C. N. STARCKE, of the University of Copenhagen.

66. PHYSIOLOGY OF BODILY EXERCISE. By FERNAND LAGRANGE, M. D.

67. THE COLOURS OF ANIMALS: Their Meaning and Use. By EDWARD BAGNALL POULTON, F. R. S.

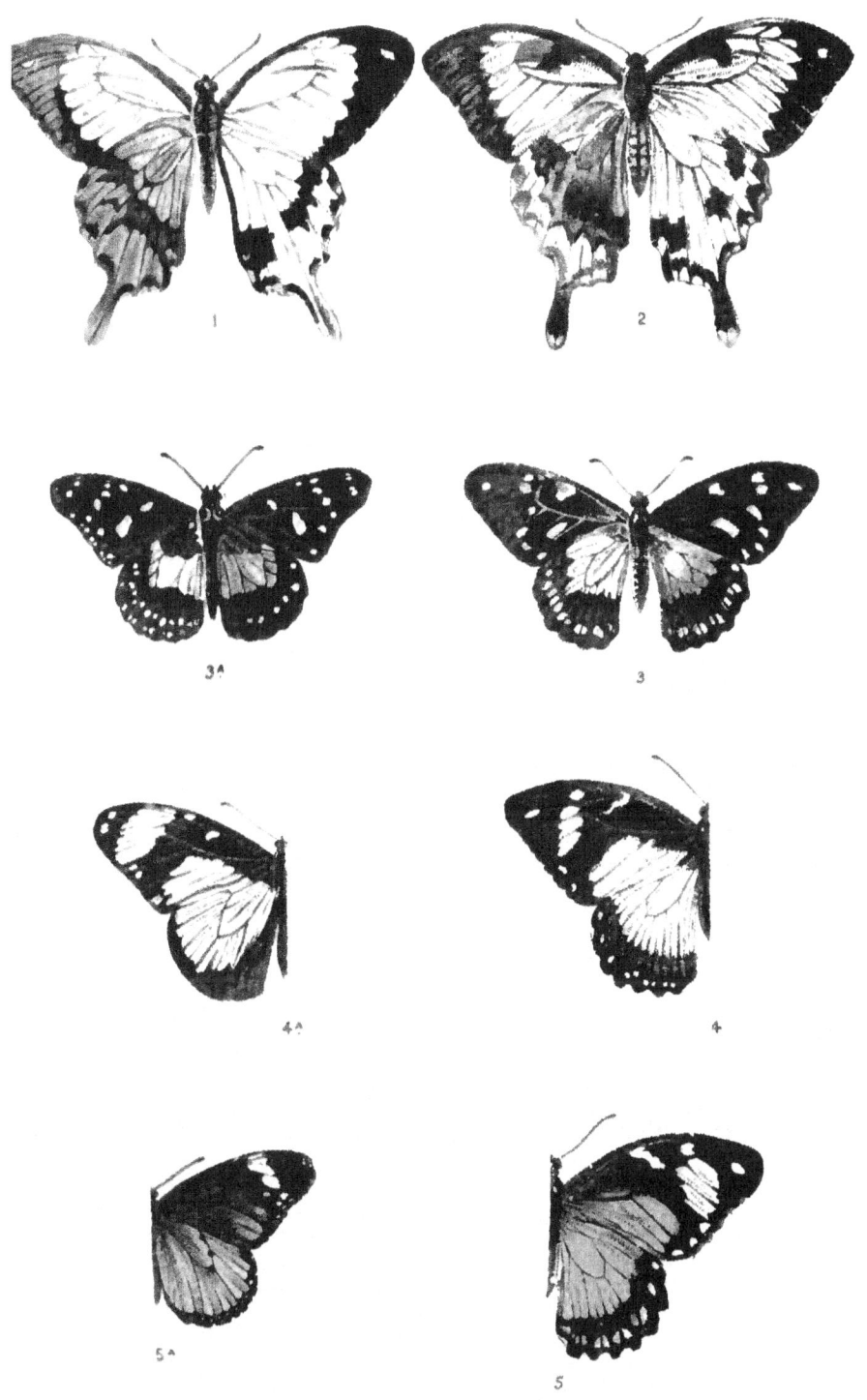

MIMICRY IN SOUTH AFRICAN BUTTERFLIES.

FIGURES 3, 4, AND 5, THE FEMALES OF A SOUTH AFRICAN *Papilio*, TOTALLY UNLIKE THE MAI
(FIGURE 1), BUT MIMICKING RESPECTIVELY THREE SPECIES OF THE UNPALATABLE GENUS, *Danais* (FIGURE
3a, 4a, AND 5a) THE FEMALE (FIGURE 2) OF A NEARLY ALLIED *Papilio*, IN MADAGASCAR, IS NOT MIMETI
AND RESEMBLES THE MALE.

DESCRIPTION OF PLATE

THE figures have been copied, by kind permission of the author, and the council of the Linnean Society, from the plates accompanying Mr. Roland Trimen's paper, 'On some Remarkable Mimetic Analogies among African Butterflies.' ('Linn. Soc. Trans.' vol. xxvi. pp. 497, *et seqq.*)

All figures are represented one-half of their natural size. The appearance of the under side of the wings is shown on the left hand of the four upper figures.

Figure 1.—The male of *Papilio merope* (now called *P. cenea*; the name *P. merope* being restricted to the West African form), from Knysna, Cape Colony. A closely allied butterfly (*P. meriones*), with a very similar male, is found in Madagascar.

Figure 2.—The female of *Papilio meriones*, from Madagascar. The male is almost exactly like Figure 1. The black bar on the costal margin of the fore wing of the female probably represents the beginning of the darkening which has been carried so far in the females of the African *P. merope* and *P. cenea*.

Figure 3.—First or *cenea*-form of female of *Papilio merope* (now called *P. cenea*), from Knysna, Cape Colony. The female is totally unlike the male of the same species (Figure 1), but closely mimics an unpalatable butterfly, *Danais echeria*, prevalent in its locality. The appearance of the latter is shown in Figure 3a. The mimetic resemblance is seen to be very striking on both upper and under sides of the wings. A local variety of the *Danais* is also mimicked by a corresponding variety of the *Papilio*.

Figure 4.—Second or *hippocoon*-form of female of *Papilio merope* (now called *P. cenea*), from Graham's Town, Cape Colony. This variety mimics the southern form of the unpalatable *Danais niavius*, shown in Figure 4a.

Figure 5.—Third or *trophonius*-form of female of *Papilio merope* (now called *P. cenea*), from Knysna, Cape Colony. This variety mimics the abundant and unpalatable *Danais chrysippus* shown in Figure 5a.

In a closely allied species of Papilio from West Africa (the true *Papilio merope*) the male closely resembles Figure 1, while there are two mimetic varieties of female. The *hippocoon*-form is like Figure 4, except that it is larger and the white patch on the hind wing is smaller; corresponding in both these respects to the West African variety of *Danais niavius*. The *trophonius*-form resembles Figure 5. There is no *cenea*-form of this species. For further details see pp. 234–38.

THE INTERNATIONAL SCIENTIFIC SERIES

THE

COLOURS OF ANIMALS

THEIR MEANING AND USE, ESPECIALLY CONSIDERED
IN THE CASE OF INSECTS

BY

EDWARD BAGNALL POULTON, M.A., F.R.S.

*WITH CHROMOLITHOGRAPHIC FRONTISPIECE
AND SIXTY-SIX FIGURES IN TEXT*

NEW YORK
D. APPLETON AND COMPANY
1890

PREFACE

I HAVE adopted a general title, 'The Colours of Animals,' in order to indicate the contents of this volume, although the vast majority of the examples are taken from insects, and indeed almost invariably from a single order, the Lepidoptera. The examples are, however, employed merely to illustrate principles which are of wide application.

I have purposely abstained from multiplying instances when a little observation or even reflection will supply them in large numbers. For example, the ordinary Protective Resemblances of mammals and birds are barely alluded to, on this account. On the other hand, more difficult problems, such as the change of colour in arctic mammals, or the meaning of the colours of birds' eggs, are treated at far greater length. My object in both cases is the same : to stimulate observation in a subject which will amply repay investigation, from the scientific value of the results, and the never-failing interest and charm of the inquiry.

Variable Protective Resemblance in insects is treated in considerable detail, for the reasons given above, and because much of the work is so recent that no complete account can be found outside the original memoirs.

My chief object has been to demonstrate the utility of colour and marking in animals. In many cases I have attempted to prove that Natural Selection has sufficed to account for the results achieved; and I fully believe that further knowledge will prove that this principle explains the origin of all appearances except those which are due to the subordinate principle of Sexual Selection, and a few comparatively unimportant instances which are due to Isolation or to Correlation of Growth.

In support of these views I have endeavoured to bring together a large amount of experimental evidence in favour of the theories as to the various uses of colour. Further experiments are still greatly needed.

In the chapters on 'Sexual Selection' I have argued in favour of Darwin's views, and have attempted to defend them against recently published attacks.

At the conclusion of the volume I have brought forward a detailed classification of the various uses of colour, in which new, and, I believe, more convenient terms are suggested. Definitions and examples are also given in the classification, which is, in fact, a brief abstract of the whole book.

I have to thank the Councils of various scientific societies for the courteous permission to copy figures from their respective publications. The figures in the coloured plate are copied from the plates accompanying Mr. Roland Trimen's paper in the 'Transactions of the Linnean Society,' vol. xxvi. pp. 497–522. Figures 18, 19, 20, 21, and 22 are copied from the plate accompanying Mr. R. Bowdler Sharpe's paper in the 'Proceedings of the Zoological Society,' 1873, pp. 414 *et seqq.* Figures 3, 4, 5, 6, 7, 8, 11, 14, 58, 60, 61, 62 are copied from the plates and woodcuts accompanying my papers in the 'Transactions of the Entomological Society,' 1884, 1885, 1887, and 1888. Figures 25, 26, and 27 are copied from the plate accompanying Mrs. Barber's paper in the 'Transactions of the Entomological Society,' 1874, pp. 519 *et seqq.* Figures 29 and 30 are copied from the plate and woodcuts accompanying my paper in the 'Philosophical Transactions of the Royal Society,' vol. 178 (1887), B, pp. 311–441. Figures 15, 16, 53, 54, 63, 64, 65, 66 are copied from the woodcuts and plates accompanying G. W. and E. G. Peckham's paper in the 'Occasional Papers of the Natural History Society of Wisconsin,' vol. i. (1889), Milwaukee. Figures 55 and 56 are copied from the plates accompanying Professor Weismann's 'Studies in the Theory of Descent,' translated by Professor Meldola. Figure 10 is copied from one of the plates accompanying Dr. Wilhelm Müller's 'Südamerikanische Nymphalidenraupen' ('Zoologische Jahrbücher,' J. W. Spengel, Jena, 1886). Figure 42 is copied from Vogt ('The Natural History of Animals': English translation: Blackie and Son). Figures 44 and 45 are copied from the plates accompanying Curtis's 'British Lepidoptera.' The remaining figures are original. Figure 17 was kindly lent me by Dr. A. R. Wallace, to whom it had been sent by Mr. Wood-Mason. In preparing the drawings of the original figures I have been greatly assisted by my wife, my sister Miss L. S. Poulton, Miss Horman Fisher, Mr. Alfred Sich, Mr. Alfred Robinson, and especially by Miss Cundell.

I have almost invariably referred to original papers from which facts or conclusions have been adopted; so that any reader having access to a scientific library may easily gain possession of further details. Not wishing to overburden the book with such notes, I have abstained from referring constantly to my own papers, although most of the examples are taken from them. A list of my papers which deal with the colours of insects is therefore printed below.

'Transactions Entomological Society,' London, 1884, pp. 27–60

"	"	"	"	1885, " 281–329
"	"	"	"	1886, " 137–179
"	"	"	"	1887, " 281–321
"	"	"	"	1888, " 515–606

'Philos. Trans. Royal Society,' vol. 178 (1887), B, pp. 311–441

Abstract of the above in 'Proceedings Royal Society,' 1887, vol. xlii. pp. 94–108

'Proceedings Royal Society,' 1885, vol. xxxviii. pp. 269–315

" " " 1886, vol. xl. pp. 135–173

'Proceedings Zoological Society,' 1887, pp. 191–274

Short papers or notes (exclusive of those which are mere abstracts of the above) :—

'Proceedings Entomological Society,' London, 1887, pp. l–li
,,   ,,   ,,   ,,   1887, ,, lxi–lxii
,,   ,,   ,,   ,,   1888, p. v
,,   ,,   ,,   ,,   ,, pp. viii–x
,,   ,,   ,,   ,,   ,, ,, xxvii–xxviii
,,   ,,   ,,   ,,   1889 ,, xxxvii–xl
'Journal of the Victoria Institute,' 1888, vol. xxii., 'On Mimicry.'

It is my pleasant duty to thank many friends for their kind assistance. I owe to Professor Meldola more than I can possibly express : his writings first induced me to enter upon this line of investigation, and I have had the benefit of his great experience and wise advice during the whole of the time that I have been at work. Nearly every subject touched upon in this volume has been discussed with him.

Professor Westwood has always been most kind in helping me with the literature of the subject, with which he has so intimate an acquaintance, and in giving me the free use of the Hope collection at Oxford. Professor E. Ray Lankester has read the proof-sheets dealing with the classifications of the uses of colour, and has offered valuable suggestions. Several beautiful examples were suggested to me by Professor C. Stewart. Dr. Günther, Mr. Roland Trimen, Mr. Oldfield Thomas, Mr. R. Bowdler Sharpe, Mr. F. E. Beddard, Mr. W. W. Fowler, and Mr. A. H. Cocks have been very kind in answering questions upon their special subjects. Sir John Conroy has kindly helped me in explaining the physical questions involved in the first chapter. I am especially pleased to speak of the help received from my former pupils Mr. W. Garstang and Mr. R. C. L. Perkins, who have supplied many valuable instances, which are specified in the volume, where other kind assistance is also duly acknowledged.

Although I have ventured to disagree with my friend Dr. A. R. Wallace upon the subject of ' Sexual Selection,' I wish to acknowledge how very much I owe to his writings, which I have very frequently quoted. I have also made great use of the late Thomas Belt's extremely interesting and suggestive ' Naturalist in Nicaragua.'

Among recent papers I wish especially to mention that by G. W. and E. G. Peckham, of Milwaukee, U.S.A. The minute observation of these authors upon the courtship of spiders of the family *Attidæ* is a model for investigation in a subject which has never before been attacked systematically.

Above all, I should wish to acknowledge, although I can never fully express, the depth of my indebtedness to the principles which first made Biology a science, the principles enunciated by Charles Darwin. It is common enough nowadays to hear of new hypotheses which are believed (by their inventors) to explain the fact of evolution. These hypotheses are as destructive of one another as they are supposed to be of Natural Selection, which remains as the one solid foundation upon which evolution rests. I have wished to express this conviction because my name has been used as part of the support for an opposite opinion, by an anonymous writer in the 'Edinburgh Review.'[1] In an article in which unfairness is as conspicuous as the prejudice to which it is due, I am classed as one of those 'industrious young observers' who 'are accumulating facts telling with more or less force against pure Darwinism.'[2] On the strength of this and other almost equally strange evidence, the Reviewer triumphantly exclaims, 'Darwin, the thanes fly from thee!' In view of this public mention of my name, I may perhaps be excused for making the personal statement that any scientific work which I have had the opportunity of doing has been inspired by one firm purpose—the desire to support, in however small a degree, and to illustrate by new examples, those great principles which we owe to the life and writings of Charles Darwin, and especially the pre-eminent principle of Natural Selection.

E. B. P.

Oxford: *Dec.* 28, 1889.

---

[1] *Edinburgh Review.* Article V. April 1888, pp. 407–47.

[2] p. 443. The bias of the writer appears in a most singular manner upon this page. In the short space of seventeen lines the following adjectives are divided between five writers and their works — industrious, illustrious, gifted, well-read, acute, intelligent, brilliant, thoughtful. I need hardly say that all five writers are believed by the Reviewer to oppose the theory of Natural Selection.

CONTENTS

THE

COLOURS OF ANIMALS

————•◦•————

CHAPTER I

THE PHYSICAL CAUSE OF ANIMAL COLOURS

Colours due to absorption

THE colours of animals are produced in various ways. By far the commonest method is the *absorption* of certain elements of light by means of special sub-stances which are called *pigments*, or *colouring matters*. The colour of each pigment is due to those elements of the light which it does not absorb, and which can therefore emerge and affect the eye of the spectator. Black is, of course, caused by the absorption of all the constituents of light, so that nothing reaches the eye. The colour of red pigment, like that of red glass, depends upon the fact that red is less absorbed than any other element of the light which passes through. If a sheet of red glass be placed upon white paper, the light traverses the glass, is reflected from the surface of the paper, re-traverses the glass, and emerges. Similarly, in painting, bright effects are produced by covering a surface of Chinese white with the desired colour. The light passing twice through the thickness of the colour, absorption is far more complete than when only one thickness is traversed, as in a piece of red glass held up to the light. Absorption being more complete, the red colour is deeper. Animal pigments are nearly always twice traversed by the light, and therefore a very thin layer produces a considerable effect.

Animal colours are therefore generally due to precisely the same optical principle which causes the colour of a wall-paper, a carpet, or a picture. Certain transparent animals are, however, for the most part coloured by light which passes but once through them, upon the same principle as the colours of a stained-glass window. The beautiful transparent blue of many pelagic animals, such as the Portuguese Man-of-war (*Physalia*), is caused in this way.

It would be out of place to discuss the details of the causes of colour by absorption. I may, however, mention that vibrations of very different rates are started in the luminiferous ether by the sun, the electric light, &c. A certain series of these vibrations causes the effect of white light when it falls on our retina ; but there are vibrations above and below this visible series—vibrations which we cannot see. We can, however, prove their existence in other ways ;

and it is certain that some animals can see vibrations which do not affect our eyes.[1] The slowest vibrations that we can see, produce the effect of red, the most rapid the effect of violet, while the intermediate vibrations cause the other well-known colours of the rainbow or the spectrum.

The absorption of certain elements of light therefore means the disappearance of ethereal vibrations with a certain speed. It is believed that these vibrations disappear because their motion has been communicated to the particles of the absorbing body. It is also believed that these particles are in a state of constant vibration, and that the vibrations of ether, which are timed to those of the body, are used up in increasing the motion of the latter.

A white appearance due to light being scattered

The production of white is due to a different principle, for we know that when light passes through a body without any absorption, the body is transparent and invisible rather than white.   When all the light passes through, the body is completely invisible. Whiteness is due to reflection of the whole visible series of vibrations, unaccompanied by the absorption of a part of them, as in the production of colours. But regular reflection, viz. reflection from

[1] Sir John Lubbock, *The Senses of Animals*, Chapter X. (International Scientific Series).

a polished surface like that of a mirror, does not cause whiteness : it renders the surface itself invisible, but produces images of surrounding objects. A white appearance is produced by irregular reflection, which causes the light to be scattered or reflected in all directions. To produce such a result there must be an immense number of surfaces in an immense number of different directions. If a coloured substance be reduced to powder of various degrees of fineness, the colour will diminish in intensity, and the whiteness will increase, according to the fineness of the powder ; this is because the number of reflecting surfaces is increased, while the thickness of the grains is diminished. This will be clear from the following consideration. When a beam of light falls on a sheet of glass, a known fraction (about 4 per cent.) of the light is reflected back from the first surface : the larger portion, however, enters the glass, and, after suffering a certain amount of absorption, reaches the second surface and is again partially reflected. If the glass be powdered, the number of surfaces will be so immensely increased that all the light will be reflected by a small thickness of the powder. The light reflected from the second surface of each grain of coloured glass will still be coloured by absorption, but not sufficiently to produce any visible results, when the thickness of the grain is very small.

Reflection is the *immediate* cause of whiteness, and the amount of reflection is due to the difference between the refractive powers (viz. the power of changing the direction of rays of light) possessed by the grains of glass and the substance, such as air or water, which lies between them. Thus the refractive powers of glass and water are much nearer than those of glass and air: hence a dry powder will reflect far more than a wet one, and will appear much whiter.

To take a few familiar examples: snow is white, because of the minute globules of air which refract very differently from the crystals between which they are entangled; ice, on the other hand, is transparent. If snow be compressed the air is driven out, and the mass becomes transparent; if ice be powdered it becomes white like snow. The froth of a coloured liquid is not coloured like the latter, but is white. Milk and fat are white because light is scattered from the surfaces of the countless oil globules, which refract very differently from the substance which lies between them. The surface of well-polished glass is almost invisible, because it reflects regularly, but a scratched surface is very visible, because there are surfaces in many different directions, which therefore scatter the light, while the far more numerous surfaces of ground glass scatter the light far more effectually and produce a white appearance.

The white markings of animals are produced in various ways. White hairs and feathers owe their appearance, like snow, to the number of minute

2

bubbles of gas which are contained in their interstices. Fat is also made use of to give a white
appearance; and the same result may be obtained by
the presence of minute granules, probably akin to
pigment, but differing widely from it in optical properties, in that no absorption takes place.

Colours due to thin plates

It has been stated already that when light traverses
a sheet of glass surrounded by air, a certain proportion of it is reflected back at the first surface and
a certain proportion at the second surface. The
light will be reflected in the same direction from
both surfaces. It is believed that the vibrations of
ether, some of which affect us as light, are in the form
of undulations of different lengths; if, therefore, the
sheet of glass be sufficiently thin, some of the undulations reflected from the second surface will interfere
with those started from the first surface. This will
happen when the sheet is of such a thickness that the
wave of light reflected from the second surface is half
an undulation behind that reflected from the first
surface; for then the two sets of undulations will be in
opposite directions, and will therefore neutralise each
other.

This will be quite clear if we apply the same
reasoning to those visible undulations from which
the name itself has been borrowed—the waves on the
surface of water. If a set of ripples is started by the

motion of an object in still water, and then another
set is started from another object moved, so that the
ripples succeed each other at exactly the same rate
as the preceding set, and if the second set is begun
when the first has advanced half a complete ripple
(viz. a movement up *and* down), it is clear that the
upward movement of the second will correspond to
the downward movement of the first and *vice versâ*,
so that, if the objects are so placed that the two sets
of ripples are traversing the same sheet of water,
they will neutralise and destroy each other.

If we compare a number of sheets of glass which
are successively thinner and thinner, interference will
first occur among the longest undulations of light,
because half an undulation will of course require a
greater distance (or thickness) than when the undulations are shorter.   As thinner and thinner sheets are
examined interference will gradually pass through
the whole spectrum from red to violet, destroying
sets of waves with shorter and shorter undulations.
The colour seen in each case will be due to the other
sets of waves which are not destroyed.

The amount of reflection, and therefore of interference and of colour produced, depends upon the
difference between the refractive power of the thin
sheet and the substance on each side of it.

Such interference colours are seen in a soap-
bubble, and the colours change as the bubble becomes larger and the film thinner : they differ, too,

on the various parts of the bubble, because the thinness also varies. A bubble of melted glass may be blown thin enough to produce the same effects, which are also well seen when a thin layer of air is enclosed between two sheets of glass or between the plates of some crystals, or when a drop of oil is allowed to spread out into a thin film on the surface of water. When a substance has a laminated structure, and sufficiently thin films are enclosed between the laminæ, very marked effects are seen. Thus the metallic appearance of the laminated flakes which are formed on the surface of glass which has been long buried in the earth, is accounted for. If these brilliant flakes are wetted the colour fades away, because the thin films of air between the laminæ are displaced by water, with a refractive power much nearer to that of the glass, and the amount of reflected light is therefore diminished.

Interference colours due to thin films are certainly very important among animals, but the extent to which they occur is imperfectly known. The iridescent colours of many beetles' wings are probably due to thin films of air included between layers of a horny consistence   Such colours are unaltered in dried specimens. In other cases the chinks between the layers are kept open by films of less powerfully refractive liquids. When the tissue becomes dry the films evaporate and the colour disappears. We must suppose that the denser layers come together, obliterating the chinks and excluding the air; otherwise the colours would be more brilliant than ever, because the refractive power of air is even lower than that of the liquids. The brilliant metallic appearance of many chrysalides, especially in the genus *Vanessa*, is caused by a large number of films of liquid enclosed between the laminæ of the dense outer layer. If the pupa be kept in spirit or water the colour remains, but disappears directly it is dry, although it can be renewed any number of times by wetting. This may even occur in a living animal, for Dr. Sharp has just directed my attention to an interesting observation made by Dr. Nickerl, who found that a brilliantly golden beetle (*Carabus auronitens*) lost all its lustre after hybernating in captivity, but entirely regained it after drinking some water.

Colours due to diffraction

When white light falls upon a surface on which there are a number of fine parallel grooves the reflected light appears coloured, the colour varying with the angle at which the light falls on the surface, and with the angle at which it is seen. This is due to the light reflected from different portions of the surface having different distances to travel before reaching the observer : and when (as occurs when the grooves are very close together) these differences amount to half a complete undulation for any particular length of vibration, interference is caused, and the vibration of that particular rate is wanting from the reflected light, which therefore appears coloured.

Opinions differ as to the relative importance of animal colours due to thin plates and to diffraction. Many which were believed to result from the latter are in all probability due to the former. The iridescent colours on the inner surface of many shells (mother-of-pearl) are at any rate partially caused by diffraction, for an accurate cast of the surface exhibits traces of the colours.[1] The shell is, however, a laminated structure, and the colours may therefore in part be caused by thin plates.

Colours due to refraction (prismatic colours)

When light passes through a wedge-shaped transparent substance (or prism) with greater refractive power than the surrounding medium, it is bent in the same direction at both surfaces, but its different constituents are bent unequally. The slowest vibrations (red) are bent least, the most rapid (violet) most ; and when the substance possesses a sufficiently high refractive power, all the colours of white light are seen arranged like the rays of a fan in the order of their rates of vibration. Prismatic colours like those of the diamond are due to refraction.

---

[1] Professor C. Stewart informs me that he has repeated Brewster's original experiment, upon which the above statement depends. He found that the colour was due to a thin layer of shell which had been stripped off and adhered to the surface of the wax.

It is doubtful how far the colours of animals are caused by this principle; but Dr. Gadow has given strong reasons for supposing that the metallic colours of birds' feathers are produced in this way,[1] and there are scales on the wings-cases of certain beetles (*Pachyrhynchus*) which also may owe their colours to refraction.

All these causes of animal colours may be conveniently grouped under two heads—(1) *pigmentary*, and (2) *structural*.　The first head includes colours caused by absorption, and the effects produced vary with the chemical nature of the substance (pigment).　The second head includes the colours or appearances produced in all other ways, the efficient cause being the structure of the substance rather than its chemical nature.

[1] *Proc Zool. Soc.* 1882, pp. 409 *et seq.*

CHAPTER II

THE USES OF COLOUR

I. Non-significant colours

COLOUR, as such, is not necessarily of any value to an organism. Organic substances frequently possess a chemical and physical structure which causes certain light-waves to be absorbed; or the elements of tissues may be so arranged that light is scattered, or interference colours are produced. Thus blood is red, fat is white, and the external surface of the air-bladder in certain fishes has a metallic lustre, like silver. In such cases there is no reason why we should inquire as to the use or meaning of the colour in the animal economy; the colour, as such, has no more meaning than it has in a crystal of sulphate of copper or iron. Such colours are the incidental results of chemical or physical structure, which is valuable to the organism on its own account. This argument will be still further enforced if we remember that the colours in question are, strictly speaking, not colours at all. Blood and fat are so constituted that they will be red and white, respectively, in the presence of light, but they cannot be said to possess these colours in their normal position, buried beneath the opaque surface of an animal.

The existence of non-significant colours is, nevertheless, most important, for they form the material out of which natural or sexual selection can create significant colours. Thus, the colour of blood may be made use of for 'complexion,' while fat may be employed to produce white markings, as in certain insect larvæ. The yellow, brown, and red fatty matters of the connective tissue are accumulated beneath the skin in patches, so as to produce patterns.

All colour originally non-significant

All animal colour must have been originally non-significant, for although selective agencies have found manifold uses for colour, this fact can never have accounted for its first appearance. It has, however, been shown that this first appearance presents no difficulty, for colour is always liable to occur as an incidental result. This is even true of the various substances which seem to be specially set apart for the production of colour in animals; for pigments occur abundantly in the internal organs and tissues of many forms. The brilliant colours of some of the lower organisms are probably also non-significant. In all higher animals, however, the colours on the surface of the body have been significant for a vast period of time, so that their amount, their arrangement in patterns, their varying tints, and their relation to the different parts of the body, have all been determined by natural selection through innumerable generations. Because the origin of all pigments is to be found in the incidental result of the chemical and physical nature of organic compounds, it by no means follows that incidental or non-significant colours would have appeared at all on the surface of most animals. And we find as a matter of fact that such colours tend to disappear altogether, directly they cease to be useful, as in cave-dwelling animals. On the other hand, the non-significant colour of blood or of fat would persist undiminished in such forms.

Colours may be destroyed by natural selection

Just as natural selection may develop an appearance which harmonises with the surroundings, out of the material provided by non-significant colour, the same agency may lead to the disappearance of the latter when it impedes the success of an animal in the struggle for existence. Thus the red colour of blood has disappeared in certain transparent fishes, which are thereby concealed from their enemies. Among the manifold possible variations of nature is that of a fish with colourless blood, which can, nevertheless, efficiently perform all the duties of this fluid. While such a variation would be no advantage to the great majority of vertebrates, it would be very beneficial to a fish which was already difficult to detect on the surface of the ocean on account of its transparency.

II. Significant colours

Colours may be useful in many ways, and are therefore always liable to be turned to account in one direction or another. They may be of direct physiological value to the organism, or may assist in the struggle for existence by deluding other species, or by aiding the individuals of the same species, or they may be intimately connected with courtship.

1. The Direct Physiological Value of colour

The colour of chlorophyll, which causes the green appearance of vegetation, must be intimately connected with the important changes which take place in this substance in the presence of light. It is well known that under these circumstances carbon dioxide (popularly called ' carbonic acid ') can be split up, and its carbon made to unite with the elements of water, forming organic substance. Although this process has been much studied it is still very imperfectly understood. It is clear, however, that the colour of chlorophyll, involving the special absorption of certain light-waves, has some direct bearing upon the changes which occur.

No equally clear instance has been proved to occur in the animal kingdom, except in those few forms which resemble plants in possessing chlorophyll. Dr. Hickson, however, believes that among corals 'the most widely distributed colours will eventually be proved to be allied to chlorophyll . . . and perform a very similar if not precisely identical physiological function.' It is much to be desired that this interesting suggestion, which Dr. Hickson supports by many arguments, may be thoroughly tested as soon as possible.[1]

In the very common association of coloured substances with the important function of respiration, it is clear that the colour is not more than incidental; while the fish with transparent blood shows that colour is not indispensable for the due performance of the function. Pigment is, however, of direct importance for vision: it is always present in the eyes of animals, except in the case of albinos, and it is said that even they possess the essential visual pigment associated with the termination of the optic nerve (retinal purple).

The difference between the physiological importance of colour in animals and plants is well shown by the fact that a true albino variety (not merely a variegated example) of a green plant could not live for any length of time.

There are, however, certain cases among animals in which it is extremely probable that colour is of direct physiological value. It is well known that dark colours readily absorb radiant heat, while light

[1] *A Naturalist in North Celebes* (Hickson, 1889), pp. 149-51.

colours do so with difficulty. For this reason black clothes are most trying, and white most comfortable, in the hottest weather. Conversely, a dark surface readily parts with heat by radiation, while a white surface retains heat far more effectually.

A few writers had suggested that these principles may explain the colours of certain animals, but the question was first fully entered upon in Lord Walsingham's presidential address to the Yorkshire Naturalists' Union in 1885.[1] The predominance of *dark* varieties of insects and *white* varieties of birds and mammals in northern latitudes is connected with these facts. 'Birds and animals living through the winter naturally require to *retain* in their bodies a sufficient amount of heat to enable them to maintain their existence, with unreduced vitality, against the severities of the climate. Insects, on the contrary, require *rapidly to take advantage* of transient gleams of sunshine during the short summer season, and may be content to sink into a dormant condition so soon as they have secured the reproduction of their species; only to be revived in some instances by a return of exceptionally favourable conditions.'

It would be fatal for the temperature of one of the higher vertebrates to sink a few degrees below the normal, except in the case of certain species, such as the dormouse, &c., which have the power of hybernating in a dormant condition; such animals were once

[1] See *Entomological Transactions* of the Union for 1885.

called 'warm-blooded,' but are now more correctly termed 'homothermic,' because it is the *constancy* of the temperature which is so important, and which must be maintained whether the surrounding medium be colder or warmer than themselves. Other animals with an inconstant temperature are now correctly called 'poikilothermic' rather than 'cold-blooded.'

Lord Walsingham's conclusions appear to be supported by the fact that young dark-coloured caterpillars, like those of the Emperor Moth (*Saturnia carpini*), or Tortoiseshell Butterfly (*Vanessa urticæ*), seek the light side of a glass cylinder, and always change their position when the cylinder is turned round. The question needs further investigation, and much might be learnt by interposing various screens between such larvæ and the light, thus cutting off different sets of light-waves.

The most important support to the hypothesis is found in an experiment made by Lord Walsingham, in which several Lepidoptera of different colours were placed on a surface of snow exposed to bright sunshine; in half an hour the snow beneath the darker insects showed distinct signs of melting, but no effects were seen beneath the others. The differences were further brought out in the course of two hours, when the darkest insect of the lot, a black Geometer, the Chimney-Sweeper (*Odezia chærophyllata*), 'had decidedly won the downward race among them.'

It is therefore certain that the absorption of

radiant heat is favoured by the dark colours of northern insects, and it is in every way probable that they are benefited by the warmth received in this way. We cannot, however, as yet assert that such dark colours are not also advantageous for concealment or some other purpose.

The white appearance of Arctic birds and mammals must be advantageous for concealment in a region so largely covered with snow, but it is very probable that advantage is also secured by checking the loss of heat through radiation.

Thus Lord Walsingham's experiments and conclusions seem to prove that colours are sometimes of direct physiological value to animals, although a great deal more work must be done before we can safely estimate the proportion which this advantage bears to others also conferred by the same colours (see also pages 92–104).

2. Protective and Aggressive Resemblance

By far the most widespread use of colour is to assist an animal in escaping from its enemies or in capturing its prey ; the former is *Protective,* the latter *Aggressive.* It is probable that these were the first uses to which non-significant colours were put. The resemblances are of various kinds ; the commonest cases are those of simple concealment. The animal passes undetected by resembling some common object which is of no interest to its enemies or prey respectively, or by harmonising with the general effect of its surroundings ; the former is *Special*, the latter *General Resemblance*, and both may be *Protective* or *Aggressive*. Among the most interesting *Special Aggressive Resemblances* are the cases of *Alluring Colouring*, in which the animal, or some part of it, resembles an object which is attractive to its prey.

3. Protective and Aggressive Mimicry

Mimicry is in reality a very important section of *Special Resemblance*. The animal gains advantage by a superficial resemblance to some other, and generally very different, species which is well known and dreaded because of some unpleasant quality, such as a sting or an offensive taste or smell, &c., or it may even be protected from the animal it resembles : this is *Protective Mimicry*. When, however, the animal resembles another so as to be able to injure the latter or some other form which accompanies it or is not afraid of it, the *Mimicry* is *Aggressive*. Although, strictly speaking, *Mimicry* should fall under the last heading, it is so important and so different from the other examples of *Special Resemblance* that it is more convenient to consider it separately. In the complete classification at the end of the book it will be shown in its true position.

4. Warning colours

When an animal possesses an unpleasant attribute, it is often to its advantage to advertise the fact as publicly as possible. In this way it escapes a great deal of experimental ' tasting.' The conspicuous patterns and strongly contrasted colours which serve as the signal of danger or inedibility are known as *Warning Colours*. In other cases such colours or markings enable individuals of the same species easily to follow those in front to a place of safety, or assist them in keeping together when safety depends upon numbers.

It is these *Warning Colours* which are nearly always the objects of *Protective Mimicry*, and it will therefore be convenient to describe the former before the latter.

5. Colours produced by Courtship

Finally, in the highest animals, the vertebrata and many of the most specialised invertebrate groups, we have some evidence for the existence of an æsthetic sense. Darwin believed that this sense was brought into play in courtship, and that colours and patterns have been gradually modified by the preference of the females for the most beautiful males ; he believed that such *Sexual Selection* accounts for many of the most beautiful features possessed by animals, viz. those which are especially displayed during courtship.

Although this hypothesis has been rejected by A. R. Wallace, I shall endeavour to support it by some striking observations of recent date, and by as far as possible answering the objections which have been raised, and the hypotheses which have been believed to account for the same facts.

Display in courtship is probably the most recently developed of all the various uses of colour among animals, and as such, its consideration is best deferred until all the others have been described.

It must not be supposed that the colours of each animal will be found to possess but a single use. Thus *Protective Resemblances* are often supplemented by *Warning Colours* or attitudes, which give the animal an extra chance of escape after its first line of defence has been broken through. It is also the general rule for the colours displayed in courtship to be hidden beneath protective tints when the animal is at rest.

The colours of animals may be recapitulated as follows :

I. Non-significant Colours.

II. Significant Colours.

    1. *Colours of Direct Physiological Value.*

    2. *Protective and Aggressive Resemblance.*

    3. *Protective and Aggressive Mimicry.*

    4. *Warning Colours.*

    5. *Colours displayed in Courtship.*

The rest of this volume will be occupied with the further consideration of the last four classes of colours. It will be remembered that the third class is but a special example of the second, which it is convenient to treat separately, and to defer until after the fourth class has been considered.

CHAPTER III

PROTECTIVE RESEMBLANCES IN LEPIDOPTERA

THE first and most important use of colour is to enable an animal to conceal itself from its enemies or to approach its prey unseen.[1]

Special and General Resemblances

These results may be achieved in one of two ways: either the animal may more or less exactly resemble some object which is of no interest to its enemies, or it may harmonise with the general artistic effect of its surroundings, so that it does not attract attention. We may therefore distinguish *Special Resemblance*, in which the appearance of a particular object is copied in shape and outline as well as in colour, and *General Resemblance*, in which the general effects of surrounding colours are reproduced.

In the latter case it is often difficult to believe,

---

[1] This was thoroughly appreciated by Erasmus Darwin, who says : ‘The colours of many animals seem adapted to their purposes of concealing themselves, either to avoid danger or to spring upon their prey.’—*Zoonomia*, 1794, vol. i. p. 509.

when we look at the animal by itself, that the protection is effective and real. We cannot appreciate the meaning of the colours of many animals apart from their surroundings, because we do not comprehend the complicated artistic effect of the latter. A caterpillar in the midst of green leaves may have many brilliant tints upon it, and yet may be all the better concealed because of their presence; the appearance of the foliage is really less simple than we imagine, for changes are wrought by varied lights and shadows playing upon colours which are in themselves far from uniform.

Francis Galton noticed this fact with regard to the higher animals in 1851. ' Snakes and lizards are the most brilliant of animals ; but all these, if viewed at a distance, or with an eye whose focus is adjusted, not exactly at the animal itself, but to an object more or less distant than it, become apparently of one hue and lose all their gaudiness. No more conspicuous animal can well be conceived, according to common idea, than a zebra ; but on a bright starlight night the breathing of one may be heard close by you, and yet you will be positively unable to see the animal. If the black stripes were more numerous he would be seen as a black mass ; if the white, as a white one ; but their proportion is such as exactly to match the pale tint which arid ground possesses when seen by moonlight.' [1]

[1] Galton's *South Africa*, p. 187 (Minerva Library).

We shall see that it is common for an insect to be protected by Special Resemblance at one time of its life, and by General Resemblance at another, or to be concealed at different periods of its life by different kinds of Special or General Resemblance respectively.

Each of these forms of Resemblance may be *Protective* or *Aggressive* according as they are made use of to defend from attack or to assist in capture. We shall also see that Protective and Aggressive Re semblances may be either Constant or Variable ; in the latter case, the appearance is capable of adjustment in order to correspond with changes in the environment. This, the highest form of Resemblance, will be deferred until the examples of the other form have been considered.

The Larvæ of Geometræ as examples of Special Protective Resemblance

There is no better instance of Special Protective Resemblance than that afforded by the larvæ of *Geometræ,* 'stick caterpillars' or 'loopers,' as they are often called. These caterpillars are extremely common, and between two and three hundred species are found in this country ; but the great majority are rarely seen because of their perfect resemblance to the twigs of the plants upon which they feed. They possess only two pairs of claspers, or legs which are peculiar to the caterpillar stage, while in nearly all other caterpillars there are five pairs.   These claspers are placed at the hind end of the body, which is long, thin, and cylindrical, and stands out like a side twig at an acute angle with the stem to which the claspers are tightly fixed.   The body also often possesses little humps which resemble buds or irregularities of the bark.   The caterpillar sits motionless

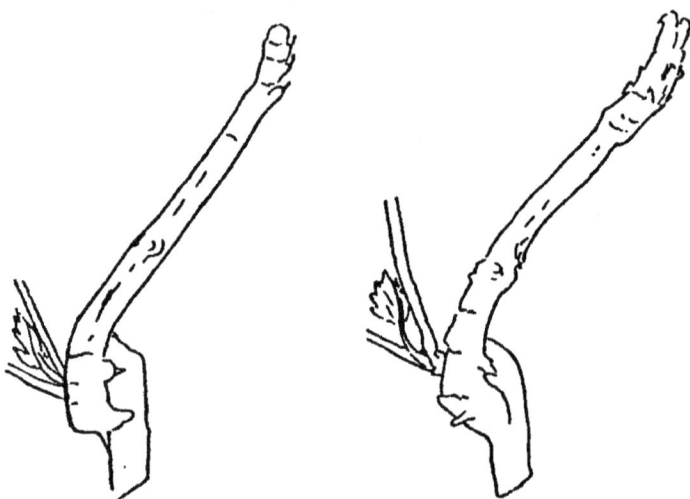

FIG. 1.—The larva of Swallow-tail Moth (*Ourapteryx sambucaria*); last stage; natural size.

FIG. 2.—Twig of currant; the general appearance much like that of fig. 1.

for hours together, and the only alteration of the attitude is brought about by feeding, which generally takes place in the evening or at night.   The general appearance of one of these larvæ and its resemblance to a twig is shown in figs. 1 and 2, for which I am indebted to the kindness of Mr. Alfred Sich.

The strain on the body during these long periods

of absolute stillness would be far too great to be
borne did not the caterpillar spin a thread of silk,
which is attached at one end to the stem, while the
other end remains fixed to the head of the animal.
How great the strain would be without such a support
may be well understood by any one who has tried to
hold out the arm straight at right angles to the body
for five minutes. There is considerable tension upon

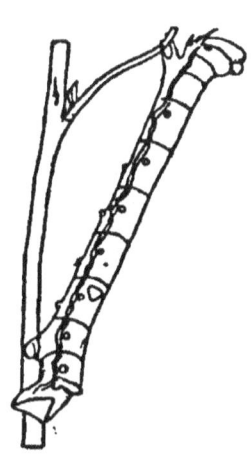

the thread of silk, so that, if it be
cut, the larva falls back with a jerk,
making a more obtuse angle with
the stem ; and it then tries to remain
rigid in the new position : this is impossible because of the strain, and
after again falling backwards once or
twice, and making one or two more
attempts to keep firm and motionless,
it is obliged to give up the twig-like
position while it fixes a new supporting thread. In some cases the
caterpillar gains support by holding
a leaf or twig with one of its three

Fig. 3.—The larva of
Peppered Moth (*Am-
phidasis betularia*);
last stage ; natural
size.

pairs of true legs, or legs which will persist in the
perfect insect (see fig. 3; also figs. 40 and 41, page 152).
These pairs of legs are placed one on each of the
body-rings behind the head.

It is very interesting to notice how the head of
these caterpillars is modified from the usual shape
into one which suggests the end of a twig. It is very

common for the crown to be deeply notched, thus producing two humps which make a very natural end to the apparent twig.   In the caterpillar of the Small Emerald Moth (*Hemithea thymiaria*) there are two additional humps on the body-ring (prothorax) behind the head, and the latter is bent forwards and inwards, so that the end of the caterpillar is made up of four blunt projections, forming perhaps the most suggestive of all the resemblances to the end of a twig.

In the larva of the Early Thorn Moth (*Selenia illunaria*) the head and first two body-rings are bent backwards at right angles to the rest of the body.   The supporting thread of silk passes between the third pair of true legs, which are borne by a high ridge projecting from the angle. The ridge continues the line of the body, and is coloured like it, while the head and first rings are of a

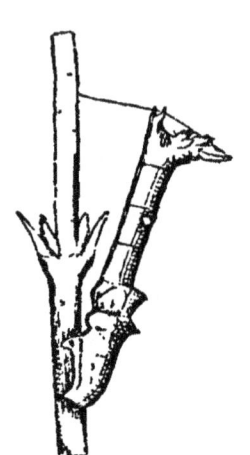

FIG. 4.—The larva of Early Thorn Moth (*Selenia illunaria*); adult; natural size.

different colour.   The whole effect is exceedingly un-caterpillar-like, and very suggestive of some eccentric vegetable growth (see fig. 4).

In order that the resemblance may be complete, it is essential that the caterpillar should appear to grow out of the branch in a natural manner.   The two pairs of claspers assist in producing this effect, for they partially encircle the branch, and appear to be

3

continuous with it (see fig. 7, page 31). Between the
two pairs there is necessarily a furrow, where the body
of the larva lies along the cylindrical branch. This
furrow, which, if apparent, would greatly interfere with
the resemblance, is rendered inconspicuous in the following manner. The under side of the caterpillar is
somewhat flattened, so that it is in contact with a
small part of the circumference of the branch, and
the furrow on each side is partially filled up, at any

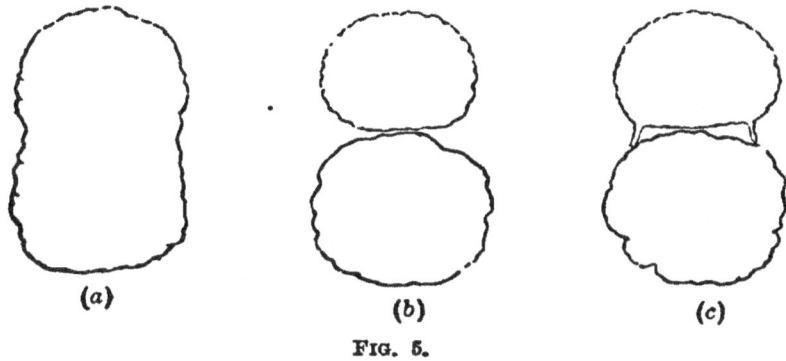

(a)   (b)   (c)

FIG. 5.

rate in certain species, by a number of fleshy tubercles.
The shadow which would betray the furrow is also
neutralised by the light colour of the tubercles. The
effect will be clear on comparing a, b, and c in fig. 5 :
a is a section of a branch just below the point where
a lateral twig comes off ; b a diagrammatic section of
a branch and the caterpillar's body ; c the same with
the addition of the tubercles, which render the outline
more like that of a.

I will illustrate the extraordinary degree of resemblance attained in *Geometræ*, by a description of the larva of one of our most abundant species—the Brimstone Moth (*Rumia cratægata*). The appearance of the larva when seated among the twigs of its commonest food-plant—hawthorn—is shown in fig. 6. It will be observed that some of the twigs are slightly bent in the middle, and that a projection is placed on the angle; these appearances are exactly reproduced in

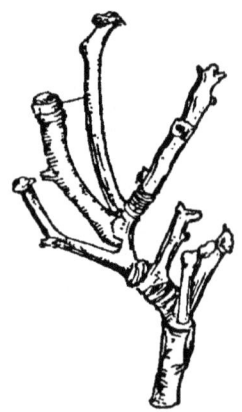

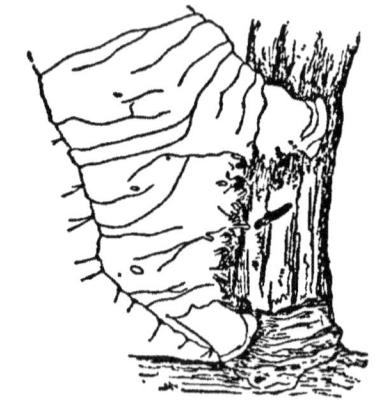

FIG. 6.—The larva of Brimstone Moth (*Rumia cratægata*); last stage; natural size.

FIG. 7.—The hind part of the larva of Brimstone Moth (*Rumia cratægata*), seen from right side, showing junction with branch; adult.

the larva. The hind part of the larva is represented in fig. 7 (magnified 4·5 diameters), showing the claspers and the fleshy projections which occupy the furrow between the larva and the stem.

The harmony of colour is quite as perfect as the resemblance of shape. The smaller branches of the hawthorn are partially covered by a thin superficial layer of a bluish-grey colour (the cuticle), while the deeper layers beneath are brown or green, or mixed brown and green; these tints become visible over a large part of the surface, owing to the breaking away of the thin layer. Hence the colour of the branches is brown or green, mottled with grey, and not only are these the exact tints of the larva, but the way in which the colours are blended is precisely similar in the animal and the plant. The marvellous fidelity with which the details are thus reproduced, probably implies that the relation between the larva and this species of food-plant is extremely ancient. It will be shown below that this caterpillar can also adjust its colour to that of its individual surroundings, so that it would become greenish if it passed its life among young green shoots, and brown if it lived upon the older twigs. It is altogether one of the most perfectly concealed forms in existence.

When, however, such 'stick caterpillars' are young, they do not sit upon the branches, but upon the leaves of their food-plant, and the twig-like attitude would then be inappropriate, for we do not see twigs projecting from leaves. In some cases the caterpillars are green (e.g. *Ephyra omicronaria*), and so possess a general harmony with the colour of the surface behind them; but in other cases they are brown, and then the attitude is often modified into a different form of Special Resemblance. The caterpillar twists itself into a very irregular spiral (e.g. *Ephyra pendularia*, &c.), or into an exceedingly angular zigzag (e.g. *Selenia illunaria*; see fig. 8), thus resembling a dead and crumpled piece of leaf, or the spiral leaf-case made by other insects, or the excrement of birds or snails. The caterpillar of *Selenia illunaria* has a very similar structure and colouring at the times when it resembles such very different objects as a twig and the excrement of a bird, the whole difference being made by a modification of attitude alone (compare figs. 4 and 8). I have seen the larva of the Brimstone Moth twisted into a spiral, resting motionless close to the notch which it had eaten out of a leaf; in this position it forcibly suggested the appearance of a small piece of leaf which had been accidentally torn, and had

FIG. 8.—The young larva of Early Thorn (*Selenia illunaria*), seated on a leaf; natural size.

turned brown and curled up, remaining attached to the uninjured part of the leaf by one end.

We may well suppose that the acquisition of a form and attitude which lend themselves so readily to the purposes of concealment, was very advantageous to the ancestral *Geometræ*, and enabled them to spread over the vegetable world, dividing into an immense number of species, and ousting many larvæ with less perfect methods of concealment. In their widening range certain *Geometræ* have thus come to feed upon low-growing plants which are altogether without twigs or branches. The attitude is then modified, and suggests some object which might be expected to occur upon the plant. Thus the caterpillar of the Straw Belle (*Aspilates gilvaria*), feeding upon such plants as yarrow and plantain, coils up the anterior part of its body into a flat spiral, with the head in the centre. Hence the attitude and the whitish colour of the larva produce a very considerable resemblance to a small

Fig. 9. — The larva of Large Emerald Moth (*Geometra papilionaria*); a green variety ; last stage; natural size.

bleached and empty snail-shell, which would be of no interest to any insect-eater. If the colour of the caterpillar were darker it might be mistaken for a living snail, and it is doubtful how far such a resemblance would be to its advantage, in the case of birds.

Another larva, that of the Large Emerald Moth (*Geometra papilionaria*), feeding upon catkin-bearing trees, birch and nut, resembles the catkins rather than the twigs (see fig. 9). It is short and stout, and the manner in which the body-rings succeed each other forcibly suggests the overlapping scales of a catkin. Some of the larvæ are green and some brown, like catkins of different colours.

Protective Resemblance to bark and lichen in Lepidoptera

Certain caterpillars belonging to other groups are concealed by their resemblance to the bark of tolerably

thick branches.   They lie flattened and closely pressed
against the bark ; while the furrow which would lead
to their detection is partially filled up, and the
shadow neutralised, by a row of fleshy protuberances
in the caterpillars of the Red and Crimson Underwing Moths (*Catocalidæ*; see figs. 38 and 39, page
151), and by hairs in the larva of the December Moth
(*Pœcilocampa populi*).   This interpretation was first
offered by Meldola, and it is strongly supported by
the previously mentioned fact that similar protuberances occur in *Geometræ*, and are strictly confined to
the comparatively short line of contact between the
larva and the branch.   The lichens on the bark are
very commonly resembled rather than the bark itself.
This is the case with the last-named larva.   The
caterpillar, chrysalis, and moth of the Black Arches
(*Psilura monacha*) are beautifully protected in this
way.   The black pupa is fixed in a chink in the bark
by a few inconspicuous threads ; its dark colour harmonises with the shadow in the chink, while the long
tufts of greyish hair project and exactly resemble the
appearance of lichen.   Both larva and moth are
coloured so as to resemble common appearances presented by lichens, and both habitually rest on lichen-
covered bark.   A lichen-feeding Geometer (*Cleora
lichenaria*) is wonderfully protected in the same
manner ; the larva often twists itself among the
irregularities of the lichen, so that it is completely

invisible. The moth is also similarly concealed, and rests on tree-trunks.

A caterpillar which makes its surroundings resemble itself

In all the examples hitherto described, and countless others, the insect is defended by resembling its surroundings; the very interesting caterpillar of a South American butterfly. (*Anaea sp. ?*), described by Wilhelm Müller, acts differently and makes its surroundings resemble itself. It gnaws the leaf in such a manner as to leave a number of rough models of itself attached to the

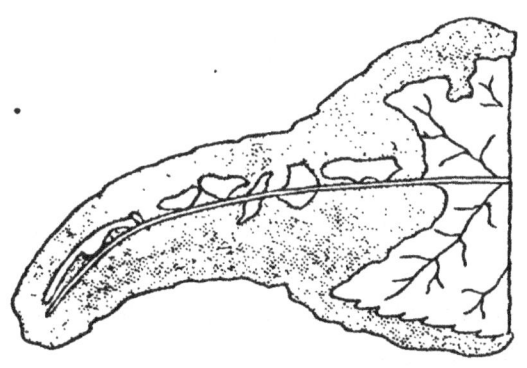

Fig. 10.—The larva of *Anaea sp. ?* on the mid-rib of a leaf on which are many pieces of leaf of the general appearance of the larva; third stage; natural size; after Wilhelm Müller.

mid-rib, and then sits down beside them. The caterpillar is green above and dark beneath, although the former colour interrupts the latter at certain points and comes into contact with the mid-rib on which the insect is resting. The dark colour is not distinguishable from the deep shadow behind the leaf, and therefore the appearance is that of an elongated patch of green connected with the mid-rib by two narrow stalks. The larva, in eating, leaves several pieces of leaf attached to the mid-rib by one or two stalks, which, therefore, present a very similar appearance to that of the larva itself. The concealment which is thus effected is sufficiently indicated in fig. 10.

An appearance of leaf-like flatness conveyed by arrangement of colour

Another very interesting example, in which the effect of shadow is gained by arrangement of colour, is afforded by the chrysalis of the Purple Emperor Butterfly (*Apatura iris*). The large green pupa resembles a leaf in the most perfect manner, mid-rib and oblique veining being represented. I showed a small twig of sallow, to which a pupa was suspended, to several friends, but it was almost invariably overlooked; even when it was pointed out, the observer frequently failed to see any difference between it and a sallow leaf. The most extraordinary thing about this resemblance is the impression of leaf-like flatness conveyed by a chrysalis, which is in reality very far from flat. In its thickest part the pupa is 8·5 mm. across, and it is in all parts very many times thicker than a leaf. The dorsal side of the pupa forms a very thin sharp ridge for part of its length, but the slope is much more pronounced in other parts and along the whole ventral side. But exactly in these places, where the obvious thickness would destroy the resemblance to a leaf, the whole effect of the roundness is neutralised by increased lightness, so disposed as just to compensate for the shadow by which alone we judge of the roundness of small objects. The degree of whiteness is produced by the relative abundance of white dots and a fine white marbling of the surface, which is everywhere present mingled with the green. The effect is, in fact, produced by a process exactly analogous to stippling. The degree of lightness produced in this way exactly corresponds to the angle of the slope, which, of course, determines the depth of the shadow. By this beautiful and simple method the pupa appears to be as flat as a leaf which is only a small fraction of 1 mm. in thickness.

Although the effect which I have just described could not have been surpassed by the efforts of an artist, it is precisely the result which can be most readily explained by the unaided operation of natural selection. The minute white markings are present over the whole surface, and their number and size must be subject to continual variation ; in fact, it is quite certain that no two individuals are alike in these respects. The increased protection afforded by their more appropriate distribution in certain individuals would clearly lead to the survival of the latter, while the same process continued in each generation would lead to the elaborate and beautiful form of adaptation which is now witnessed in this species.

An analogous effect is produced by the larva of a Saw-fly (a plant-eating Hymenopterous insect), which rests stretched along the edge of a leaf.   In this position the larva (*Nematus curtispina*) would be detected if it covered the notched edge of the leaf; it has, however, the habit of resting along the curved edge of the gap made by its own exertions.   From the side its green ground colour is alone apparent, and it is very difficult to detect.   When, however, the leaf is looked at edgeways, it would seem that the larva must be conspicuous, because its thickness is much greater than that of a leaf.   From this point of view the back of the larva is, of course, seen; along the middle line the tubular heart is more distinct than usual because of the transparent skin.   The green blood within makes the heart appear

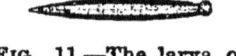

Fig. 11.—The larva of *Nematus curtispina*; in last stage; natural size.

as a fine dark line against a white border on each side, which is entirely due to an accumulation of fat beneath the skin.   The white band with the fine dark line down its middle produces the effect of the edge of the leaf, while the rest of the body on each side is green, shaded with dark pigment so as to appear much flatter than it really is.   The appearance of the larva is shown in fig. 11.

The case is also of special interest, because the colouring is chiefly derived from internal tissues or organs showing through a transparent skin.   The ground colour is due to the green fluids of the body and the green contents of the alimentary canal. The dark shading is the only part of the appearance caused in the usual way by superficially placed pigment. Nearly all the colours of this animal are non-significant in many other insects.

Reply to objection that methods of concealment would certainly be detected

It has been sometimes objected that these methods of concealment cannot be intended as a means of defence, because insect-eating animals would be sharp-sighted enough to penetrate the disguise. Of course, the progressive improvement in the means of concealment has been attended by a corresponding increase in the keenness of foes, so that no species can wholly escape. But so long as a well-concealed form remains motionless, it is easy to prove by experiment that enemies are often unable to recognise it. Thus I have found that the insect-eating, wood-haunting Green Lizard (*Lacerta viridis*) will generally fail to detect a 'stick caterpillar' in its position of rest, although it is seized and greedily devoured directly it moves. The marvellous resemblance of *Cleora lichenaria* (see p. 35) even deceived one of these lizards after the larva had moved more than once. The instant the caterpillar became rigid the lizard appeared puzzled, and seemed unable to realise that the apparent piece of lichen was good to eat.   After a few moments, however, the lizard was satisfied, and ate the caterpillar with the keenest relish.

Furthermore, the fact that all well-concealed forms are good for food, and are eagerly chased and devoured by insectivorous animals, while unpalatable forms are conspicuously coloured, points strongly towards the conclusion that the object of concealment is defence from enemies.

CHAPTER IV

PROTECTIVE RESEMBLANCES IN LEPIDOPTERA
(continued), DIMORPHISM, ETC.

General Protective Resemblance and changes of colour corresponding to changes in the surroundings

ALL the examples hitherto described illustrate Special Protective Resemblance. A good instance of General Resemblance is afforded by the large and common caterpillar of the Privet Hawk Moth (*Sphinx ligustri*). Although the caterpillar looks so conspicuous, it harmonises very well with its food-plant, and is sometimes difficult to find. The purple stripes increase the protection by breaking up the large green surface of the caterpillar into smaller areas. This caterpillar also affords a good example of a rapid change of colour corresponding to a change of environment. When full grown it descends to the ground and hurries about in search of a spot to bury in, and, being very large and bright green, it would be exceedingly conspicuous against the brown earth if it retained the usual colour. But just before it descends the back begins to turn brown, and becomes finally dark brown, so that the caterpillar harmonises well with the colour of its new surroundings. The significance of this change was first pointed out by Professor Meldola. Other nearly allied caterpillars feeding upon trees, such as willow or poplar, which grow in damp situations where the ground is covered with green vegetation, do not turn brown to anything like the same extent.

A very interesting instance of exactly the opposite change at a corresponding period is afforded by the caterpillar of the August Thorn Moth (*Ennomos angularia*), a brown 'stick caterpillar,' protected by a very perfect Special Resemblance to the dark twigs of the elm on which it feeds. When full-fed it constructs a very loose cocoon of elm leaves, so loose and open that it is easily seen within, and its brown body would be conspicuous against the background of green leaves. But at the same time the dark brown colour of its surface entirely disappears, and the animal is tinted by its green blood, which is seen through the transparent skin; it is thus well concealed by General Resemblance to its new surroundings.

Another exceedingly interesting case of the same kind of change is witnessed in the caterpillar of the Miller Moth (*Acronycta leporina*), which sits motionless on the under side of the leaves of the birch and alder, and is covered with very long beautiful hair which is brilliantly white, and bends over on all sides so as to touch the leaf, forming a wide margin round the caterpillar. Hence all we can see is an oval convex mass of a substance resembling white cotton wool, an appearance very suggestive of a cocoon (see fig. 12). The caterpillar's body is almost invisible; but on looking carefully we can just make out a dim curved shape beneath the white covering, just as a caterpillar or chrysalis appears through the walls of its cocoon:

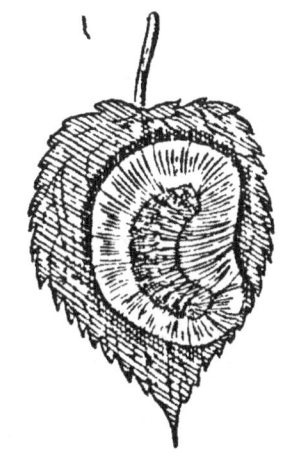

FIG. 12.—The larva of Miller Moth (*Acronycta leporina*), at rest on a birch leaf; adult; natural size.

FIG. 13.—The larva of Miller Moth (*Acronycta leporina*), wandering about on bark before forming cocoon; natural size.

furthermore, the larva is very short and thick, and thus resembles the contracted state of a caterpillar before turning to a chrysalis. This perfect Special Resemblance is kept up until the caterpillar is full-fed, when it wanders over the bark and finally burrows in it. But a cocoon is a motionless object, and the resemblance, if continued, would be fatal, for it would attract attention. But as soon as the larva is mature, the hairs become black and the body of a much darker tint, and the animal is then well protected by General Resemblance to the dark surface over which it moves (see fig. 13).

Although the bark of large birch trees is chiefly white, the caterpillar is, upon the whole, better concealed by becoming dark-coloured. It lives on small birches and alders with dark bark, as well as on large birches, and in the latter case it probably wanders among the wide dark chinks rather than over the smooth wide expanses, for it would certainly burrow in the former rather than the latter.

Just before pupation the colours of caterpillars nearly always become dull, and it is in every way probable that such incidental changes have been seized upon by natural selection, and have been rendered advantageous to the species. Such alterations of colour are entirely different from those which will be described below, in which an animal can modify its appearance into correspondence with its individual surroundings. The larva of the Privet Hawk Moth almost invariably wanders over the earth when it has come down from its food-plant ; but if it were to descend upon turf, the brown colour would still be assumed, although green would conceal it more effectually. The change to brown is, however, far safer for the average caterpillar, and is beneficial to the species on the whole, although it must lead to some individual failures. In the far higher form of Variable

Protective Resemblance, which will be described in Chapters VII., VIII., and IX., the individual can adjust its appearance to any of the various environments it is likely to meet with in nature.

The consideration of changes in colour very naturally leads to the subject of Dimorphism.

Dimorphism in Lepidopterous larvæ

It has been already mentioned that the caterpillars of the Large Emerald Moth are sometimes green and sometimes brown. The same is true of many larvæ, and in some of the Mocha Moths (*Ephyridæ*) the chrysalides are the same colour as the larvæ from which they develop. These colours have nothing to do with sex, and the appearance of the perfect insect does not seem to be influenced in any way by the larval dimorphism. It is noteworthy that *both* colours of dimorphic larvæ are invariably of protective value : they are, in fact, nearly always the two chief tints of nature— green and brown.

If we breed from moths developed from the green larvæ of, *e.g.*, the Large Emerald, the larvæ in the next generation are chiefly green, and after several generations there is little doubt that the brown form would become excessively rare ; so also the green form would disappear if we bred from the brown varieties. But in nature both forms are common, and therefore it is certain that both must be advantageous to the species, or one of them would quickly disappear. I believe that it is a benefit to the species that some of its larvæ should resemble brown and others green catkins, instead of all of them resembling either brown or green. In the former case the foes have a wider range of objects for which they may mistake the larvæ, and the search must occupy more time, for equivalent results, than in the case of other species which are not dimorphic.

Dimorphism is also valuable in another way: the widening range of a species may carry it into countries in which one of its forms may be especially well concealed, while in other countries the other form may be more protected. Thus a dimorphic species is more fully provided against emergencies than one with only a single form. To take an example: the green colour of the young caterpillars of the Convolvulus Hawk Moth (*Sphinx convolvuli*) sometimes persists, and is sometimes replaced by brown in the later stages. In Europe the latter form predominates, because the creeping food-plant (*Convolvulus arvensis*) is so small that it is safer for a large caterpillar to resemble the earth beneath rather than the small leaves on its surface. In the Canary Islands and Madeira, where the larva feeds on many large-leaved species of *Convolvulus*, the green form predominates, for it is far better protected than the other against a continuous green background.

This result appears to have been brought about by

the ordinary operation of natural selection, leading to the extermination of the less protected variety. I have experimented with all the dimorphic larvæ mentioned above, and could not find any trace of susceptibility to the influence of surroundings, so as to lead to the production of the appropriate form. When such susceptibility is present, of course the dimorphism has a far higher protective value. The description of such cases is reserved for a future chapter.

Occasionally the two forms of a dimorphic species appear at different times and correspond to the tints which successively predominate in the surroundings. At one time I thought the brown form of the Large Emerald caterpillar might appear rather later than the other, when the green catkins had been replaced by brown ; but further examination did not confirm the observations which pointed in this direction. Dr. Alexander Wallace, of Colchester, has, however, found that the moths of *Bombyx cynthia* which are the first to emerge from the pupæ possess, as a rule, an olive-green ground colour, while those which emerge in September are generally of a yellow tint. These colours harmonise with the appearance of the *Ailanthus* leaflets at corresponding times of the year.

Dimorphism in the Perfect Insect

Dimorphism is also met with in perfect insects, and it is especially frequent in the females (see page

302 for an example of a dimorphic male among spiders). Its meaning is obscure, but one of the two forms is generally much rarer than the other, and probably the older. The facts seem to point towards the replacement of an older by a younger form, because the latter is more attractive to the opposite sex, or because it is better concealed, or because the appearance is accompanied by other benefits to the species. The dark variety of the female Silver-washed Fritillary (*Argynnis paphia*, var. *valezina*), and the white variety of the female Clouded Yellow (*Colias edusa*, var. *helice*), are examples of dimorphism among British butterflies. I exclude that form of dimorphism, or polymorphism, which is caused by one sex 'mimicking' two or more species which are specially protected (for a good example see pp. 234–38).

An extremely important form of di- or polymorphism occurs among the females of the social Hymenoptera. In this case, however, the different forms are specially fitted for certain duties, and the consequent division of labour is beneficial to the society and therefore to the species.

Seasonal Dimorphism

Finally, a species which passes through two or more cycles of development in a year, viz. one that is 'double' or 'treble-brooded,' is often characterised by 'seasonal dimorphism,' in which the first brood is different in appearance, and often in size, from the later ones. Professor Weismann has investigated this question, and he finds that while the later broods can be readily made, by the application of ice in the pupal stage, to assume the form of the first or winter generation, the latter cannot be made to assume the form of the summer brood by the application of warmth. He infers that such species were single-brooded in the short summers which succeeded the Glacial Period, and that the appearance was that of the present winter form. As the summers became longer, other newer generations with a different appearance were added (summer broods), but the species always tends easily to revert to the more ancient form. An important part of the evidence consists in the proof that such species are now single-brooded in the northern part of their range, and that the one form is that of the winter brood of more southern localities.[1]

I have given a very brief sketch of dimorphism, hardly alluding to polymorphism, which is only an extension of the same principle. Although the subject is only touched upon, enough has been said to show that there are many distinct kinds of dimorphism, some of which are very obscure. By far the most important kind of di- or polymorphism remains to be described below (see Chapters VIII. and IX.), in which

---

[1] See *Studies in the Theory of Descent*, by August Weismann. English translation by Professor Meldola.

each individual has two or more appearances, as it were, at its command, and can develop that one which is most suited to its own peculiar surroundings.

A reason for the wonderful concealment of Lepidopterous larvæ

In the remarkable abundance and variety of methods by which concealment is effected in Lepidopterous larvæ, we probably see a result of their peculiarly defenceless condition. A larva is a soft-walled cylindrical tube which owes its firmness, and indeed the maintenance of its shape, to the fact that it contains fluid under pressure, which is exerted by the sides of the body. This construction is extremely dangerous, for a slight wound entails great loss of blood, while a moderate injury must prove fatal. Hence larvæ are so coloured as to avoid detection or to warn of some unpleasant attribute, the object in both cases being the same—to leave the larva untouched, a touch being practically fatal (see also pp. 175–76).

The concealment of Pupæ

Protective Resemblance, either Special or General, is seen in nearly all exposed pupæ, but most chrysalides are buried in the earth or protected by cocoons. The cocoons are often sufficient defence, because the silk is very unpleasant in the mouth; but such protection

only applies in the warmer weather when there is
an abundance of insect food. In the winter, insectivorous animals are pinched by hunger, and would devour
the pupa in spite of the cocoon. We therefore find
that all cocoons which contain pupæ during the winter
are well concealed, either spun between leaves which
fall off and become brown, or hidden under bark or
moss, or constructed on the surface of bark with a
colour and texture which renders them extremely
difficult to detect. It is very common for particles of
the bark to be gnawed off by the larva and fixed on to
the outside of the cocoon. It will be shown below
that many larvæ can also control the colour of their
cocoons.

Protective Resemblances in Butterflies and Moths

The perfect insect is also commonly defended by
very efficient methods of concealment. The under
sides of the wings of butterflies are generally coloured
like the surface on which the insect habitually rests,
and they are the only parts seen during repose. We
can form some idea of the perfection of this concealment when we remember the entire disappearance of
common butterflies in dull weather. Many of them
creep far down among thickly set leaves, while others
rest freely exposed upon surfaces which harmonise
with their colours.

Perhaps the most perfect concealment attained
by any butterfly is seen in the genus *Kallima*, found

in India, the Malay Archipelago, and Africa.   The way in which the insect is concealed has been described by Wallace in his 'Malay Archipelago,' and also in the 'Essays on Natural Selection.'   The tip of the fore-wing is pointed like the apex of a leaf, and the hind-wing has a short tail like a leaf-stalk, while the outline of the folded wings between these extremities is exactly like that of a withered and somewhat shrivelled leaf.   At rest the wings are held upright over the back, the head and antennæ are concealed between them, while the tails touch the branch to which the insect clings by its almost invisible legs. Along the supposed leaf runs a distinct mark like a mid-rib, with oblique veining on either side.

But dead and withered leaves are not all alike ; they may be almost any shade of brown, grey, or yellow, while they are often attacked by fungi of different colours and in different places.   Similarly the under sides of the wings of the butterfly are excessively variable, the different colours and markings only agreeing in that they all represent some familiar appearance presented by withered or decayed leaves.

Dead leaves are often pierced by insect larvæ, and a detail of great interest is added to the disguise in the semblance of a small hole.   The scales are absent from both sides of a certain spot on each fore-wing, which is therefore only covered by the thin transparent wing membrane.   These spots come opposite to each other in the position of rest, and the effect produced

4

is exactly that of a hole, for the two membranes are so transparent that they are completely invisible. The size of the apparent hole varies very greatly in the numerous specimens of *Kallima inachis*, in the Hope Collection at Oxford.

The upper sides of the wings, concealed during rest, are dark, with a deep orange bar across the fore-wings. I have heard a naturalist, who is acquainted with the Indian species (*Kallima inachis*) in its natural surroundings, object to the interpretation afforded by Mr. Wallace, on the ground that he has often seen the butterfly displaying the conspicuous upper sides of its wings when settled, and has seen it resting on inappropriate surfaces. I do not think that this objection is fatal; for butterflies only display their brilliant tints during the short pauses between the successive flights, when they are on the alert and can evade their enemies by wariness and by the swiftness of their flight. Our own beautiful Red Admiral (*Vanessa atalanta*), Peacock (*V. Io*), and Small Tortoiseshell (*V. urticæ*) similarly display their brilliant colours when pausing on a flower or even on the ground. But during prolonged rest, when the insects are often semi-torpid and would be easily captured if detected, the wings are invariably held so that the sombre tints of the under sides are alone visible. Hence the display of bright colours by the Indian *Kallima* is no argument against the protective value of the leaf-like appearance of the under sides; for the latter acts as a disguise when it is most necessary. for the butterfly to be concealed. It appears that the Malayan species (*Kallima paralekta*) is more cautious during the brief pauses between the flights; for Mr. Wallace states that it frequents dry woods and thickets, and that it invariably settles on bushes with dry or dead leaves. He never saw one of these butterflies settle upon a flower or green leaf.

A recent paper by Mr. S. B. J. Skertchly [1] entirely supports Mr. Wallace's statements. The author calls attention to the fact that leaf-mimicking butterflies, of several genera in addition to *Kallima*, settle in an entirely different manner from that of other butterflies. While the latter gradually slacken their speed and settle deliberately, the leaf butterflies ' fly rapidly along, as if late for an appointment, suddenly pitch, close their wings, and become leaves. It is generally done so rapidly that the insect seems to vanish.'

Certain English moths are also protected by their resemblance to dead leaves. One of the most beautiful examples is afforded by the Herald Moth (*Gonoptera libatrix*), which suggests the appearance of a decayed red leaf sprinkled with a few white spots of fungoid growth; the irregularly toothed margin of the wings adds to the effect. The bright eyes of the moth might expose the deception, but they are covered during rest by a tuft of hair which springs from the base of

[1] *Ann. and Mag. Nat. Hist.* Sept. 1889, pp. 209 *et seq.*

the antennæ (see fig. 14). When the moth is about to fly the antennæ are brought forward, and the same action raises the tufts and uncovers the eyes. The moth appears in the autumn and lives through the winter, so that the resemblance to dead leaves is peculiarly appropriate.

The Angle-shades (*Phlogophora meticulosa*) is also

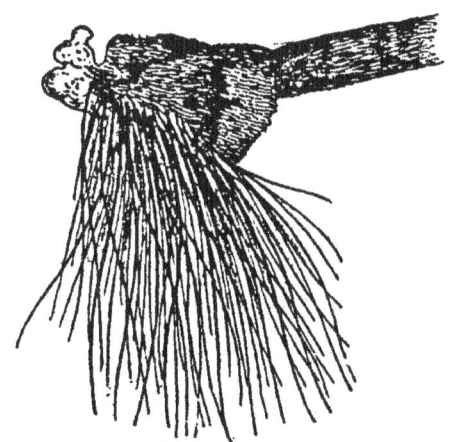

beautifully concealed by resembling a withered and crumpled leaf. The colours of the Yellow Underwing (*Triphæna pronuba*), as seen during flight, strongly suggest the appearance of a yellow leaf whirled along by the wind and then suddenly dropping. The sudden swift rise and rapid descent are very unlike the flight of a

Fig. 14.—The base of left antenna of Herald Moth (*Gonoptera libatrix*), showing the tuft of hair which covers the eyes of the moth in the position of rest; × 24·5 diameters.

moth. When at rest, it hides deeply amid thick foliage or among dead leaves on the ground; it is extremely difficult to detect, and instantly rises when disturbed.

The Rev. Joseph Greene has pointed out that the various shades of yellow and brown are especially characteristic of autumn moths, while grey and silvery tints predominate in the winter species; such tints harmonise with those that are most characteristic in the corresponding seasons.

The Buff-tip Moth (*Pygæra bucephala*) is very perfectly concealed by resembling a broken piece of decayed and lichen-covered stick. The cylindrical shape is produced by the wings being rolled round the body. A friend [1] has raised the objection that the moth resembles a piece of stick cut cleanly at both ends, an object which is never seen in nature. The reply is that the purple and grey colour of the sides of the moth, together with the pale yellow tint of the parts which suggest the broken ends, present a most perfect resemblance to wood in which decay has induced that peculiar texture in which the tissue breaks shortly and sharply, as if cut, on the application of slight pressure or the force of an insignificant blow.

The excreta of birds are also very commonly resembled by moths as well as by caterpillars. This is the case with the little Chinese Character (*Cilix spinula*),[2] and with many grey and white Geometers which rest on the upper sides of leaves with their wings extended as if 'set.' In this position they forcibly suggest the appearance of birds' excrement which has fallen on to a leaf from a great height, and has therefore become flattened into a wide patch. In spite of a faithful resemblance to such an object, these moths possess very great beauty.

[1] Dr. C. M. Chadwick, of Leeds.
[2] Arthur Sidgwick, *Journ. of the Rugby School Nat. Hist. Soc.*

The appearance of splinters of wood is also often suggested by moths such as the 'Sharks' (*Cucullia*) or Goat Moth (*Cossus*). Others resemble the surfaces of rock upon which they habitually rest (*Bryophila*, many Geometers, &c.).

I have merely given a few striking instances of resemblance to objects which are of no interest to insect-eating animals. Numerous other examples might have been added, but my object is merely to illustrate from the Lepidoptera a principle of colouring which is of extremely wide application, viz. its use in aiding an organism to escape from enemies by the method of concealment. Abundant examples of this principle will be recognised by every one interested in natural history, among other orders of insects as well as the Lepidoptera, among vertebrate animals no less than among the invertebrate sub-kingdoms.

Protective Resemblances in other Insects and in Spiders

In the other orders of insects, the Orthoptera (locusts, grasshoppers, &c.) will be found to include the most beautiful examples of Protective Resemblance. The tropical 'leaf insects' and 'walking-stick insects' belong to this order. The latter hold their limbs irregularly, so that the resemblance to a dead branch with lateral twigs is rendered all the more perfect.

Spiders are often protectively coloured; many excellent examples are given by Elizabeth G. Peckham.[1] One of the most remarkable is *Cærostris mitralis*, from Madagascar, which sits motionless on a branch and resembles a woody knot. Its appearance is shown in fig. 15. A common Wisconsin spider, *Epeira prompta,*

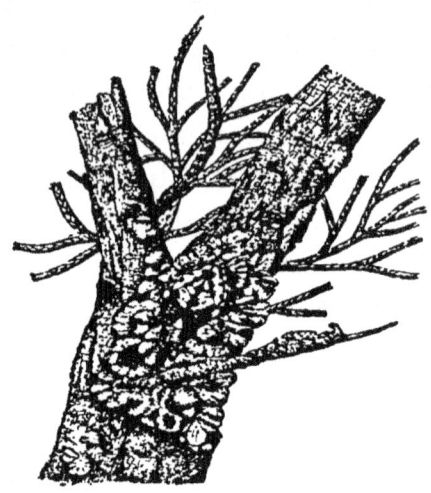

Fig. 15.—*Cærostris mitralis* in profile; from Peckham; after Vinson.

Fig. 16.—*Epeira prompta*, resting on lichen - covered tree - trunk; from Peckham.

generally rests on the branches of cedar bushes, and closely resembles lichen (see fig. 16). Spiders are especially relished by insectivorous animals, so there is every reason for the faithfulness of these resemblances. In many other cases, however, the resemblance is chiefly aggressive, enabling the spider to approach its prey.

[1] *Occasional Papers of the Natural History Society of Wisconsin,* vol. i. 1889, Milwaukee, pp. 61 *et seq.*

CHAPTER V

PROTECTIVE RESEMBLANCES IN VERTE-BRATA, ETC.

MANY of the lower Vertebrata have the power of rapidly modifying their colour according to the environment, and these will be described in a future chapter. Such a power appears to be possessed by few reptiles, and by no bird or mammal.

Protective Resemblances among Reptiles

Our two English snakes are well concealed by their colours; the olive-green Grass Snake (*Tropidonotus natrix*) harmonising well with the grassy banks which it chiefly frequents; while the brown viper (*Pelias berus*) is difficult to detect upon the dry heaths where it is most commonly found. Our lizards are also well protected in the same manner.

Protective Resemblances among Birds

Wallace has directed attention to the protective colours of female birds which build open nests, and he points out that the males are similarly protected when they undertake the duties of incubation.   The same necessity does not apply to species which construct covered nests or build in holes.

The Colours and Markings of Birds' Eggs

The protective value of the tints and markings of eggs are of great interest, and have not been sufficiently investigated.   The fact that eggs are protectively coloured was fully recognised by Erasmus Darwin, who places them under ' colours adapted to the purpose of concealment.'   He says ' the eggs of birds are so coloured as to resemble the colour of the adjacent objects and their interstices.   The eggs of hedge-birds are greenish with dark spots ; those of crows and magpies, which are seen from beneath through wicker nests, are white with dark spots ; and those of larks and partridges are russet or brown, like their nests or situations.' [1]   This description of the eggs of crows and magpies is incorrect.   The eggs of crows are greenish with umber markings ; those of magpies pale greenish with dark markings.   It is probable that Erasmus Darwin correctly explained the appearance of the eggs of the wood-pigeon (see p. 62), and inadvertently illustrated this principle of colouring by erroneous instances.   The special mention of the interstices between the parts of surrounding objects, as well as the objects themselves, is

---

[1] *Zoonomia*, 1794, vol. i. p. 510.

of great interest; protective colouring can never be fully understood until this principle is taken into account.

In order to make out the true meaning of the colours of eggs they must be observed in their natural surroundings, and must be looked at from all points of view and at varying distances. It is very probable that the bright blue colour of certain eggs will be explicable under these conditions.

The fact that concealed eggs are almost invariably white strongly confirms the conclusion that the colours of exposed eggs are of value to the species, and are maintained by the operation of natural selection. Certain exposed eggs may, however, be white, as in the wood-pigeon, but in these cases the eggs are protected from enemies beneath; for the holes in the loosely constructed nest through which they are seen cannot be distinguished from others through which the bright sky appears.

The whiteness of eggs hidden in holes or in covered nests, or buried under leaves, is of a very different nature, for it is due to the cessation of natural selection, perhaps aided by reversion to the ancestral colour, which is still preserved in the eggs of reptiles. All useful characters are kept up to a high pitch of efficiency by the continual elimination of the unfittest, and as soon as such elimination ceases, the level of efficiency must fall. This interpretation is confirmed by the fact that the eggs of certain species which now nest in the dark still retain traces of patterns which are well developed upon the eggs of their nearest allies with other habits. Thus the egg of the puffin, which nests in a burrow, would be called white at a little distance, but closer examination reveals the presence of very faint spots, which are distributed as in the very distinctly marked egg of the razor-bill.[1] Certain other species still lay strongly marked eggs in the dark, and in their case the change of habit presumably took place at a comparatively recent date. Such a conclusion can be tested by an investigation of the habits of closely allied species. Although white must have been the ancestral colour of birds' eggs, it has probably been re-acquired in species which nest in the dark. It would be very difficult to believe that such a habit has persisted continuously since the time when all birds' eggs were white.

The strongest confirmation of this explanation of the whiteness of hidden eggs is, however, to be found in the colours of the eggs in the various breeds of domestic fowls. If the gradual disappearance of colour is due to the cessation of natural selection, we must expect it to occur, however the cessation has been brought about. Natural selection cannot operate to preserve the colour of eggs laid in the dark, and it

[1] This interesting example attracted my attention while looking over a collection of eggs in the possession of my friend, Mr. E. H. Greenly. Mr. H. Seebohm informs me that he has no doubt about the validity of this interpretation, which was suggested in his work on *British Birds*, 1885, vol. iii. p. 367.

is equally inoperative when enemies are artificially excluded from eggs laid in open nests. And the eggs laid in our poultry-yards afford conclusive evidence that colour disappears as surely under the latter condition as under the former. The brown colour must be a very important protection to the eggs of the ancestor of our domestic breeds, the Asiatic jungle fowl (*Gallus bankiva*); while a white appearance would greatly add to the danger of discovery by egg-eating animals. But there is no such difference between the value of white and brown in confinement, and we accordingly find that the colour is disappearing. Certain fowls lay white eggs, and the tint of those which still lay coloured eggs varies considerably, 'the Cochins laying buff-coloured eggs, the Malays a paler variable buff, and Games a still paler buff. It would appear that dark-coloured eggs characterise the breeds which have lately come from the East, or are still closely allied to those now living there.'[1]

Erasmus Darwin further suggested that the colours of eggs, in common with other protective colours, may be due to the effect of the imagination of the female.[2] This suggestion has been still further elaborated by A. H. S. Lucas,[3] but no real proof of it is brought forward in his paper. That eggs resemble their sur-

---

[1] Darwin, *Variation of Animals and Plants under Domesti ation*, 1875, vol. i. p. 261.

[2] *Loc. cit.* p. 511.

[3] *Royal Society of Victoria*, 1887, pp. 52–60.

roundings is explicable by the operation of natural selection, while the gradual loss of colour when natural selection ceases to operate, is in opposition to Mr. Lucas's hypothesis, which assumes that the colour of the shell is determined by the influence of surrounding tints upon the retina of the female.   If the rusty spots on the eggs of birds of prey are due, as Mr. Lucas supposes, to the sight of blood, eggs laid in the dark should still be affected by the memory of some colour either predominant in the surroundings, or of especial interest to the female.   The hypothesis might easily have been tested by surrounding birds with unusual colours and observing the tints of their eggs : and, had this been done, I believe that the paper would not have been written.

Since the last paragraph was printed, a letter from the Rev. F. F. Grensted has been communicated to ' Nature ' by Mr. A. R. Wallace.[1]   The writer believes that the colour of the egg of the red-backed shrike varies with the tint of the lining material of the nest. Mr. E. B. Titchener maintains that there is not sufficient evidence for this opinion.   At one time Mr. Titchener believed that Variable Protective Resemblance was exhibited by the eggs of the yellowhammer and spotted fly-catcher as well as by those of the red-backed shrike.   Further observation convinced him that the evidence was insufficient.[2]

[1] *Nature*, vol. 41, Nov. 21, 1889, p. 53.
[2] *Ibid.*, Dec. 12, 1889, pp. 129–30.

The strongest argument used by Mr. Lucas is the fact that cuckoos at first sight appear to have the power of adjusting the colour of their eggs to those of the birds which are so successfully imposed upon. It seems to be certain, however, that the cuckoo carries her egg to the nest in her beak ; for there are numerous instances of the cuckoo's egg having been found in a nest which the bird itself could not possibly enter, and Mr. Lucas gives examples of the same kind from Australia. The cuckoo has therefore the chance of seeing the colour of her egg, and of carrying it to the appropriate nest. It is also possible that different individuals lay eggs of a different shade, and deposit them in the nests of species with eggs of a corresponding appearance. The whole relation of the cuckoo to the birds it deludes is most interesting, but very difficult to decide satisfactorily, because of the extreme shyness of the bird. I do not think, however, that the facts which are now at our disposal afford sufficient justification for the opinion that the female cuckoo can control the colour of her eggs.

I have discussed the colours of birds' eggs at some length in the hope that those readers who are interested in the subject may be induced to observe for themselves, and assist in obtaining a far more complete knowledge of the meaning of the colour and marking of eggs than we at present possess.

I know of no more inspiring subject than the colours of birds' eggs. The most superficial glance over a collection of eggs reveals hosts of interesting problems which require solution. I look forward to the time when any description of colour and marking will be considered incomplete unless supplemented by an account of their meaning and importance in the life of the species.

Protective Resemblances among Mammalia

Among the Mammalia it would be hardly possible to meet with a better example of protective colouring and attitude than that of the hare as it sits motionless, exactly resembling a lump of brown earth, for which indeed it is frequently mistaken. The dark brown or grey colours of all our smaller quadrupeds are also highly protective. The change of colour in northern mammals in the winter will be described in Chapter VII.

Protective Resemblances among Fish

The power of colour adjustment is very widely distributed among fish and Amphibia, and will receive attention in a later chapter. I will therefore only say a few words about the Protective Resemblance of the former.

Professor Stewart has shown me a beautiful example in the Australian Sea Horse (*Phyllopteryx eques*), a fish which is covered with numerous cutaneous appendages, most of which are supported by a bony core. The appendages are flat, and are alternately banded with dusky brown and orange, exactly resembling the form and colour of the sea-weed to which the fish clings with its tail.   There also are many bony spines without the flat folds of skin, and these are doubtless defensive.

The general arrangement of colour on porpoises, most fish, &c., has been well explained by Wallace.

Looking *down* on the dark back of a fish it is almost invisible, while, to an enemy looking *up* from below, the light under-surface would be equally invisible against the light of the clouds and sky.'[1]

The white colour of one side of such fish as the sole, turbot, &c. (*Pleuronectidæ*), viz. the side which is in contact with the sand or mud, cannot be explained in this way.   In such a case we see the disappearance of colour in consequence of the cessation of natural selection, as in the white eggs laid in the dark, while the white bellies of many fish may be compared to the whiteness of the eggs of the wood-pigeon, an appearance produced by the operation of natural selection.

It has been already pointed out that natural selection may not only remove the pigment from an animal, but may even replace the red blood of a vertebrate by a colourless fluid.   The transparency

---

[1] *Tropical Nature*, p. 171.

of the surface swimming fish, *Leptocephalus*, is increased in this way.[1]

Protective Resemblances among Marine Animals

Before leaving this part of the subject I must allude to Protective Resemblances among marine animals. Although large numbers of isolated cases are understood, the principles of colouring in marine forms have been very incompletely worked out. The difficulties are far greater than in land animals, because it is often nearly impossible to observe the species in their natural environment, and it has been already shown that this is essential if we are fully to understand the meaning of all details in their appearance and attitudes. It is, however, very satisfactory to know that the whole subject of the colouring of marine mollusca is being undertaken in a systematic manner by Mr. W. Garstang,[2] assisted by all the appliances of the laboratory of the Marine Biological Association at Plymouth.

Protective Resemblances among Marine Mollusca

E. S. Morse has shown, contrary to Darwin's opinion,[3] that the appearances of many mollusca are such as to afford concealment. An extremely

[1] E. Ray Lankester, ' On the Distribution of Hæmoglobin,' *Proc. Roy. Soc.* No. 140, 1873.

[2] *Journ. Mar. Biol. Assoc.*, New Series, vol. i. No. 2, Oct. 1839, pp. 173 *et seq.*

[3] *Descent of Man*, vol. i. p. 316.

interesting example was brought before me by Mr. Garstang, viz. that of the Opisthobranch mollusc, *Hermæa*, which is transparent and therefore invisible, except for the ' hepatic ' canals, which simulate in form and colour the reddish weed (*Griffithsia*) on which the animal usually lives. Mr. Garstang finds that the colour is purely adventitious, being due to the food undergoing digestion (see pp. 79, 80). Another English species of *Hermæa* is green, and lives on green weeds.

Mr. H. L. Osborn has published a very interesting note on the resemblance between the colour of a coral on the North American coast and the mollusc which habitually lives upon it.[1] He states that Dr. E. B. Wilson, working in 1879 in Dr. Brooks's laboratory at Beaufort, N.C., found an orange-yellow coral (*Leptogorgia virgulata*) invariably attended by a gastropod of the same colour (*Ovulum uniplicatum*), which was never seen apart from the coral. Dr. Wilson's coral occurred in shallow water. In 1884, Mr. Osborn, also working at Beaufort, found a *Leptogorgia* in ten fathoms of water, of the same general habit as *L. virgulata*, but of a deep rose colour, almost purple. The ground-colour was mottled with white round the openings of the polypes. A large number of molluscs were found on the coral, and these had red-brown shells, with the surrounding skin of a deep rose colour mottled with white. Except for this difference in colour the molluscs exactly resembled *O. uniplicatum*, and Mr. Osborn con-

[1] H. L. Osborn, *Science*, New York, 1885, vi. pp. 9–10.

siders that they were undoubtedly of the same species. When placed in an aquarium the molluscs always sought their own corals, but if red molluscs and yellow corals were put together the former took no notice of the latter.

It is very interesting to find that Mr. Garstang notices a similar association between species allied to the above at Plymouth. A reddish coral (*Gorgonia verrucosa*) is attended by a gastropod (*Ovula patula*), adapted in form and colour for concealment on the stems of the *Gorgonia*.

It might be argued that these are cases of Protective Mimicry, inasmuch as one animal resembles a portion of another for the purpose of protection. Similar examples are to be found in certain parasites which resemble the colour of the hair or skin of the animal they infest. Protective Mimicry, however, leads one animal to be mistaken for another, and thus to live upon the reputation of the latter. Protective Resemblance simply renders an animal difficult to detect. Animals defended in the former manner are almost invariably conspicuous; in the latter they are admirably concealed. Mr. Garstang tells me that *Gorgonia* is exempt from the attacks of fishes, so that the molluscs gain additional advantage by resembling an inedible form. Inasmuch as concealment appears to be the chief object of the form and colour, the example falls under Protective Resemblance, although it leads in the direction of true Mimicry.

CHAPTER VI

AGGRESSIVE RESEMBLANCES—ADVENTITIOUS PROTECTION

Aggressive Resemblances

PASSING now to Aggressive Resemblances, the appearance of the larger Carnivora harmonises well with their surroundings, enabling them to approach their prey. The colours of snakes, lizards, and frogs are doubtless Aggressive as well as Protective. Certain carnivorous insects, such as the *Mantidæ*, are well-concealed by their colour ; and this, although chiefly Protective, is probably also of value in enabling them to creep upon their prey. Aggressive, like Protective, colouring may be either Special or General.

Alluring Colouration

Special Aggressive Resemblance sometimes does more than hide an animal from its prey ; it may even attract the latter by simulating the appearance of some object which is of special interest or value to it. Such appearances have been called Alluring Colouration by Wallace, and they are some of the most interesting of all forms of Aggressive Resemblance.

An Asiatic lizard, *Phrynocephalus mystaceus*, is a good example.   Its general surface resembles the sand on which it is found, while the fold of skin at each angle of the mouth is of a red colour, and is produced into a flower-like shape exactly resembling a little red flower which grows in the sand.   Insects, attracted by what they believe to be flowers, approach the mouth of the lizard, and are of course captured. Professor C. Stewart kindly brought this instance before me, and showed me a specimen of the lizard in the Museum of the Royal College of Surgeons.

Similar examples are to be found among fishes. The Angler, or Fishing Frog (*Lophius piscatorius*), possesses a lure in shape of long slender filaments, the foremost and longest of which has a flattened and divided extremity.   The fish stirs up the mud so as to conceal itself, and waves these filaments about : small fish are attracted by the lure, mistaking it for worms writhing about in the muddy water ; they approach and are instantly engulphed in the enormous mouth of the Angler.   This interesting habit has been known since the days of Aristotle.   Certain deep-sea forms allied to *Lophius* behave in a similar manner, but as the depths of the sea are dark, they have a special ' phosphorescent organ, which probably illuminates the play of the tentacles which serve to allure other creatures.'   In some of these fish (certain species of *Ceratias*) the foremost tentacle bears a luminous organ which is suspended as a lure in front of the mouth.[1] The prey are attracted by the light into this convenient position for effecting their capture.

An Indian *Mantis* (*Hymenopus bicornis*) feeds upon other insects which it attracts by its flower-like

Fig. 17.—*Hymenopus bicornis* in active pupa stage.

shape and pink colour. The apparent petals are the flattened legs of the insect. The appearance of the *Mantis* in the active pupa stage is shown in fig. 17. The figure has been copied from a drawing sent by

[1] A. Günther, *Challenger Reports*, vol. xxii. p. 52, and Introduction, p. xxx. The function of the luminous organ was first suggested by Lütken.

Mr. Wood-Mason to Mr. Wallace, who kindly lent it to me.

Another beautiful example of Alluring Colouring was discovered by Mr. H. O. Forbes in Java. Butter-flies are often attracted by the excreta of birds, and a spider (*Ornithoscatoides decipiens*) takes advantage of this fact to secure its prey. The resemblance to a bird's dropping on a leaf is carried out with extraordinary detail. Such excreta consist of a ' central and denser portion, of a pure white chalk-like colour, streaked here and there with black, and surrounded by a thin border of the dried up more fluid part, which, as the leaf is rarely horizontal, often runs for a little way towards the margin ' and there evaporates, forming a rather thicker extremity. The margin is represented by a film-like web, with a thickened part to represent the fluid which has run to the edge or apex of the leaf ; the central mass is represented by the spider itself with white abdomen and black legs, lying on its back in the middle of the web, and held in position by the spines on its anterior legs which are thrust under the film.[1] The whole combination of habits, form, and colouring afford a wonderful example of what natural selection can accomplish. In such a case there is no necessity for calling in the aid of any other principle, for the addition of each new feature and the improvement of every detail would at once

[1] H. O. Forbes : *A Naturalist's Wanderings in the Eastern Archipelago*, pp. 63–65.

give an advantage to the possessor in the constant struggle for food.

Adventitious Protection

Before proceeding to describe the power of Variable Protective Resemblance possessed by many animals, it is necessary to point out that effects similar to those described above may be gained by means which supplement the acquisition of any special colour and form, or which may entirely replace these methods of producing concealment. Many animals cover themselves with objects which are prevalent in their surroundings and are of no interest to their enemies. Sometimes the meaning of this habit is concealment alone, but in other cases objects of great strength are selected and bound firmly together so as to form a resistant armour.

Many Lepidopterous larvæ live in cases made of the fragments of the substance upon which they live. The cases of the larvæ of Clothes Moths are only too well known; those of the *Psychidæ* are made of leaf or brown grass stems. The larva of the Essex Emerald Moth (*Geometra smaragdaria*) covers itself with a loose case made of fragments of leaves spun together with silk. The cocoons of Lepidoptera are frequently concealed by containing fragments of wood or bark gnawed off the surface on which the cocoon is constructed (*Cerura, Cilix, Hemerophila,* &c.). Birds' nests are often similarly concealed ; the lichen-covered nest of the chaffinch is an obvious instance. ˉ

The well-known cases of Caddice-worms (*Trichoptera*) are partly for concealment and partly for defence; they are built of grains of sand, small shells (often alive), vegetable fragments,—in fact, of any suitable objects which are abundant at the bottom of the stream in which they happen to be.

Some of the best examples are to be found among marine animals. Certain sea-urchins cover themselves so completely with pebbles, bits of rock, shell, &c., that one can see nothing but a little heap of stones.

Many marine mollusca have the same habits, accumulating sand upon the surface of the shell or allowing a dense growth of algæ to cover them.[1] The best example of the kind was shown me by Professor C. Stewart, and is all the more interesting because of the transition observed in the habits of different species of the same genus, *Xenophora*. Many of these gastropods include pieces of shell, rock, coral, &c., in the edge of the growing shell. The effect is probably to obscure the junction between the shell and the surface on which it rests, and thus to assist in rendering the organism difficult of detection. Thus the growth of the shell may be traced by a spiral line of included fragments (*X. calculifera*). In *X. solaris* the habit is only maintained during the early stages of growth,

[1] E. S. Morse: *Proc. Boston Soc. Nat. Hist,* vol, xiv, April 5, 1871, p. 7.

and the spiral line of fragments extends for a certain distance, and is then suddenly replaced by spines which are doubtless of value as a defence. In *X. cerea* and *X. solaroides* the size of the adventitious particles is so great as to nearly conceal the shell, while in *X. conchyliophora* nothing can be seen but a heap of fragments. Specimens of *Xenophora* and of the crabs mentioned below are to be seen in the Museum of the Royal College of Surgeons, as part of a beautiful series intended by Professor Stewart to illustrate the various uses of the colours of animals.

The tube of certain well-known marine worms (*Terebellidæ*) is constructed of sand-grains cemented together.

One of the most interesting examples of adventitious protection is afforded by certain crabs (*Stenorhynchus, Inachus, Pisa, Maia*), which fasten pieces of sea-weed, &c., on their bodies and limbs. Bateson has watched the process in *Stenorhynchus* and *Inachus*. ' The crab takes a piece of weed in his two chelæ, and, neither snatching nor biting it, deliberately tears it across, as a man tears paper with his hands. He then puts one end of it into his mouth, and, after chewing it up, presumably to soften it, takes it out in the chelæ and rubs it firmly on his head or legs until it is caught by the peculiar curved hairs which cover th m. If the piece of weed is not caught by the hairs, the crab puts it back in his mouth and chews it up again. The whole proceeding is most human and purposeful. Many substances, as hydroids, sponges, Polyzoa, and weeds of many kinds and colours, are thus used, but these various substances are nearly always symmetrically placed on corresponding parts of the body, and particularly long, plume-like pieces are fixed on the head, sticking up from it. . . . Not only are all these complicated processes gone through at night as well as by day, but a *Stenorhynchus* if cleaned and deprived of sight will *immediately* begin to clothe itself again, with the same care and precision as before.'[1] Bateson states that *Stenorhynchus* does not betray any disposition to remain in an environment which harmonizes with its dress.

Adventitious Colouring

The protective colouring of many animals may be due to the food in some part of the digestive tract, seen through the transparent body. This is important in many transparent caterpillars, such as the *Noctuæ*, and probably in many marine organisms. If a larva, such as that of the Angle-shades (*Phlogophora meticulosa*), be fed on the orange-coloured marginal florets of the marigold, the passage of food along the alimentary canal can be distinctly traced by the progressive change in the colour of the caterpillar.

The green colour of the blood of most larvæ is

[1] *Journ. Mar. Biol. Assoc.*, New Series, vol. i. No. 2, Oct. 1889, pp. 213-14.

adventitious in origin, having been derived from the chlorophyll of the leaves ; it is, however, much modi-fied in constitution by the time it reaches the blood. The green colouring matter passes from the blood into the cells of the surface of the body in many caterpillars, but is re-dissolved in the blood of the chrysalis. It is then made use of, in certain species, to tinge the eggs, and, after this, is absorbed into the body of the young larvæ which afterwards hatch from them, protecting them with a green colour before they have had time to acquire fresh chlorophyll from the leaves. The passage of an adventitious colouring matter on into a second generation is a very remark-able phenomenon. There does not, however, seem to be any doubt about its occurrence in certain species (e.g. *Smerinthus ocellatus*),[1] and I have a good deal of unpublished evidence on the subject.

[1] See 'Proceedings of Physiological Society,' pp. xxv and xxvi, in *Journal of Physiology*, vol. viii. 1887.

CHAPTER VII

VARIABLE PROTECTIVE RESEMBLANCE IN VERTEBRATA, ETC.

PROTECTIVE Resemblance in its highest and most perfect form must not be fixed, but capable of adjustment, so that the animal is brought into correspondence with each of the various tints which successively form its environment, as it moves about. An active and wide-ranging animal will be benefited by the power of resembling the tints of many different environments, and by that of changing its colour rapidly.

More sluggish animals only require the power of bringing their appearance into harmony with a single environment, although the capability of adjustment is still of great value, because the environments of the different individuals vary, at any rate to a slight extent. Thus a moth lays some of its eggs upon one tree of a certain shade of green, and others upon another with leaves of a rather different shade; so that the caterpillars would not have same environment, and would gain by possessing the power to adapt their colours. At the same time there would be no imperative necessity for the change to be extremely rapid.

In other cases it will be of advantage to the animal to possess the power of changing twice in its life, once for the peculiar surroundings of the caterpillar, and once for the peculiar surroundings of the chrysalis. There is indeed some ground for the belief that in certain cases the colours of the perfect insect also may be adjusted to correspond with the peculiar environment.

Variable Protective Resemblance in Fishes

Instances of the power of rapid adjustment are very common, although most people are not aware of them. Nearly all fishermen know that the trout caught in a stream with a gravelly or sandy bottom are light-coloured, while those caught in a muddy stream are dark. It is also well known that the same fish will soon change in colour when it passes from one kind of background to the other. Thus Mr. E. D. Y. Pode tells me that all the trout in a stream near Ivy Bridge have become unusually light ever since the pollution of the stream by white china clay.

The same facts are true of many other freshwater and sea fishes. The interior of a minnow-can is painted white in order that the bait may become light-coloured and thus conspicuous in the dark water where the pike or perch is likely to be found. The change of colour occupies an appreciable time, and the fisherman knows that he stands an extra chance of catching his fish while the bait remains unadapted to its environment.   This experience serves to prove in a practical way that the power of changing the colour is essentially protective.

Variable Protective Resemblance in Amphibia

Other animals possess the same power. The Common Frog (*Rana temporaria*) can change its tints to a considerable extent.   Thus Sir Joseph Lister states that ' a frog caught in a recess in a black rock was itself almost black ; but after it had been kept for about an hour on white flagstones in the sun, was found to be dusky yellow with dark spots here and there.   It was then placed again in the hollow of the rock, and in a quarter of an hour had resumed its former darkness.   These effects are independent of changes of temperature . . .' [1]   The Green Tree Frog (*Hyla arborea*), so common in the South of Europe, is bright green when seated among green leaves, but becomes dark-brown when resting on the earth or among brown leaves.   It is very interesting to notice that when this frog turns brown, irregular spots become conspicuous upon its skin, spots which evidently correspond to those upon the Common Frog (*Rana*), but which are invisible when the green tint is assumed.

[1] Lister : *Phil. Trans.*, 1858, vol. 148, p. 628.

Variable Protective Resemblance in Reptiles

The power of Variable Protective Resemblance is therefore present among fish and Amphibia, but the most remarkable and well-known example is afforded by a reptile, the Chamæleon. The rapidity with which the change of colour takes place, and the wide range of tints which the animal has at its command, have caused this lizard to be regarded as a type of everything changeable. But the same power is also present in certain of the South American lizards. belonging to the family *Iguanidæ*, and it is probable that Variable Protective Resemblance is much more common than has been generally supposed.

The changes of colour depend upon the eye

The physiological mechanism by means of which these rapid changes of colour are effected has been investigated by Lister in this country, by Brücke in Germany, and by Pouchet in France. At first sight it appears likely that the light may directly determine the distribution of colouring matter in the pigment cells in or immediately beneath the skin. Each of the various surroundings of an animal would, according to its colour, reflect light of a certain constitution, and it might well be supposed that each kind of reflected light would produce a different effect upon the pigment cells. It is, however, now well known that the action is extremely indirect; certain kinds of reflected light act as specific stimuli to the eye of the animal, and differing nervous impulses pass from this organ along the optic nerve to the brain. The brain being thus indirectly stimulated in a peculiar manner by various kinds of reflected light, originates different impulses, which pass from it along the nerves distributed to the skin, and cause varying states of concentration of the pigment in the cells. The highest powers of the microscope, assisted by all the varied methods of histology, have failed to detect the connection between the nerves and the pigment cells in the skin, and yet such connection appears to be rendered certain by the fact that light falling on the eye modifies the distribution of the pigment granules.

The pigment cells in the skin are often of various colours, and are arranged in layers, so that very different effects may be produced by concentration in certain cells, leading to the appearance of those of another colour, or to a combined effect due to the colours of two or more kinds of cells.

Blind animals cannot vary their colour protectively

It has been shown by experiment that blinded frogs have no power of altering their colour so as to correspond with surrounding tints. The same facts also have been proved in a most interesting manner by the observation of living animals in their natural surroundings. Thus Pouchet noticed that one single plaice out of a large number upon a light sandy surface was dark-coloured, and thus unlike its surroundings. Examination showed that this individual was blind, and therefore unable to respond to the stimulus of reflected light.[1]

Another very interesting example of the same kind was brought under my notice by my friend, Mr. H. Nicoll. This gentleman had observed that in addition to the light-coloured trout usually seen in a chalk stream in Hampshire (a tributary of the Test), very dark individuals are occasionally met with. He was puzzled for a long time, but the fact that the dark fish could never be induced to rise to a fly finally led him to examine them, when he found that they were invariably blind, the crystalline lens being opaque. Sometimes the fish were blind in one eye, but this did not affect their colour. The darkness appears to come on gradually with increasing blindness, for the depth of the tint varies in different individuals, and sometimes only part of the body (e.g. the tail) is affected. The blindness probably comes on with age, for the dark fish are always large, generally between one and two pounds in weight.

[1] Quoted by Semper, *Animal Life*, International Scientific Series, pp. 95-96.

The power of varying the colour essentially protective

The protective value of the change of colour in normal trout was especially well seen when contrasted with these blind individuals. As it has been sometimes asserted that protection is not the meaning of resemblance to the environment, I was anxious to observe so striking a contrast for myself. Mr. Nicoll kindly gave me the opportunity of seeing the fish in his stream, and I can in every way confirm his statement that a person unaccustomed to the observation of animals would certainly fail to detect any trout except the black ones. No one who had the opportunity of comparing the changing colours of the normal fish — ever harmonising with their surroundings,—with the unvarying conspicuous darkness of the blind individuals, could hesitate for a moment in admitting that concealment is the one object of the adjustment of colour.

The change of colour may also be voluntary or may follow from mental excitement. Thus the colours of fish often become much brighter while they are feeding.[1]

The food of blind trout

It may be objected that the dark fish still continue to live in the same stream with the more perfectly

[1] For a curious change of colour in the conger, see Bateson, *l.c.* pp. 214–15.

concealed individuals. This is sufficiently explained by the facts that the waters are carefully preserved, and that the blindness only comes on when the fish are large, and are therefore exposed to the attacks of comparatively few enemies.

Mr. Nicoll informed me that the black fish were usually in very poor condition, and I was very anxious to ascertain the kind of food which was still accessible to them. We therefore caught two fine specimens which were in fair condition. I opened them and found their stomachs quite full of caddice-worms, cases and all, together with a few fresh-water shrimps (*Gammarus*). These animals are doubtless hunted by scent and touch, while the insects on the surface of the water can only be obtained by sight.[1]

Loss of power of varying colour in a chamæleon before death

The changes which took place in a chamæleon in my possession probably show the dependence of the power of adjustment upon the state of the nervous system. In the summer, while the lizard was healthy and had an abundance and variety of insect food, it was dark-coloured by day, when it rested on some dark branches or walked about in its shaded cage. Placed upon a leafy branch in strong light it became

[1] Certain fish habitually seek their food by the olfactory and tactile senses. See Bateson, *l.c.* p. 214.

yellowish-green in a very short time, the change beginning in a few seconds. At night when it was asleep it became light and straw-coloured. In the winter it died, probably on account of the scarcity and monotony of the only insect diet which could be obtained for it. For many days before its death it became almost black and lost all power of changing its colour. Its weakened nervous system either ceased to respond to the influence of light, or was unable to produce any effect upon the pigment cells, which were thus paralysed, with their pigment permanently diffused. Green frogs also generally become dark before they die.

Explanation of darkness of blind animals

Some authorities have maintained that an animal of a kind which possesses the power of altering its colour should, when blind, become light- instead of dark-coloured. When the skin is light-coloured the pigment in the cells is strongly contracted, so that the coloured surface contributed by each cell occupies but a small space, and produces but little effect; when the skin is dark the coloured parts of the cells are relaxed, and stretch out into the long branching processes, so that each dark surface becomes as large as possible. The latter is evidently the condition of rest, while concentration is the state of activity. It is therefore to be expected that when the coloured parts of cells are cut off from all stimuli, they will be permanently relaxed, so that the skin will be dark; and we have seen that such a result actually occurs. When a muscle is cut off from nervous stimuli it also enters a condition of permanent rest or relaxation. Thus when the face is paralysed on one side, the muscles are relaxed and unable to balance the contraction of those on the other, so that the face is drawn over towards this latter side. The contractions of a muscle cell and those which take place in a pigment cell are not essentially different; the former are far more specialised and powerful, but both of them exhibit manifestations of that contractile power which is possessed by the simplest cells. It is therefore of interest that both should behave in a similar manner when cut off from the nervous system which provides the stimuli under which both normally contract. In 1858, Sir Joseph Lister showed that the coloured part of a pigment cell contracts independently of the cell itself. Cells are now recognised as composed of a network containing a glassy substance in its meshes; pigment granules are only contained in the network, and, as this contracts, it carries them inwards from the long branching processes towards the centre of the cell.

Loss of colour in cave-dwelling animals

On the other hand it has been argued that the *Proteus*, a blind amphibian living in the underground rivers of Carniola and Carinthia, is light-coloured,

and that other blind animals living in dark caverns
are often white.   In the majority of cases this result
is undoubtedly due to the gradual disappearance of
the useless pigment, and not to the excessive contraction of the structures in which it is usually contained.   Just as the useless eye has become rudimentary in these animals, so has the useless colour
gradually disappeared from the skin.   The energy
necessary for the production and maintenance of such
structures has been diverted, either wholly or in
part, to other and more useful ends.   In the *Proteus*,
however, the degeneration is as yet incomplete, for the
skin still retains pigment cells.   An individual now in
my possession has gradually become much darker since
its removal from the cave at Adelsberg.   It is probable
that this result has followed from the direct effect of
light upon the skin ; for it is known that superficial
pigment cells are sensitive to light, although the
changes of colour thus induced differ from those caused
indirectly through the nervous system, in the absence
of any harmony with the colours of the environment.
The skin of the *Proteus* is probably extremely sensitive
to light.   By day the animal in my laboratory always
lies concealed beneath a plate at the bottom of the
aquarium, while it comes out every night and swims
freely about.   As the eyes are very degenerate and
buried beneath the surface, it appears certain that the
difference between light and darkness is appreciated
by the skin.   W. Bateson has shown that blind

shrimps and prawns bury themselves in the sand by day and swim about at night, exactly like the uninjured animals.[1]

The seasonal change of colour in northern mammals

The well-known fact that many northern quadrupeds become white in winter has given rise to a great deal of discussion as to the manner in which the change is brought about.   Some have maintained that the animals simply acquire a new coat of white hair which conceals the darker fur beneath, while the long hairs of the summer coat are believed to be shed. Others believe that these latter actually change and become white, and that, although an abundance of new hairs also appear, nothing is shed.   Most observers agree that the white hair is shed at the close of winter : this is of course independently necessary, in order to reduce the thickness of the winter coat.

I shall bring forward what appears to be conclusive evidence that the latter view is the right one, at any rate for certain species.   But however the change is brought about, it will be rightly considered in this part of the subject, if it can be proved that it is called up either directly or indirectly by the stimulus provided by the external conditions, and is not merely a contemporaneous change, harmonising with those in

[1] *L.c.* p. 212.

the surroundings. The simplest view to take of the matter would be to suppose that natural selection has favoured an extra growth of hair of a white colour for the winter season, so that if an animal were transported to the equator, a similar change would take place at a corresponding time. If the change was thus merely contemporaneous and without any actual physiological relation to the surroundings, it would require discussion in the previous chapters, for it would be precisely parallel to the darkening of the larva of the Privet Hawk Moth, which takes place whether it will descend upon brown earth with which it will harmonise, or green turf against which it will be conspicuous (see pp. 42–43). It is possible that the change of certain purely Arctic animals is of this kind; but it must be remembered that many such animals range southward into districts where the white coat would be conspicuous in winter, so that the higher power of Variable Protective Resemblance would be very beneficial.

The question is, however, one of evidence, and I shall show that in certain species the change in colour is physiologically associated with the conditions, like the change in the colour of a fish which depends on the reflected light entering its eye. A discussion of the probable nature of the physiological association is better deferred until after considering the evidence.

Sudden change of colour determined by sudden exposure to extreme cold

A classical experiment made by Sir J. Ross, considerably over fifty years ago, seems decisive on the above-mentioned point, as far as the species experimented upon is concerned. A Hudson's Bay Lemming kept in the cabin, and thus shielded from the low temperature, retained its summer coat through the winter: 'It was accordingly placed on deck in a cage on February 1, and next morning, after having been exposed to a temperature of 30° below zero, the fur on the cheeks and a patch on each shoulder had become perfectly white. On the following day the patches on each shoulder had extended considerably, and the posterior part of the body and flanks had turned to a dirty white; during the next four days the change continued but slowly, and at the end of a week it was entirely white, with the exception of a dark band across the shoulders, prolonged posteriorly down the middle of the back. . . .' No further change took place, and the lemming died of the cold on February 18, the thermometer having been between 30° and 40° below zero every night. 'On examining the skin it appeared that all the white parts of the fur were longer than the unchanged portions, and that the ends of the fur only were white so far as they exceeded in length the dark-coloured fur; and by removing these white tips with a pair of scissors it again appeared in its dark summer dress, but slightly changed in colour, and precisely the same length as before the experiment.' [1]

This experiment conclusively proves,—(1) that the external condition itself provides the cause which brings the appropriate change in colour; for the animal did not change until subjected to the condition; [2] (2) that in all probability the cause is a lowered temperature acting upon the skin; (3) that the existing dark hairs become white at the tips; for we cannot well believe that a fresh growth could have overtopped the existing hair in a single night; (4) that the whitening hairs grow suddenly and rapidly.

Nature of the change of colour in the American Hare

The same conclusions are also supported by some extremely careful observations conducted by F. H. Welch upon the American Hare (*Lepus Americanus*) in New Brunswick.[3] In the latter district the animal keeps its winter coat till May, when it is gradually shed, the change being complete in June. The winter coat gradually develops in October and November, and

---

[1] Sir J. Ross: *Appendix to Second Voyage, Nat. Hist.* p. xiv. 1835.

[2] This conclusion is also supported by the fact that such changes occur earlier when the winter is exceptionally early. Concerning the Alpine Hare, see Tschudi, *Thierleben der Alpenwelt*, p. 300.

[3] *Proc. Zool. Soc.* 1869, p. 228.

is retained from December till the end of April. The appearance of the back and sides in summer is ' glistening fawn-colour interspersed with black, especially over the vertebral ridge.' The colour is conferred by long thick hairs (the pile) covering a woolly undergrowth of a slaty colour.

Early in October the first changes appear ; the whiskers become white at the tip or in some part of the shaft, and a few of the longer hairs on the back also become white at the tip or throughout. At this time there is no addition to the summer coat, only a change in the colour of existing hairs. The changes advance during November, and on separating the fur a new growth of stiff white hairs is seen over the sides and back : these grow rapidly, while the long hairs of the summer coat also grow and become white very quickly as soon as the new hairs appear on the surface. ' The shaft of the hair of the new growth is invariably white, a circumstance which renders it easily distinguished from the autumnal hair in process of change.' This change is most frequent at the tip, proceeding downwards, but it sometimes begins in the middle, and occasionally at the base. ' The whiskers, which apparently do not lengthen but merely alter in colour, will demonstrate each variety.

' Thus the winter hue would appear to be brought about by a change of colour in the pile of the autumnal coat, combined with a new hybernal white crop, the latter undoubtedly playing no small part in the colouring process and in the thickening of the fur. There is no indication of shedding : an increase in length ensues over the whole body.'

There is considerable individual difference in the time of change : it sometimes commences before the first fall of snow, indicating that the stimulus is the fall of temperature affecting the skin rather than the colour affecting the eyes.   Great differences are seen when the same species is followed into other localities. ' On the seaboard it (the winter change) is postponed in comparison with inland districts in the same latitudes.'   In Hudson's Bay Territory it changes early and carries the winter coat till June, while no change of colour takes place in the winter in the southern parts of the United States.   An individual kept in a warm barn at St. John's, New Brunswick, retained the summer colours.

The consideration of the Hudson's Bay Lemming and the American Hare lead to the conclusion that all species in which the northern change does not occur in the southern individuals, possess the power of Variable Resemblance.   It is possible that the change is merely contemporaneous when it occurs uniformly in *all* individuals of the species, and it is at any rate probable that it would soon become so, because the extreme complexity of the mechanism by which Variable Resemblance is brought about would need the constant operation of natural selection to keep it in a state of efficiency. This consideration is better deferred until after the probable nature of the mechanism has been discussed.

The physical cause of the change of colour

It is now necessary to inquire into the actual physical cause of the change in appearance. It has already been explained that the dark colour depends upon absorption, while the whiteness depends upon scattering of light. The former is occasioned by pigment granules, the latter by included gas bubbles. When the latter are sufficiently abundant, the hair becomes white in spite of the pigment; if then the gas were absorbed the dark colour would be restored.[1] It appears to be well authenticated that in certain cases patches of human hair have become white during some nervous attack, again becoming dark at its cessation. Such changes can be explained by the evolution of gas (probably carbon di-oxide) at the base of the hair, and its subsequent absorption (probably by some alkaline fluid). It is therefore probable that the nervous system can so modify the processes taking place in the cells at the base of the hair as to cause

[1] This explanation only applies to the existing dark hairs which become white. It is very improbable that any pigment exists in the new hairs which make up the great part of the winter coat. Hence, in testing the explanation offered above, the hairs must be selected with the greatest care, and the investigation should be conducted in connection with an experiment like that of Sir J. Ross (see pp. 94–95).

the formation of gas bubbles. The many recorded cases of hair turning white in a few hours as the result of some strong nervous shock are to be explained in the same manner.

That the change in the long autumnal hairs of *Lepus Americanus* is due to the appearance of large numbers of bubbles is rendered probable by an examination of Welch's figures and descriptions. He speaks of the white part of a hair being much broader than the coloured part, and containing additional rows of 'cells.' His 'cells' appear to be bubbles of gas, and he draws them with the characteristic dark borders. It must be remembered that the dark parts of a hair also contain bubbles, although in smaller amount.

The change in the hair is indirectly caused by the change of temperature

It is extremely improbable (to say the least) that such changes as the evolution of bubbles, and above all, the growth in length, are the *direct* result of a lowered temperature on the hair itself. That they are *indirect* results, through the nervous system, is in every way probable, and is furthermore in harmony with certain well-known facts concerning the regulation of temperature.

The *direct* tendency of cold is clearly to diminish the activity of those processes upon which the production of heat depends, just as it would tend to diminish rather than promote the growth of hair. This *direct* effect is obvious in animals which are un-injured by variations of temperature. 'The body of a cold-blooded animal behaves in this respect like a mixture of dead substances in a chemist's retort: heat promotes and cold retards chemical action in both cases.' But the higher vertebrates are warm-blooded (homothermic), and such direct effects of cold would be fatal. 'In these animals there is obviously a mechanism of some kind counteracting, and indeed overcoming, those more direct effects which alone obtain in cold-blooded animals.' The influence of cold upon the nerves of the skin constitutes a stimulus to that part of the central nervous system which regulates the production of heat: thus cold *indirectly* increases the amount of heat, and the temperature of the body remains constant. I may mention that the amount of heat produced in the body at any one time may be gauged by the amount of oxygen ab-sorbed in respiration.[1]

It is in every way probable that such changes in colour as that of Sir J. Ross' Lemming and the American Hare are also *indirectly* caused by the cold, which we may suppose acts as a stimulus to that part

[1] For a further account of the regulation of temperature see Professor Michael Foster's *Physiology*, from which the quoted sentences are taken. I owe the correct understanding of the physical cause of the change of colour to a conversation with Professor Foster.

of the nervous system which presides over the nutritive and chemical changes involved in the growth of hair and the appearance of the bubbles.

Probable variation in susceptibility to stimulus of cold in different districts

In the northern part of an animal's range, natural selection would favour great delicacy in the adjustment of the mechanism by which such changes are produced, so that the winter coat would be ready in time to harmonise with the mantle of snow. Conversely, extreme delicacy would be a disadvantage in the southern part of the range, if the climate were such that the snow did not lie on the ground for any great part of the winter. There is abundant evidence of variations in the delicacy of adjustment, upon which natural selection could operate.

Mr. F. E. Beddard has directed my attention to three Arctic Foxes (*Canis lagopus*) from Iceland, which have been in the Zoological Gardens since 1887. One [1] of these turns perfectly white every winter, while the other two remain dark.

The stoat always becomes white in the alpine districts of Scotland, frequently in the north of Eng-

[1] When I examined this fox on October 14, 1889, the change in colour was nearly complete : there was, however, a grey patch of hair on the back which was certainly moulting. It is possible, therefore, that the change is effected in an entirely different manner in this species.

6

land, occasionally in the Midlands, and Mr. Couch
has seen two white stoats in Cornwall.[1] It would be
extremely interesting to take a number of Scotch
stoats to Cornwall and an equal number of Cornish
stoats to Scotland, in order to test whether the
southern individuals are less susceptible to change
than the northern. It is likely that the great difference is not wholly to be explained by the relation of
northern to southern temperature, but at any rate
partially by the fact that the change is disadvantageous
in most parts of England ; for it would render the
animal conspicuous against the prevalent tints of a
midland or southern winter. Of course, any such
disadvantage implies that natural selection would
gradually blunt the susceptibility of the apparatus by
which the change is produced. The rare cases of
a change of colour in Cornwall are probably examples
of a formerly beneficial susceptibility, as yet unaltered
by natural selection.

Loss of susceptibility to stimulus of cold in animals which remain white all the year

Such a nervous mechanism as that to which I have
alluded, would be of the highest intricacy and complexity, and would speedily lose its efficiency unless
constantly preserved by natural selection. Thus
certain Arctic animals which remain on the snow

[1] Bell : *British Quadrupeds*, second edition, pp. 196–201.

nearly all the year retain the white coat permanently, and there is no need for the mechanism by which the change is produced.   And yet in certain species we may feel sure that such a mechanism existed under former conditions.   Thus the Arctic Hare (*Lepus glacialis*) usually remains white all the summer; occasionally, however, it becomes greyish, the change of colour being limited to the points of the hair: the young are born grey, but change to white at their first winter (Welch).   The latter change appears to be independent of cold, for Sir J. Ross speaks of a young hare turning white as early as those running wild, although in a temperature not much below freezing.   This observation forms an interesting contrast with the behaviour of species possessing an efficient nervous mechanism (the Hudson's Bay Lemming and the American Hare) when shielded from a low temperature.

The white winter coat chiefly for concealment, but may also help to retain heat

Certain northern animals, especially those frequenting trees, do not become white in winter: this is true of the Glutton (*Gulo luscus*).   Occasionally dark winter individuals occur in species which as a rule change their colour regularly: thus, a black Arctic Fox is well known, but its rarity (Sir J. Ross found three individuals out of fifty white ones) probably indicates that it is, as we should expect, at a disadvantage, and that it will disappear. Mr. Wallace considers that the dark colour of arboreal northern animals, which is clearly for concealment, disproves the theory that the white colour is of value in retaining animal heat. But it does not follow that such benefits are wholly non-existent, because they must be dispensed with under the pressure of a stronger necessity. Mr. Wallace's argument shows that concealment is the paramount necessity; but this does not disprove the opinion that other advantages also may be conferred by one particular mode in which concealment is attained.

The seasonal change of colour in northern birds

The same convincing evidence as to the nature of the change, and the manner in which it is brought about, has not yet been brought forward in the case of birds. Mr. A. H. Cocks, who has had a very wide experience of northern animals, believes that it is at least partially due to a change in the autumnal feathers. He writes: 'I have some specimens of *Lagopus* (various species) showing brown feathers with white tips, and in one species, at any rate, the converse.' Mr. R. Bowdler Sharpe does not however think that the evidence of a winter change in existing feathers is sufficient.[1] He has nevertheless proved

[1] H. Seebohm thinks it 'possible that the white winter feathers

that other changes of colour do occur, as will be seen in the following passage from his most interesting paper.[1]

'Let any one who doubts the possibility of markings such as those on the Greenland Falcon becoming gradually changed without an intermediate moult, study the changes exhibited by the common Sparrow Hawk in its progress towards maturity.   The general characteristic of the species of *Accipiter* is to have a

   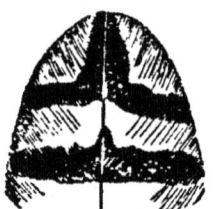

FIG. 18.   FIG. 19

striped plumage when young and a barred dress when old.   But it is not generally known that this is effected by a gradual change in the markings of the feather, and not by an actual moult.   On the first appearance of the feathers from the downy covering of the nestling, the markings on the chest are longitudinal drops (fig. 18) of a pale rufous-brown colour. The gradual dissolution and breaking up into three bars is shown in fig. 19.   Hence, when the bars are perfectly developed a shade of darker brown over-

(of Ptarmigan) gradually change colour in spring, only those being moulted which have been injured in winter.'—*British Birds*, vol. ii. p. 427, *n.*
[1] *Proc. Zool. Soc.* 1873, pp. 414 *et seq.*

spreads the upper margin, gradually eclipsing the rufous-brown shade, which remains the evidence of the previous plumage (fig. 20). Hence are shown two successive stages of the development of the dark brown shade which at last removes all traces of the reddish tint (figs. 21 and 22).'

If the winter change does not occur in the autumnal feathers, it by no means follows that the power of Variable Resemblance is absent. The growth of new white feathers may be indirectly due

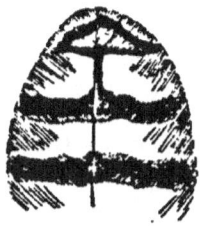 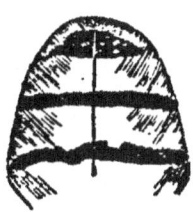 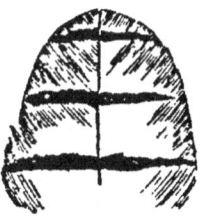

FIG. 20.   FIG. 21.   FIG. 22.

to the cold, acting through the medium of the nervous system. This is, however, very far from being proved ; for it does not appear to be certain that there is a single species becoming white in winter which retains its dark colour at this time of the year in the southernmost part of its range.

Mr. A. C. Billups, of Niagara, Ontario, tells me that during an exceptionally mild winter, about seven or eight years ago, neither the ' snow bird ' nor the American Hare acquired the winter dress. Hence the power of Variable Resemblance appears to be possessed by certain birds.

Variable Resemblance of northern animals most nearly related to that of certain insects

The acquisition of a special winter covering as a response to the stimulus of cold is most nearly related to the Variable Resemblance exhibited by many caterpillars and chrysalides. It will be shown in the next chapter that these latter changes are similar to the above in that the stimulus (of reflected light) acts upon the skin ; that the results are in all probability indirect, and take place through the part of the nervous system which regulates the production of colour ; finally, that far greater time is required for the accomplishment of the change than in those animals in which the stimulus acts upon the eye, and in which existing pigments are arranged instead of new substances elaborated.

Rapid adjustment of Colour in certain invertebrate animals

Certain invertebrate animals, however, possess the power of rapidly adjusting their colour to that of their surroundings. It is well-known in Crustacea, and is probably very common among them. The power has been proved to depend upon the eye as among the vertebrates. Some cuttle-fish also can modify their colours in the same manner, with remarkable precision and rapidity. The resemblance between certain individuals of *Ovulum* and the rose-coloured coral, and between other individuals and the yellow coral (see pp. 70–71), is probably due to the existence of a power of adjustment; but this suggestion needs experimental verification. A fact mentioned by Morse is even more convincing : he states that individuals of the same molluscan species occupying different stations are differently coloured, and he quotes from Dr. A. A. Gould the observation that the colour of all the shells found in the sandy harbour of Provincetown is remarkably light.[1] There is no evidence as to whether the change in colour, if produced at all, takes place rapidly or slowly ; but the latter is the more probable in these animals.

Professor Stewart found four or five bright red individuals of the Nudibranchiate mollusc *Archidoris tuberculata* in a mass of bright red sponge (*Hymeniacidon sanguinea*) upon which they were feeding.[2] The colour was very different from that of individuals taken upon another sponge (*Halichondria*). The observation strongly suggests the existence of a power of Variable Protective Resemblance, although it is possible that the colour of the food may be made use of.

It is very likely that Variable Resemblance will be found to occur far more generally than has been hitherto supposed.

---

[1] *Proc. Boston Soc. Nat. Hist.* vol. xiv. April 5, 1871.
[2] W. Garstang, *l.c.* p. 177.

Variable Resemblance, Protective and Aggressive

As in so many other cases, the specialised form of concealment by the organism resembling its surroundings treated of in this chapter may be either Protective or Aggressive; it may enable an animal to escape its enemies or to approach its prey unseen. Frequently it may be turned to both uses by a single animal. Thus the green tree frog is probably aided in capturing the insects on which it feeds because of its close resemblance to the leaves around it; but it is also protected in the same manner from the animals which prey upon it. Thus Mr. E. A. Minchin tells me, from his experience in India, that tree frogs are sought for with especial eagerness by snakes, which greatly prefer them to others. It is probable that this power when possessed by a vertebrate animal nearly always bears a double meaning, although a consideration of the different instances will show that it is especially Protective in some and especially Aggressive in others. In the next chapter we shall meet with a large number of cases briefly alluded to at the beginning of this chapter, in which the power is in many respects different, and possesses an entirely Protective meaning.

CHAPTER VIII

VARIABLE PROTECTIVE RESEMBLANCE IN INSECTS

No insect is known to possess the power of rapidly adjusting its colour to the tints of its surroundings, and it has not long been known that any power of adjustment exists. There is still a great deal to be done in finding out the extent to which the power is present, and in further investigating the physiological processes which are involved in its operation. Up to the present time the Lepidoptera (butterflies and moths) alone have been made the subjects of inquiry, and we know nothing of other insects in this respect.

Many caterpillars and chrysalides have been proved to be capable of adjusting their colours to those of the surroundings, and it is also known that certain caterpillars can construct cocoons of different colours, so as to harmonise with the environment. The latter extremely interesting example of Variable Protective Resemblance has been very insufficiently investigated. It is also probable that a relatively small number of perfect insects possess the same power; but in this case no experimental researches have been conducted. I will first consider the chrysalides, because they were first found to possess the power, and because it has been more completely investigated in them than in the other cases.

Variable Protective Resemolance in Lepidopterous Pupæ.

The capability of adjusting the colour to that of the surroundings is only present in exposed chrysalides, and has not been found hitherto among the pupæ of Heterocera (or moths), nearly all of which are either buried in the earth or concealed in opaque cocoons. In both cases the chrysalides are generally reddish-brown in colour, the shade varying greatly in different species. The dark colour is of pro-

FIG. 23.—The pupa of Swallow-tailed Moth, showing colour assumed when the larva has been placed on white paper before pupation.

FIG. 24.—The pupa of Swallow-tailed Moth (*Uropteryx sambucata*); the usual dark colour assumed in cocoon; natural size.

tective value when the chrysalis is accidentally exposed upon the surface of the earth.

Since this last paragraph was written, I have found that the chrysalis of the Swallow-tailed Moth

(*Uropteryx sambucata*) becomes light-coloured when the caterpillar has been placed upon white paper shortly before pupation (see fig. 23). The chrysalis is usually dark (see fig. 24), and is contained in a cocoon which is formed of the brown fragments of leaves or twigs spun together with threads of silk. The cocoon, which is suspended from the food-plant and swings freely, is so loose and open in texture that the enclosed pupa is easily seen, and is in fact as exposed as that of many butterflies.

The chrysalides of butterflies are generally freely exposed, and many species have been proved to possess the power of adjusting the pupal colour to that of the adjacent surface. Such pupæ are often suspended head downwards from a boss of silk, to which the hooks at the posterior end are affixed; or they are frequently attached horizontally, or in a vertical position with the head upwards, by similar posterior hooks and a strong silken girdle, which is fixed on either side to the supporting surface, and which sinks into a groove across the back of the pupa. The group which includes the Tortoiseshell and Peacock Butterflies adopts the former mode of suspension; that to which the 'Garden Whites' belong adopts the latter.

The History of the Discovery of Variable Protective Resemblance in the pupæ of Butterflies

In 1867 Mr. T. W. Wood exhibited to the Entomological Society of London [1] a number of chrysalides of the Swallow-tailed Butterfly (*Papilio machaon*), and of the large and small Garden White Butterflies (*Pieris brassicæ* and *P. rapæ*), which corresponded in colour to the surfaces to which they were attached. Dark pupæ had been found on tarred fences and in subdued light; light ones on light surfaces; while green leaves were shown to produce green chrysalides, at any rate in certain cases. Mr. Wood's inclusion of the chrysalis of the Swallow-tail, with which he states that he was imperfectly acquainted, was most unfortunate, and doubtless prevented his suggestive paper from gaining the success it deserved. It is quite true that this chrysalis appears in two forms, being sometimes green and sometimes dark grey; but, without sufficient evidence, it was unwise, although most natural, to assume that these colours could be adjusted to green or dark surroundings respectively. I have since tested the chrysalis, and as far as my experiments (which were with small numbers) are conclusive, they show that it has no power of adjustment.[2] In the discussion which followed Mr. Wood's paper, Mr. Bond stated that 'he

[1] *Proc. Ent. Soc.* 1867, pp. xcix.–ci.
[2] *Phil. Trans* vol. 178 (1887), B. p. 406–408.

had had thousands of pupæ of *Papilio machaon*, and had often had the brown variety of pupa on a green ground colour, whilst in some seasons he had obtained no brown specimens at all.'

In spite of this unfortunate mistake, Mr. Wood adduced quite sufficient evidence concerning the Garden Whites to show that the subject was worth investigation. But the great example and the great principles of Darwin had not penetrated far into the mass of naturalists; and distinguished entomologists preferred the expression of an adverse opinion, to making an easy experiment upon one of our commonest insects.

Mr. Wood also stated that the chrysalis of the Large Tortoiseshell Butterfly (*Vanessa polychloros*) was coloured like a withered elm-leaf, when suspended among the foliage of the elm on which its caterpillar feeds. Its colour was then light reddish-brown with a cluster of metallic silvery spots, but when suspended from a wall, the metallic spots were not produced, and the pupa was of a mottled greyish colour. This observation led Mr. Wood to conclude 'that by the proper use of gilded surfaces the gilded chrysalides of *Vanessa*, and perhaps of other genera, would be obtained'; and he added, 'I hope to be able to try the experiment next season.' If this intention had been carried out, such startling results would have been obtained that opposition would have broken down before them, and the combined researches of many naturalists would have been brought to bear upon the subject. The experiment, however, was not made till nineteen years later, when I was led to do as Mr. Wood had proposed, although unaware at the time of his suggestion.

Nevertheless, during these nineteen years, gradual confirmation of Mr. Wood's central position was afforded. In 1873 Professor Meldola supported the observations upon the chrysalides of the 'Garden Whites.' He compared large numbers of individuals, and found that the pupæ upon black fences were darker than those upon walls.[1]

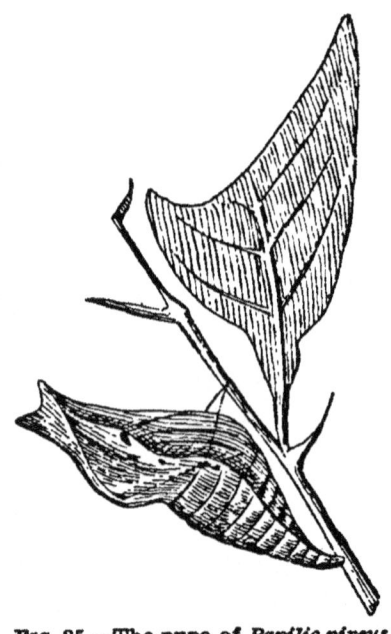

In 1874 a paper by Mrs. M. E. Barber, and communicated by Mr. Darwin to the Entomological Society of London, was printed in the Transactions of that society.[2] Mrs. Barber had experimented with a common South African Swallow-tailed Butterfly (*Papilio nireus*), and had found the chrysalis wonderfully sensitive to the colours of its environment. When the pupæ were attached among the deep green leaves of

FIG. 25.—The pupa of *Papilio nireus* attached to orange tree; natural size.

[1] *Zool. Soc. Proc.* 1873, p. 153.   [2] 1874, p. 519.

the food-plant, Orange, they were of a similar colour
(see fig. 25); when fixed to dead branches covered
with withered, pale yellowish-green leaves, they resembled the latter (see fig. 26).   One of the caterpillars 'affixed itself to the wooden frame of the case,

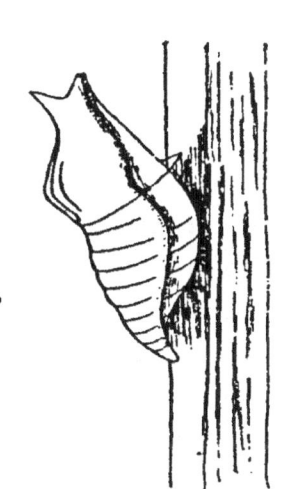

FIG. 26.—The pupa of *Papilio nireus*
attached to plant (*Vepris lanceo-
lata*) with withered yellowish-green
leaves.

FIG. 27.—The pupa of *Papilio nireus*
attached to woodwork.

and then became a yellowish pupa of the same colour
as the wooden frame' (see fig. 27).   The case was
made partly of purplish-brown brick and partly of
wood, and one of the pupæ, attached close to the
junction, was believed by Mrs. Barber to have assumed

both colours, that of the brick upon its back and that of the wood upon its under surface. My experiments upon the chrysalis of the Small Tortoiseshell Butterfly, to be described below, do not support this conclusion, and it is a common thing for the colours of pupæ to differ greatly in the dorsal and ventral regions. Mrs. Barber also tried the effect of scarlet cloth, but little if any influence was exerted.

Mr. Mansel Weale also showed that the colour of certain other South African pupæ can be modified,[1] and Mr. Roland Trimen made some experiments upon another African Swallow-tail[2] (*Papilio demoleus*, common at Cape Town), confirmatory of Mrs. Barber's observations. He covered the sides of the cage with bands of many colours, and found that green, yellow, and reddish-brown tints were resembled by the pupæ, while black made them rather darker. Bright red and blue had no effect. The larvæ did not exercise any choice, but fixed themselves indiscriminately to colours which their pupæ could resemble and those which they could not. In the natural condition the latter would not exist, for the pupæ can imitate all the colours of their normal environments.

Finally, Fritz Müller experimented upon a South American Swallow-tail (*Papilio polydamus*),[3] and found

---

[1] *Trans. Ent. Soc. Lond.* 1877, pp. 271, 275.
[2] Described in a letter to me, published in my paper already referred to, p. 316.
[3] *Kosmos*, vol. 12, p. 448.

that its pupæ, although appearing in two forms, dark and green, like those of our own Swallow-tail, also resemble the latter in having no power of adjusting their colours to the surroundings.

Theories as to the manner in which the colours of such pupæ are determined

These observations and experiments had been made when I began to work at the subject in 1886: they appeared to prove that the power certainly exists, but nothing was really known as to the manner in which the adjustment is effected. Mr. T. W. Wood's original suggestion, that 'the skin of the pupa is photographically sensitive for a few hours only after the caterpillar's skin has been shed,' was accepted by most of those who had worked at the subject. And yet the suggestion rested upon no shadow of proof; it depended upon a tempting but overstrained analogy to the darkening of the sensitive photographic plate under the action of light. But the analogy was unreal, for, as Professor Meldola stated in the discussion which followed Mrs. Barber's paper, 'the action of light upon the sensitive skin of a pupa has no analogy with its action on any known photographic chemical. No known substance retains permanently the colour reflected on it by adjacent objects.' The supposed 'photographic sensitiveness' of chrysalides was one of those deceptively feasible suggestions which are not tested because of their apparent probability. It would have been very easy to transfer a freshly formed pupa from one colour to another which is known to produce an opposite effect upon it; and yet if this simple experiment had been made the theory would have collapsed, for the pupa would have been found to resemble the first colour and not the second. Furthermore, Mr. Wood's suggestion raised the difficulty that chrysalides which had become exposed in the course of a dark night would have no opportunity of resembling the surrounding surfaces, for the pupal colours deepen very quickly into their permanent condition. In working at the subject I determined to pay especial attention to such questions.

Experiments upon the chrysalis of the Peacock Butterfly

I began work with the common Peacock Butterfly (*Vanessa Io*), of which the chrysalis appears in two forms, being commonly dark grey (see fig. 28), but more rarely, bright yellowish-green (see fig. 29) : both forms are gilded, especially the latter. The gilding cannot be represented in the woodcuts. Only six caterpillars could be obtained, and these were placed in glass cylinders surrounded by yellowish-green tissue paper. Five of them became chrysalides of the corresponding colour; the sixth was removed immediately after the caterpillar skin had been thrown off, and was placed in a dark box lined with black paper, but it subsequently deepened into a green

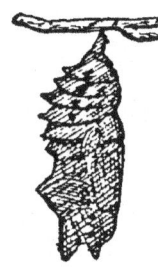
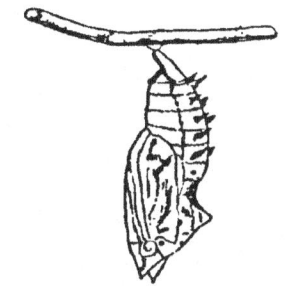

FIG. 28.—The pupa of Peacock Butterfly ; dark form ; natural size.

FIG. 29.—The pupa of Peacock Butterfly ; light yellowish-green form.

pupa exactly like the others. Obviously the surroundings had exercised their influence before the pupa was removed.

Experiments upon the chrysalis of the Small Tortoise-shell Butterfly

Being unable to obtain more larvæ of the Peacock, I worked upon the allied Small Tortoiseshell Butterfly (*Vanessa urticæ*), which can be obtained in immense numbers. In the experiments conducted in 1886, over 700 chrysalides of this species were obtained and their colours recorded. Green surroundings were first employed in the hope that a green form of pupa, unknown in the natural state, might be obtained. The results were, however, highly irregular, and there seemed to be no susceptibility to the colour. The pupæ were, however, somewhat darker than usual, and this result suggested a trial of black surroundings, from which the strongest effects were at once witnessed: the pupæ were as a rule extremely dark, with only the smallest trace, and often no trace at all, of the golden spots which are so conspicuous in the lighter forms. These results suggested the use of white surroundings, which appeared likely to produce the most opposite effects. The colours of nearly 150 chrysalides obtained under such conditions were very surprising. Not only was the black colouring matter as a rule absent, so that the pupæ were light-coloured, but there was often an immense development of the golden spots, so that in many cases the whole surface of the pupæ glittered with an apparent metallic lustre. So remarkable was the appearance that a physicist, to whom I showed the chrysalides, suggested that I had played him a trick and had covered them with gold-leaf.

These remarkable results led to the use of a gilt background as even more likely to produce and intensify the glittering appearance. By this reasoning I was led to make the experiment which had been suggested by Mr. Wood nineteen years before. The results quite justified the reasoning, for a much higher percentage of gilded chrysalides, and still more remarkable individual instances, were obtained among the pupæ which were treated in this way.

The following table shows the results of some experiments in which the above-mentioned colours were employed :—

Degrees of colour	(1) The darkest forms; no gilding or only a trace	(2) Less dark, but still very dark; little gilding	Dark (3) Dark normal forms; sometimes gilded	(3) Normal forms, less dark, and with more gilding	Light (3) Light normal forms, often with considerable amount of gilding	(4) Very light; often extremely golden; sometimes light pink	(5) The lightest; often golden all over	Totals
Green surroundings	2	8	—	25	—	1	3	= 3
Black „	11	29	27	22	14	2	—	= 105
White „	—	7	21	37	44	25	11	= 145
Gilt „	—	1	2	7	16	27	14	= 67
								356

In order to realise these results it must be remembered that the appearance represented by (4) or (5) is *very rarely* seen in nature, except when the pupa is diseased. By far the commonest varieties met with are those represented by (3), which are therefore called normal forms.

Special advantages of the Small Tortoiseshell for purposes of experiment

From the results expressed in the tabular form given above, it was clear that this species was very susceptible to surrounding colours, and that black and gold produced the most opposite effects. Another advantage in the use of this species is the fact that the caterpillars live in companies, each of which develops from the eggs laid by a single butterfly. Hence by keeping the companies separate, the varying hereditary tendencies, due to different parentage, are eliminated ; for a company of moderate size would contain over one hundred larvæ, and would therefore furnish the material for several experiments. Considering also the abundance of the species, I determined to employ it for the investigation of the process by which the change of colour is effected.

The pupæ darker when crowded together

Very early in the investigation a possible source of error was detected. It seemed probable, when many individuals were collected together at the susceptible period, which will be shown to occur towards the end of larval life, that each of them would be affected by that part of the surroundings which was constituted by the black skins of its neighbours. It was therefore necessary to take into account the relative positions of the pupæ, and, in the most careful experiments, to place only a single individual in each coloured case. Experiment soon showed that these precautions were necessary. Many of the darker pupæ, shown in the table to be produced by white and gilt surroundings, were proved to have been influenced by mutual proximity, so that the results would have been even more striking if this source of error had been allowed for.

The period during which the colours of pupæ are determined

A very large number of experiments and the closest and most frequent observations were devoted to the determination of the time during which these organisms are sensitive to surrounding colours. It was first necessary to observe everything that happens to a caterpillar between the cessation of feeding and the change into a chrysalis, for I felt sure that the time of susceptibility lay somewhere within these limits. When one of these caterpillars is full-fed, it descends from its food-plant (nettle) and wanders about in search of some suitable surface upon which to pass the pupal period. This is stage i., and its length varies greatly, according to the proximity of suitable surfaces. Then the caterpillar, having found the surface, rests motionless upon it, generally in a somewhat curved position. This is stage ii., and it is also variable in length, but fifteen hours may be accepted as a fair average of the time spent in this position. Finally the caterpillar hangs, head downwards, suspended by its last pair of claspers (larval legs), which are attached to a boss of silk spun at the close of the second stage. This is stage iii., which lasts for about eighteen hours, at the end of which time the skin splits along the back behind the head, and the chrysalis is exposed by the skin being worked up towards the boss of silk. Then the tail of the chrysalis is withdrawn from the interior of the skin and is forced up the outside of the latter, until it comes in contact with the boss of silk. Contact immediately causes some of the numerous hooks on the end of the chrysalis to be entangled in the silk. During this apparently perilous operation the chrysalis is suspended to the larval skin, although different opinions obtain as to the exact method of its attachment. The sight is extremely interesting and beautiful, and the operation is almost always performed with precision and success. As soon as the pupa is firmly attached to the silk, it endeavours, by the most violent movements, to get rid of the skin, and generally succeeds in detaching it.

Exact determination of the period of susceptibility

The whole of the period before pupation, including the three stages, may be estimated at about thirty-six hours. Even if the caterpillars were susceptible during stage i., no effective results could be obtained; for they are then wandering over surfaces of various colours, of which few can be the same as that which will form the environment of the chrysalis. Many experiments were conducted with the object of ascertaining the exact period of susceptibility. Larvæ were exposed to one colour during stages i. and ii., and then transferred to another colour for stage iii.,

7

while other larvæ were exposed to each of the colours
for all three stages : the effects were then compared.
The results of the largest experiment of the kind are
given below :—

Degrees of colour (as before)	(1)	(2)	Dark (3)	(3)	Light (3)	(4)	(5)	Totals
In black surroundings for all three stages . . .	—	1	—	5	—	1	—	= 7
Transferred from black into gilt for stage iii. . .	—	—	—	1	5	3	—	= 9
Transferred from gilt into black for stage iii. . .	—	—	—	—	6	9	—	= 15
In gilt surroundings for all three stages . . .	—	—	—	—	5	7	8	= 20
								51

This analysis speaks for itself.   Stages ii. and iii. are
both sensitive, but stage iii. is much less sensitive
than the other.   This is proved by the fact that the
larvæ which had been exposed to gilt surroundings
during stage ii. and to black afterwards, were lighter
thrn those which had been exposed to black during
stage ii. and to gilt afterwards.   In other words, the
coloured surroundings, both gilt and black, produced
more effect during stage ii. than iii. ; but both stages
are sensitive, because the black and gilt surroundings
produced still greater effects when they operated for
the whole period before pupation.   It must be observed that the caterpillars, in the experiment summarised above, tended as a whole to produce the
lighter forms of chrysalides, so that the black did

not cause nearly such strong effects as the gilt surroundings. The tendency was evidently hereditary
and shared by all the caterpillars of the company, so
that we have a striking example of the errors which
were eliminated by keeping the companies separate.

It is almost unnecessary to point out how completely the old theory of ' photographically sensitive '
chrysalides is broken down by these experiments.
Not only is the adjustment of the pupal colours to
their surroundings due to larval susceptibility, but
the larva itself has ceased to be highly sensitive many
hours before pupation takes place. And this is to be
expected, for during the latter part of stage iii. rapid
changes are going on beneath its surface, and the
developing pupa is becoming loosened from the larval
skin which encloses it like a shell. Putting together
the results of all the experiments, it is probable that
in this species the influence of surrounding colours
operates upon the larva during the twenty hours
immediately preceding the last twelve hours of the
larval state. Hence stage ii. is the great period of
susceptibility, and this is probably the true meaning
of the hours during which the caterpillar rests motionless on the surface upon which it will pupate; while
stage iii. has other meanings connected with the rapid
pupal development which is taking place.

Determination of the part affected by surrounding colours

Having thus defined the time of susceptibility, the next question was to ascertain the organ or part of the larva which is sensitive. At first it appeared likely that the larvæ might be influenced through their eyes (ocelli), of which they have six on each side of the head. Hence in many experiments the eyes of some of the larvæ were covered with an innocuous opaque black varnish, and they, together with an equal number of normal larvæ from the same company, were placed in gilt or white surroundings. The pupæ from both sets of larvæ were, however, always equally light-coloured. It then seemed possible, although highly improbable, that the varnish itself might act as a stimulus similar to that caused by white or gilt surroundings, and therefore the experiment was repeated with black surroundings in darkness; but the pupæ of the two sets were again almost identical, so that it appeared certain that the eyes can have nothing to do with the influence.

It then seemed possible that the large branching bristles, with which the larvæ are covered, might contain some organ which was affected by surrounding colours, but experiments in which half of the larvæ were deprived of their bristles showed conclusively that the sensitive organs must have some other position, for the pupæ from both sets of larvæ were identical.

I was thus driven to the conclusion that the general surface of the skin of the caterpillar is sensitive to colour during stage ii. and part of stage iii. In order to test this conclusion I wished to subject the body of the same larva to two conflicting colours, such as black and gold, producing the most opposite effects upon the pupa. Such an experiment, if successfully carried out, would decide some important points. If the part of the body containing the head was not more sensitive than the other part, a valuable confirmation of the blinding experiments would be afforded. Mrs. Barber's suggestion that parti-coloured pupæ may be produced by the influence of two colours would be tested in a very complete manner ; if parti-coloured pupæ were obtained it seemed probable that the light acts directly upon the skin, but if they could not be obtained it seemed more probable that the light influences the termination of nerves in the skin, and that the pupal colours are produced through the medium of the nervous system.

The practical difficulties in the way of such an experiment were very great, for the conflicting colours could only be applied during stage iii., when the larva is motionless and may be disturbed with impunity. If, on the other hand, a larva be disturbed in stage ii. it begins to walk about and thus renders the experiment impossible. The only way to obtain satisfactory results in spite of the slight susceptibility of stage iii. was to employ large numbers of larvæ, and to pay careful attention to minute differences of pupal colour as well as to the time during which the conflicting colours had been applied.

The experiments were conducted in two ways. In the first the larvæ were induced to suspend themselves from sheets of clear glass, by placing them in wide shallow glass boxes so that the ascent to the glass roof was easily accomplished.. As soon as suspension (stage iii.) had taken place, each larva was covered with a cardboard tube divided into two chambers by a horizontal partition which was fixed rather below the middle. There was a central hole in the partition just large enough to admit the body of the larva. The tube was fixed to the glass sheet with glue; the upper chamber was lined with one colour, e.g. gilt, and the lower chamber with the opposite colour, e.g. black, with which the outside of the cylinder was also covered, in case the larva should stretch its head beyond the lower edge. The partition was fixed at such a height that the larval head and rather less than half of the total surface of skin were contained in the lower chamber, while rather more than half of the skin surface was contained in the upper chamber. The arrangement is shown in section in fig. 30.

The second method of conducting the conflicting colour experiments was superior in the more equal illu-

mination of the upper and lower colours. The bottom
of a shallow wooden box was covered with alternate
areas of black and gilt paper, and partitions were
fixed along the lines where the two colours came into
contact. Each par-
tition was gilt to-
wards the gilt surface
and black towards
the black, and was
perforated close to
the bottom of the
box with holes which
would just admit the
body of a larva. The
box was then placed
in a vertical position
towards a strong
light, so that the
partitions became

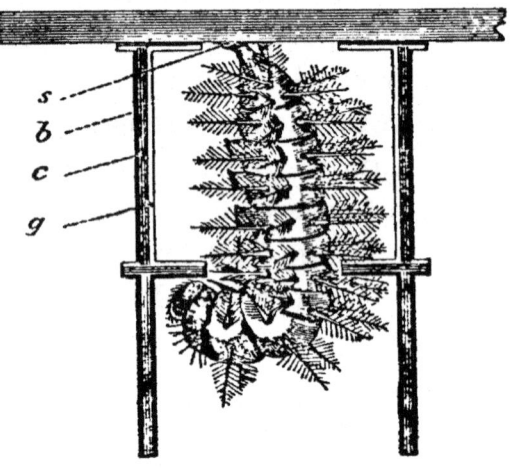

FIG. 30.—The larva of Small Tortoiseshell Butterfly suspended in a tube of which the upper
compartment is lined with gilt, the lower with
black; × 2. *s*. Boss of silk. *b*. Black. *c*. Cardboard. *g*. Gilt.

horizontal shelves, while the black and the gilt surfaces were uppermost alternately. As soon as a larva
was suspended to a glass sheet, the boss of silk was
carefully scraped off and was pinned on the upper colour
above one of the holes, so that the head and first five
body-rings passed through the hole on to the colour
beneath, which tended to produce opposite effects.
Other larvæ were similarly fixed between the shelves
upon one colour only, so as to afford a comparison
with the results of the conflicting colours.

A careful comparison of all the pupæ obtained in
the conflicting colour experiments showed that, when
the illumination of the two surfaces was equal, the
effective results were produced by that colour to
which the larger area of skin had been exposed,
whether the head formed part of that area or not.
Parti-coloured pupæ were never obtained. It therefore appears to be certain that the skin of the larva
is influenced by surrounding colours during the sensitive period, and it is also probable that the effects are
wrought through the medium of the nervous system.
This latter conclusion receives further confirmation
from other observations which will be described in the
next chapter (see pp. 142-46).

CHAPTER IX

VARIABLE PROTECTIVE RESEMBLANCE IN INSECTS (continued)

The meaning of the metallic appearance of pupæ

APART from the general physiological significance of the results described in the last chapter, they are of extreme interest in giving us a possible clue to the meaning of the remarkable metallic appearance of the pupæ of many butterflies. This wonderful appearance has given the name *chrysalis* to the second stage of Lepidopterous metamorphosis, although relatively few pupæ are really entitled to bear it. But some pupæ which deserve the name are very common, and probably have attracted attention ever since men began to look with interest on the world around them. Not only did the alchemists believe that in the appearance of these animals they received encouragement for the successful issue of the projects which were always before them, but we find that Aristotle, writing more than 2,200 years ago, mentions *chrysalis* as a word which was generally used in his time, and which had therefore been invented as descriptive of the

golden appearance at a still earlier period.   There can
be no doubt of this, for Aristotle's word is χρυσαλλίς,
identical with our own ; nor can there be any doubt
as to the stage of insect life to which Aristotle was referring, for his language is precise and descriptive.   In
fact, if a naturalist wished to convey to any one ignorant of the changes undergone in insect metamorphosis
a short and simple but perfectly accurate account of
the two first stages of a Lepidopterous insect, he could
not do better than use the very words of Aristotle:
' Caterpillars take food at first, but afterwards they
cease to take it and become quiescent, being generally
called chrysalides ; ' [1] or again in another passage :
' Afterwards the caterpillars, having grown, become
quiescent, change their shape, and are called chrysalides.' [2]

Mr. T. W. Wood suggested that the metallic
appearance was so essentially unlike anything usually
found in the organic kingdoms, that it acted as a
protection to the organisms possessing it.   Others
have thought that it has the value of a warning
colour, indicating an unpleasant taste (see Chapter
X.).   It is probable that the appearance sometimes
bears this meaning now, but it is unlikely that such
was its original use ; for the fact that metallic colours
can be called up or dismissed by the appropriate sur-

---

[1] αἵ τε γὰρ κάμπαι λαμβάνουσι τὸ πρῶτον τροφὴν, μετὰ ταῦτα οὐκέτι
λαμβάνουσιν, ἀλλ' ἀκινητίζουσιν αἱ καλούμεναι ὑπό τινων χρυσαλλίδες.

[2] μετὰ δὲ ταῦτα (αἱ κάμπαι) αὐξηθεῖσαι ἀκινητίζουσι, καὶ μεταβάλ-
λουσι τὴν μορφὴν, καὶ καλοῦνται χρυσαλλίδες

roundings shows that they are essentially protective, and as far removed as possible from conspicuous warning colours, the object of which is to render their possessors *unlike* the environment. What can be the object in nature which the glittering pupæ resemble? It is obvious that metals are not sufficiently abundant on the surface of the earth to afford models for successful imitation, and there is the same objection to certain metallic sulphides which otherwise would answer the purpose admirably.

A consideration of the darker non-glittering varieties of the same species helps us to an explanation. These certainly resemble the grey surface of weathered rocks, and the whole shape of such pupæ, with their angular projections and tubercles, combines with their colour to produce a most perfect Protective Resemblance to rough dark surfaces of rock. In fact, did we not delude the larvæ by offering them flat mineral surfaces in our walls and sides of houses, the protection would be so complete that we should hardly ever find the chrysalides; and, as a matter of fact, they are rarely seen except in such situations.

In England we very rarely see a brightly metallic pupa because in our moist climate exposed rock-surfaces quickly weather and become lichen-covered. If, however, the bright appearance of many recently fractured rocks were retained, as they are in drier countries, they would cause the production of a similar appearance in the pupæ of those larvæ which sought them.

Although metallic surfaces are not conspicuous in nature, there is a very abundant glittering mineral which is quite common enough to offer a surface against which the larvæ might often suspend themselves. I refer to the mineral mica, the substance forming the glittering flakes which are so well-known in common granite. Furthermore, any recently broken rock contains bright and glittering surfaces, although they may not be so brilliant as mica, and the bright spots of the pupæ would thus be of protective value against almost any freshly exposed mineral surface.

Hence we see that the pupæ would occur as dark or glittering forms, as the surrounding mineral surfaces are dark or glittering : they appear in two different varieties which are respectively in harmony with the two conditions of the mineral surfaces they resemble—the dark and weathered, and the bright and freshly exposed condition.

It may be that this adaptation to mineral surroundings arose when the widespread green tints of the vegetable kingdom contributed less to the total appearance of land-surfaces; or the adaptation may have followed the habit of feeding upon herbaceous plants which withered away in the hot season, changing from green to brown during the time when the insect was in the chrysalis state and could undergo no corresponding change of colour. However the adaptation arose in the ancestor of all butterflies which now emerge from gilded chrysalides, it is probable that it took place in some hot dry country, where mineral surfaces did not weather quickly but remained glittering for long periods of time.

The manner in which golden chrysalides are adapted for concealment on plants

In the origin and gradual progress of our modern aggressive forms of vegetation, less and less of the land-surface has been formed by mineral substances, until the green colour of foliage and the brown colour of stems and of withered leaves have become the predominant tints of nature and the most feasible models for Protective Resemblance. It is therefore interesting to note how the species with gilded pupæ have adapted themselves to the change.

The chrysalis of the Peacock Butterfly (*Vanessa Io*) still retains the dark variety, which is formed when pupation takes place upon dark rock surfaces ; but the golden form has been replaced by a green variety, which is produced when the chrysalis is suspended from the leaves of its food-plant. The green variety still retains the metallic appearance, and exhibits it to a much greater extent than the dark variety. During the summer of 1888 I found that the green form is produced by the surroundings which cause the appearance of the gilded form of the Small Tortoiseshell chrysalis, viz. by a gilt and by a white environment.

The chrysalis of the Red Admiral Butterfly (*Vanessa Atalanta*) has no green variety, but it appears, like the Small Tortoiseshell, as a dark or a glittering form resembling the two conditions of rock-surfaces upon which it often pupates, hanging suspended without any attempt at concealment except such as is afforded by its very perfect colour-harmony with the surroundings. I have shown that this species also is susceptible, and that either variety of pupa is produced by the appropriate environment. But this chrysalis is very commonly found attached to the food-plant, and when this is the case it hangs suspended in a tent formed of leaves carefully spun together by the caterpillar, so that it is concealed from view. The larva also often has the habit of partially biting through the leaf-stalk or stem, so that the leaves of its retreat hang down and wither. The dead brown leaves thus afford a far more harmonious background for the dark pupa, if by any chance it becomes exposed to view.

The Small Tortoiseshell has neither the green variety of the Peacock nor the protective habit of the Red Admiral, and therefore it almost invariably seeks mineral surroundings for the pupal period, and very rarely becomes a chrysalis on its food-plant. In 1886 I only found three such pupæ suspended to the food-plant, although I examined the nettle-beds where many hundreds of caterpillars had been feeding and had left for pupation. All these three pupæ were dead, being filled with the parasitic larvæ of Ichneumon flies. In 1888 I found many more pupæ upon the food-plant, but a very high percentage of these had been killed by parasites, and the hurrying on of pupation which occurred in the other cases and prevented the larvæ from wandering in a normal manner may, I think, be attributed to the state of health induced by that extraordinarily wet season.

The colours of certain dimorphic pupæ cannot be adjusted to the surroundings

I have already mentioned that I experimented upon the pupæ of the Swallow-tailed Butterfly (*Papilio machaon*), and found that they were not susceptible to the influence of surrounding colours. This is also true of the small family of Mocha moths (*Ephyridæ*) which have freely exposed pupæ, fixed like those of many butterflies by a silken girdle and boss, and often appearing in two varieties, green and brown. The caterpillars of the same species are also of two colours, and always produce pupæ of corresponding tints (see page 46).

Variable Protective Resemblance in the pupæ of the Pieridæ.

The susceptibility of the two species of Garden White Butterflies (*Pieris brassicæ* and *P. rapæ*) was also investigated in the same season (1886), and the results of previous observers were confirmed and extended. Many colours were employed, and it was found that the light reflected from yellow and orange surroundings was very potent in producing bright green varieties of the chrysalides of both species. It is therefore probable that when the light reflected from green leaves produces this effect in nature, the yellow and orange constituents of the light form the stimuli. When, therefore, these constituents are made use of nearly alone, they produce still more marked effects. Black and white backgrounds caused the pupæ of both species to become dark and light respectively, and all other colours except yellow and orange produced more or less dark pupæ.

Experiments were made upon *P. rapæ* to ascertain the susceptible period, the larvæ being transferred as in the case of the Small Tortoiseshell. The results were as in the latter: the larva is sensitive and not the pupa, and the time of chief susceptibility is during stage ii.

A few larvæ of *P. rapæ* were blinded, but the chrysalides were similar to those produced by normal larvæ.

Further experiments on the same subject

During the summer of 1888 I conducted further experiments upon the same subject. The results are as yet imperfectly worked out, and are unpublished, but I will shortly mention the chief conclusions. Other glittering metallic surfaces, such as silver or tin, do not produce anything like so striking an effect as gold upon the pupæ of the Small Tortoiseshell. It seems probable that the yellow light reflected from the gold is effective in preventing the formation of pigment, and in thus producing the gilded chrysalides, just as the yellow light also prevents the appearance of pigment and produces the bright green pupæ among the *Pieridæ*.

Two new species also were investigated, and proved to be sensitive. The pupæ of the Silver-washed Fritillary (*Argynnis paphia*) can be rendered dark or light in colour, although the metallic spots do not seem to be affected. The pupæ of the Large Tortoiseshell (*Vanessa polychloros*) were also rendered dark brown without metallic spots, or light reddish-brown with the spots, by the use of appropriate surroundings. The metallic spots could not be extended over the pupal surface as in the case of the Small Tortoiseshell.

Confirmatory results obtained by other workers

It is also interesting to record that many of these results have been since confirmed by independent workers. Mr. G. C. Griffiths worked at the chrysalis of the Small Garden White (*Pieris rapæ*), and confirmed my results in many important respects.[1] The Rev. J. W. B. Bell and Mr. Pembrey have worked at the pupæ of the Small Tortoiseshell and Peacock, and the former also at the pupæ of the Large Tortoiseshell.[2] Their results are, on the whole, confirmatory of those described above.

Variable Protective Resemblance in the colours of cocoons

It has been already mentioned that the colour of the cocoon in certain species can be adjusted to the environment. I obtained proof of this in 1886, at the suggestion of Mr. W. H. Harwood of Colchester, who had observed that the colour of the cocoon of the Emperor Moth (*Saturnia carpini*) varied, and seemed to suit its environment. I found that caterpillars of this species spun very dark brown cocoons in a black calico bag (see fig. 31), while white cocoons were

[1] *Trans. Ent. Soc. Lond.* 1888, pp. 247 *et seq.*
[2] *The Midland Naturalist*, Dec. 1889, pp. 289–90.

spun in white surroundings in a strong light (see fig. 32).[1]

In this case it seems almost impossible for the surrounding colours to influence directly the colour of the cocoon. It is necessary to assume the existence

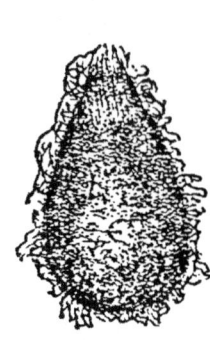

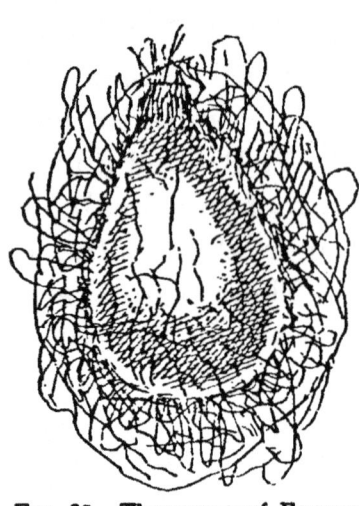

FIG. 31.—The cocoon of Emperor Moth (*S. carpini*), spun in a black calico bag ; natural size, although an exceptionally small cocoon.

FIG. 32.—The cocoon of Emperor Moth, spun on a white surface in strong light ; natural size.

of a complex nervous circle as a medium through which the stimulus of colour can make itself felt. If this conclusion be correct it is probable that the colours of the pupa and larva are adjusted in the same manner.

The observation upon *S. carpini* has been con-

[1] *Proc. Roy. Soc.* vol. xlii. p. 108. I have since found that the fact must have been known previously, for it is quoted in Mr. A. R. Wallace's *Tropical Nature.* I do not yet know the name of the naturalist who made the observation.

firmed, and has been extended to other species. Thus
Rev. W. J. H. Newman showed that the cocoons of the
Small Eggar Moth (*Eriogaster lanestris*) are creamy
white when spun upon white paper (see fig. 33), dark

Fig. 33.—The cocoon of Small Eggar
Moth (*E. lanestris*), spun upon white
paper ; natural size.

Fig. 34.—The cocoon of Small Eggar
spun among green leaves.

brown when constructed among leaves (see fig. 34).[1]
These cocoons are so compact and smooth that they resemble birds' eggs : a fact which explains the name of
the moth. In constructing the cocoon the caterpillar
leaves a few holes, which are doubtless of importance
in permitting a free exchange of air. The fact that
light reflected from green leaves is here the stimulus
for the production of a dark colour is readily intelligible
when we remember that the moth does not emerge till
the following February at the earliest, while the insect often remains in the pupal state for one or two
years longer. The leaves in contact with the cocoon
soon die and turn brown, and after this change the
dark colour is highly protective. It is also of especial
importance for the cocoon to be well concealed during
the winter months, when insect-eating animals are

[1] *Proc. Ent. Soc. Lond.* 1887, pp. l. li.

pressed for food, and are obliged to search for it with extreme care.

I have also shown that the cocoon of the Green Silver Lines Moth (*Halias prasinana*) can be modified in colour like that of the Small Eggar.[1] This species also passes the winter in the chrysalis state, when the brown colour is highly protective. One of my caterpillars had begun to spin a brown cocoon upon an oak leaf (see fig. 35). I then removed the caterpillar to a white box ; it remained motionless for several hours and then

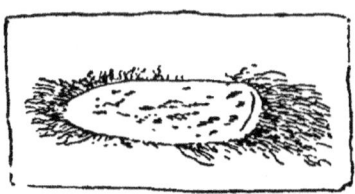

FIG. 36.—White cocoon spun by same caterpillar when transferred from oak leaf to white paper ; natural size.

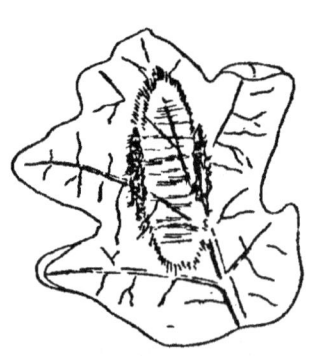

FIG. 35.—Brown cocoon begun by caterpillar of Green Silver Lines Moth (*H. prasinana*) upon an oak leaf ; natural size.

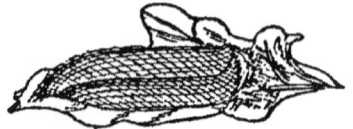

FIG. 37.—The brown cocoon of Green Silver Lines spun upon an oak leaf.

spun a white cocoon (see fig. 36). The brown cocoon of the same species is shown in fig. 37. Remembering the experiments upon the Small Tortoiseshell, it is very probable that the colour of the cocoon was deter-

[1] *Proc. Ent. Soc. Lond.* 1887, pp. l. li.

mined during the time when the caterpillar was motionless in the box.

Still later in 1888 Dr. R. G. Lynam sent me some cocoons of the Gold-tail Moth (*Liparis auriflua*) which had been also modified in a similar manner, and I found that the same power is possessed by the caterpillar of the Brimstone Moth (*Rumia cratægata*).[1] In this latter case a green tissue-paper background produced brown cocoons like those spun upon green leaves.

It is probable that this power of adjusting the colour of the cocoon is very common among species which spin in exposed situations. It may also be expected to occur in those Hymenoptera with similar habits. The investigation of the physiological processes involved in the adjustment would be of extreme interest. Last year (1888) I obtained a large number of Small Eggar caterpillars, intending to begin such an investigation, but nearly all of them died just before reaching maturity. It is to be hoped that many species will now be tested in order to ascertain whether this form of susceptibility is present.

Variable Protective Resemblance in Lepidopterous larvæ

It now remains to briefly consider the power of colour-adjustment possessed by certain caterpillars. Naturalists have long known that in certain species

---

[1] *Proc. Ent. Soc. Lond.* 1888, p. xxviii.

the colour of the caterpillars may vary according to the colour of the plant upon which they are found. This is especially true of caterpillars feeding upon brightly coloured parts of the plant, such as the anthers or petals. At the same time there has been, until recent years, hardly any systematic investigation of these interesting facts. Professor R. Meldola's editorial notes to his translation of Dr. Weismann's 'Studies in the Theory of Descent' (the essay on 'The Origin of the Markings of Caterpillars') contain many instances of this kind, together with most suggestive remarks upon them, which first induced me to work at the subject. At a still earlier date the same writer had brought together all the scattered examples of this kind, including the power of adjusting the colours of pupæ, and had drawn attention to the general principles involved.[1]

Experiments upon the larva of the Eyed Hawk Moth (*Smerinthus ocellatus*)

The instance which Professor Meldola chiefly considers in his editorial notes is that of the caterpillar of the Eyed Hawk Moth (*Smerinthus ocellatus*), which is of a whitish-green colour when it is found upon apple and certain kinds of willow, and of a bright yellowish-green when found upon other species or varieties of willow. The colours are on the whole

[1] *Proc. Zool. Soc.* 1873, p. 153.

protective; the larva resembles the under side of a rolled-up leaf, and when the food-plant bears leaves with white and downy under sides (apple, *Salix viminalis*, &c.) the larva is usually whitish; while it is generally yellowish-green upon trees of which the leaves have green under sides (*Salix triandra, S. baby-lonica, S. rubra, S. fragilis*, &c.). I remember, when a boy, finding the two varieties of larva, and being much astonished at the difference between them.

I began working at the species in 1884, and have bred large numbers of the larvæ for every season since that year. Only the results of the earlier experiments are published.[1] The eggs of each female moth were kept separate, and the caterpillars of each batch were fed upon a variety of food-plants, and manifested decided differences in their shade of green. At the same time remarkable exceptions occasionally occurred: sometimes, also, when collecting I have found bright green individuals upon apple. Blinding experiments like those upon the Small Tortoiseshell led to negative results. These experiments were very laborious, for a caterpillar changes its skin four times, and with it the covering to its eyes and the opaque varnish. Hence, before each change of skin the caterpillars were separated from the food, and, after changing it, were re-blinded before being restored.

Before this investigation had been begun, it was believed that such variability in caterpillars was due to

[1] *Proc. Roy. Soc.* vol. xxxviii. p. 269 ; vol. xl. p. 135.

the direct chemical effect of different kinds of leaves upon them after being eaten, and it was therefore called *phytophagic* variability. Many special experiments were directed toward the solution of this question. Thus, leaves were sewn together, so that the caterpillars were exposed to the colour of the upper or of the under side alone, although they ate the same leaf in both cases. In other instances the ' bloom ' was rubbed off the under sides of some leaves (*Salix fragilis*, incorrectly described as *Triandra* in my papers), while others were left normal. The results proved that the caterpillars are affected by the colour of the leaves and not by the leaves as food. Comparison with the experiments on pupæ renders it most probable that reflected light influences the skin.

Experiments upon the larvæ of other Sphingidæ

Professor Meldola had also quoted the instance of the larva of the Privet Hawk Moth (*Sphinx ligustri*), which is of a much brighter green when found upon privet than when found upon lilac. Larvæ of this species, from the same batch of eggs, were fed upon the two plants, and the above quoted observation was confirmed. The larvæ of the Lime Hawk Moth (*Smerinthus tiliæ*) were similarly modified, being made unusually light green by the use of variegated elm and a lime having leaves with very white and downy under sides.

8

Experiments upon the larvæ of Geometræ and Noctuæ

The experiments were then extended to many other dark-coloured larvæ (chiefly *Geometræ*). The method of experiment was as follows : a larva which resembles the twigs or bark of its food-plant was selected, and was surrounded by the leaves upon which it fed, and by white or green surfaces. No brown twig or anything dark-coloured was allowed to come near it during its whole life. Under these circumstances the larvæ, in the majority of the species selected for experiment, became very light brown or light grey in colour, and quite unlike the darker larvæ of the same kinds which were produced when an abundance of dark twigs had been mixed with the leaves of the food-plant.[1]

The results were certainly protective, for the lighter larvæ were far less conspicuous on the green leaves and stems than the darker ones would have been. At the same time it must be admitted that the resemblance of the darker forms to the dark branches

---

[1] These experiments have been successfully applied to the following *Geometræ* :—*Crocallis elinguaria* (for two seasons), *Ennomos angularia*, *E. lunaria*, *Boarmia rhomboidaria* (this species was investigated by my friend and pupil, Mr. R. C. L. Perkins, B.A., of Jesus College, Oxford), *B. roboraria* ; and to one of the *Noctuæ*, *Catocala sponsa*. Since this note was written, I have found, during the past summer (1889), that the Geometer *Heterophylla abruptaria*, and the Noctuas *Catocala electa* and *C. elocata*, are also sensitive, the first and last named to a marked degree.

is much stronger than that of the light varieties to the leaves (see figs. 38 and 39). Two species, however, are already known in which the green stems and

FIG 38. The larva of a continental Noctua (*Catocala elocata*) with the colour adjusted to that of the dark twigs mixed with its food-plant; nearly full-fed; two-thirds natural size.

FIG. 39.—The colour of a larva of the same species when only green twigs and leaves were supplied to it. The food-plant in both cases was black poplar (*Populus nigra*).

leaves cause the production of *green* larvæ, so that the concealment is very perfect. And we may be quite sure that there are many other species with equal powers.

Experiments upon the larvæ of the Brimstone Moth

Lord Walsingham first pointed out to me that the larvæ of the Brimstone Moth (*Rumia cratægata*) vary from brown to green, and through all intermediate shades. I found that when brown objects were entirely excluded the larvæ became greenish-brown, brownish-green, or sometimes of a decided green colour, and thus harmonised well with the leaves and young green twigs of the hawthorn. In the presence of dark twigs they became dark brown like so many other larvæ.[1]

Experiments upon the larvæ of the Peppered Moth

The second instance is even more remarkable, and has only been observed during the present year (1889).

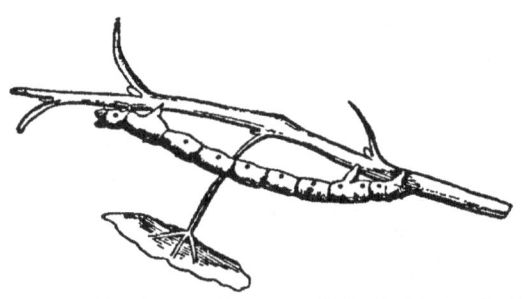

FIG. 40.—The larva of Peppered Moth (*A. betularia*) surrounded by green twigs and leaves ; full-fed ; half natural size.

FIG. 41.—The larva of Peppered Moth surrounded by abundant dark twigs as well as leaves.

I obtained some hundreds of eggs from a single wild female of the Peppered Moth (*Amphidasis betularia*), and the caterpillars which hatched were treated as in the other experiments. The larvæ reared among green leaves and shoots became bright green (see fig. 40) *without exception*, while the others in nearly all cases assumed the colour of the dark-brown twigs, which were mixed

[1] *Report of the British Association*, 1887, p. 756 ; also *Nature*, vol. 36, p. 594.

with the leaves upon which they fed (see fig. 41):
about one or two per cent., however, took their colour
from the latter. The food-plants were the same in
both experiments.

The change of colour is not due to the food seen through a transparent skin

Some authorities have supposed that the change
of colour under such circumstances is a comparatively
simple thing, that the younger green leaves eaten
and seen in the alimentary canal through the more or
less transparent tissues cause a brighter appearance,
while the older leaves produce in the same manner a
darker appearance. This cause of colour is certainly
efficient in many transparent caterpillars (see p. 79),
such as some of the *Noctuæ*, but it does not account
for any of the results obtained in my experiments.

As a precaution against such an error, I reversed
the surroundings of a few larvæ of most of the species
experimented upon. The new conditions were maintained for some days, during which the contents of the
alimentary canal must have been changed many times,
but no perceptible effect was produced. This result
also serves to show that the influences act very slowly,
and that the processes of adjustment are totally different from those which cause the rapid changes of
colour considered in Chapter VII.

The difference between slow and rapid adjustment of colour

The essential difference between the two kinds of adjustment is that, in the one case, the pigmented part of certain cells contracts in obedience to nervous stimuli, and thus alters the general appearance ; while in the other case the coloured part is actually built up of the appropriate tint, or loses its colour altogether and becomes transparent in obedience to the same stimuli.   The frog or fish has a series of ready-made screens which can be shifted to suit the environment ; the insect has the power of building up an appropriate screen.   In many cases, however, the green colour of caterpillars is due to the ready-made colour of the blood, which becomes effective when pigment is removed from the superficial cells, but which disappears when the latter are rendered opaque.   Here, however, the superficial cells form the screen which has to be built up or from which the colour must be dismissed ; and in certain species even the colour of the blood is entirely changed in the passage from a green to a dark variety or *vice versâ*.

Hence it is to be expected that the changes occurring in an insect will occupy a considerable time as compared with those which take place in a frog. Another difference between the two processes is that the stimulus from the environment falls upon the eye in the one case and probably upon the surface of the skin in the other.

Variable Protective Resemblance in insects is no explanation of the origin of colour

Many authorities have believed that, in the results of these experiments upon the colours of insects, we see an explanation of the origin of colour, by the direct influence of environment accumulated through many generations. This is a very tempting conclusion, and one which for a time appeared to me to be satisfactory. But as soon as there was clear evidence that the medium of the nervous system is necessary, the results were seen to be indirect, and to have needed the most astonishing adaptations on the part of the organism before the colour of the environment could exercise any influence upon it.

It might still be maintained that the existing colours and markings of certain caterpillars are at any rate in part due to the accumulation through heredity of the indirect influence of environment, working by means of the nervous system. To this it may be replied that the whole use and meaning of the power of adjustment depends upon its freedom during the life of the individual; any hereditary bias towards the colours of ancestors would at once destroy the utility of the power, which is essentially an adaptation to the fact that different individuals will probably meet with different environments. As long ago as 1873, Professor Meldola argued that this power of adjustment is adaptive and to be _explained by the operation of natural selection.[1]

Comparison between the varying effects of green leaves upon the different stages of an insect strongly supports the view that the results are due to adaptation. Thus the caterpillar of the Brimstone Moth remains upon its food-plant for a few weeks in the summer when the leaves are green, and green leaves cause the larva to become *green* and to lose the dark pigment. But the chrysalis remains among the leaves in winter when they have become brown, and green leaves cause the caterpillar to spin a *dark* cocoon. Hence precisely opposite effects are produced by the operation of the same force, the nature of the effects having been determined by adaptation.

Furthermore, there is no positive evidence for any of these effects becoming hereditary. I have carried on some of my experiments for more than one generation, always carefully noting the effects produced in the parents, and have never been able to detect any resulting hereditary tendencies, even when the previous generation had been powerfully influenced.

When therefore we meet with a dimorphic species which is not influenced by its environment, so as to produce the appropriate form, I do not believe that we

[1] *Proc. Zool. Soc.* 1873, p. 153.

are witnessing the results of a power of adjustment which existed in the past but is now lost. I think, on the other hand, that variability or dimorphism preceded the power of adjustment in all cases. I have already shown that these appearances possess a protective value even when they cannot be adjusted (see pp. 46–48). When Variable Protective Resemblance is present, but acts somewhat uncertainly (as in the larva of the Eyed Hawk Moth), it is probable that the power has been only recently acquired and is still imperfect. This conclusion is supported by the fact that the closely allied caterpillar of the Convolvulus Hawk Moth (*Sphinx convolvuli*) has no power of adjustment, although it is completely dimorphic [1] (see pp. 47, 48).

Before finally leaving this part of the subject I will briefly allude to facts which render it probable that certain perfect insects possess the power of Variable Protective Resemblance.

Variable Protective Resemblance probable in certain Moths

The colour of certain insects varies with the prevailing tint of the locality in which they occur. The best instance known to me is that of one of the *Geometræ*, the Annulet Moth (*Gnophos obscurata*). This moth is light-coloured in chalky localities (*e.g.* on the chalk at Lulworth), but darker when the pre-

---

[1] *Trans. Ent. Soc. Lond.* 1888, pp. 552–553.

vailing tint of the earth is dark, as in peaty districts. It is improbable that these are local races, and the only other interpretation is that the colours can be varied as the result of a stimulus. No experimental proof of this has been as yet afforded. If the view adopted here be correct, it will be of extreme interest to define the susceptible period; it will most probably be found at the close of larval life.

I have treated this part of the subject at some length and have discussed many details. I have done so because the inquiry is new, and will not be found in other books on the colours of animals;[1] and also because I hope that some of my readers may be induced to carry on investigations for themselves in a field which is easily entered, and in which further help is especially necessary.

[1] Since this sentence was written, Mr. A. R. Wallace's most interesting volume, *Darwinism*, has appeared. A short account of Variable Protective Resemblance in insects will be found in it.

CHAPTER X

WARNING COLOURS

WE now come to a class of colours with a meaning precisely opposite to that of the large class we have just been considering. The object of the latter is to conceal the possessor from its enemies, the object of the former is to render it as conspicuous as possible. As in other classes of colour, the most familiar and striking illustrations are to be found among insects.[1]

The sharp contrast between most Protective or Aggressive Resemblances and Warning Colours

It must have been obvious to any one interested in natural history that the insects met with during a walk in summer may be arranged in two great groups : those which are extremely difficult to find and excite our wonder by the perfect manner in which they are concealed, and those which at once attract our attention by their startling colours and conspicuous attitudes, the effect being often greatly increased by the habit

[1] Many of the facts and conclusions in this chapter are taken from my paper in the *Proc. Zool. Soc.* 1887, p. 191.

of living in companies. These two groups form, perhaps, the sharpest contrast in nature. We assume, almost as a matter of course, that the latter are protected in some other way, that if captured they would prove to be of little value, or even positively nauseous or dangerous.

The value of Warning Colours

At first sight the existence of this group seems to be a difficulty in the way of the general applicability of the theory of natural selection. Warning Colours appear to benefit the would-be enemies rather than the conspicuous forms themselves, and the origin and growth of a character intended solely for the advantage of some other species cannot be explained by the theory of natural selection. But the conspicuous animal is greatly benefited by its Warning Colours. If it resembled its surroundings like the members of the other class, it would be liable to a great deal of accidental or experimental tasting, and there would be nothing about it to impress the memory of an enemy, and thus to prevent the continual destruction of individuals. The object of Warning Colours is to assist the education of enemies, enabling them to easily learn and remember the animals which are to be avoided. The great advantage conferred upon the conspicuous species is obvious when it is remembered that such an easy and successful education means an education involving only a small sacrifice of life. It must not be supposed that nauseous properties are necessarily attended by Warning Colours ; there are very many instances in which they are accompanied by Protective Resemblances and habits. The common cockroach is a familiar example of this latter association.

Warning Colours in Mammalia

The highest vertebrate animals are rarely protected by the possession of the qualities which are most commonly attended by Warning Colours, viz. an unpleasant taste or smell. There is, however, at least one mammal of which this is certainly true. This example is brought forward in Belt's most interesting book, 'The Naturalist in Nicaragua.' [1] Thus he tells us that at night 'the skunk goes leisurely along, holding up his white tail as a danger-flag for none to come within range of his nauseous artillery.' He also alludes to the fœtid fluid which these animals 'discharge with too sure an aim at any assailant.' He describes the large white tail as laid over against the black and white body, producing a very conspicuous effect in the dusk, so that the animal 'is not likely to be pounced upon by any of the Carnivora, mistaking it for other night-roaming animals.' The conspicuous appearance of the skunk is shown in fig. 42.

[1] Second edition, 1888, pp. 174, 249, 250, 320, 321. See also Mr. A. R. Wallace's *Darwinism*, 1st edition, p. 233.

I know of no instance of this kind among birds, but it is probable that the gaudy and strongly-contrasted colours of certain tropical species may be found to be accompanied by some nauseous property and to be of warning significance.

FIG. 42.—The Brazilian Skunk (*Mephitis suffocans*) : showing the conspicuous black and white appearance of the animal which serves as a warning to its enemies.

The brilliant and conspicuous colours of many powerful birds are, I think, to be explained as a result of the free scope given to sexual selection (see pp. 311–12).

Warning Colours in Reptiles

Warning characters are not uncommon among poisonous reptiles. The various species of Coral Snake (*Elaps*), occurring in tropical America, are extremely venomous, and are highly conspicuous, their bodies being alternately banded with bright red and black, and often with yellow.[1] It is extremely interesting to observe that the deadly Rattlesnake (*Crotalus*) warns an intruder of its presence by sound instead of by sight, like the Coral Snake. The Cobra is protectively coloured, but, if attacked, it expands the hood with the conspicuous eye-like marks, and thus endeavours to terrify its enemy by the startling appearance. The majority of poisonous snakes, however, depend entirely upon Protective Resemblance together with the use of their fangs. This, for example, is the case with our common Viper.

It is, however, an advantage to some snakes to acquire warning characters and to live on their reputation for being poisonous; for although an animal bitten by one of them would probably die, the effects are never immediately fatal, and there would be plenty of time for the snake itself to be killed. Again, the snake possesses only a limited supply of poison at any one time, and if this had been recently drawn upon

[1] See also A. R. Wallace's *Essays on Natural Selection*, 1875, p. 101.

for purposes of defence or for killing prey, the snake would be comparatively harmless. Hence it would be to the advantage of certain snakes to advertise publicly the fact that they are dangerous, retaining the poison to use if necessary; and others would gain by concealing themselves by Protective Resemblance, while they also would use their poison fangs if detected and attacked. The question is not whether one of these methods is better than the other, but whether either of them is better than an intermediate condition; so that we can well understand why one group of poisonous snakes should adopt one method, while the other method is made use of by another group.

Warning Colours in Amphibia

Among the Amphibia a beautiful example has been afforded by Mr. Belt's acute powers of observation.[1] 'In the woods around Santo Domingo there are many frogs. Some are green or brown, and imitate green or dead leaves, and live amongst foliage. Others are dull earth-coloured, and hide in holes and under logs. All these come out only at night to feed, and they are all preyed upon by snakes and birds. In contrast with these obscurely coloured species another little frog hops about in the daytime, dressed in a bright livery of red and blue. He cannot be mistaken for any other, and his flaming vest and blue stockings

[1] *Loc. cit.* p. 321.

show that he does not court concealment. He is very abundant in the damp woods, and I was convinced he was uneatable so soon as I made his acquaintance and saw the happy sense of security with which he hopped about. I took a few specimens home with me and tried my fowls and ducks with them, but none would touch them. At last, by throwing down pieces of meat, for which there was a great competition amongst them, I managed to entice a young duck into snatching up one of the little frogs. Instead of swallowing it, however, it instantly threw it out of its mouth, and went about jerking its head, as if trying to throw off some unpleasant taste.' It is also extremely probable that the well-known European Salamander (*Salamandra maculosa*), so conspicuous with its irregular yellow blotches on a black ground, possesses some unpleasant attribute. I do not think, however, that there is any direct evidence for this, like that obtained by Mr. Belt in the case of the Nicaraguan frog.

Warning Colours in Marine Animals

Many fish are poisonous, and many possess formidable defensive spines, but I do not know that any attempt has been made to connect these characters with a conspicuous appearance. It is very probable, however, that such a connection exists in many cases.[1]

[1] Mr. Garstang suggests that the weever-fish (*Trachinus vipera*) is an example of Warning Colouration. It possesses a pair of in-

Warning Colours are probably wide-spread among marine organisms. Mr. Garstang had suspected that the bright colours of certain compound Ascidians were of warning significance, because these helpless animals are thus rendered extremely conspicuous, and because some of them emit a most unpleasant odour. He now finds that fish invariably refuse them : although sometimes tasted or even swallowed, they are never retained. The bright colours of many sea-anemones and sponges are probably to be explained in the same way. Evidence in favour of this conclusion is given on pp. 200–204.

Warning Colours in Caterpillars : the history of their discovery

Warning Colours are greatly developed in insects, and an account of the first recognition of this principle among caterpillars is of great historical interest. When Darwin was investigating the bright colours of animals, and was elaborating his theory of their explanation as of use in courtship, he came across the brilliant colours of certain caterpillars, and saw at

tensely poisonous spines on its gill-covers, and is rendered conspicuous by a deep black first dorsal fin. The body of the fish is completely buried in the sand, which it resembles in colour, the black fin alone being seen. Mr. Garstang thinks that this conspicuous character prevents such fish as gurnards from mistaking the weever for the dragonet (*Callionymus lyra*), which is similar in size and habits. He has frequently found the dragonet in the stomachs of gurnards, but the weever never.

once that they were a difficulty in the way of the
theory. For caterpillars are undeveloped organisms;
they have been described as 'embryos leading an independent life,' and there is no way of distinguishing
the sexes by external colour or structure (except in a
few instances). Here, therefore, we meet with brilliant colours, often rendering the possessors conspicuous, which cannot be of any use in courtship.
Seeing, therefore, that the bright colours must be of
use in some other way, Darwin drew the attention of
Wallace to the subject, and asked whether he could
suggest any explanation. Wallace accordingly thought
over the subject, and considered it as part of the
wider question of the varied uses (other than sexual)
of brilliant and startling colour, in other stages of
insect-life, and in numerous instances scattered over
the whole animal kingdom; and he finally ventured
to predict that birds and other enemies would be found
to refuse such conspicuous caterpillars if offered to
them. He believed, in fact, that such larvæ are protected by possessing a nauseous taste or smell, or some
other property which renders them unfit for food.
Conversely Wallace argued that inconspicuous caterpillars would be eaten and relished whenever they
were detected.

It is most inspiring to read the letter in which the
great founder of modern biology accepted this fruitful
suggestion.

'. . . You are the man to apply to in a difficulty.

I never heard anything more ingenious than your suggestion, and I hope you may be able to prove it true. That is a splendid fact about the white moths; it warms one's very blood to see a theory thus almost proved to be true.'[1]

Very soon after the suggestion was made public [2] it received confirmation by experiments conducted by Mr. J. Jenner Weir [3] and Mr. A. G. Butler.[4] At a later date experiments of the same kind were made by Professor Weismann,[5] and still later by myself.[6] It was found that while birds devoured with eagerness the well-concealed caterpillars, they refused those with conspicuous colours; it was also found that other insect-eating animals, such as frogs, lizards, and spiders, refused larvæ with warning colours, or did so after first tasting them.

Examples of Warning Colours among Caterpillars

A very common example of a caterpillar with warning colours is afforded by the larva of the Currant Moth or Magpie Moth (*Abraxas grossulariata*), which is excessively abundant in gardens (see fig. 43)

[1] *Life and Letters of Charles Darwin*, 1887, vol. iii. p. 94.
[2] *Proc. Ent. Soc. Lond.* Ser. 3, v. p. lxxx. 1867.
[3] *Trans. Ent. Soc. Lond.* 1869, Part i. April.
[4] *Ibid.* p. 27.
[5] *Studies in the Theory of Descent*, Part ii. pp. 336–340. English translation by Professor R. Meldola.
[6] *Proc. Zool. Soc.* 1887, p. 191. This paper contains an account of all previous work on the same subject.

The caterpillar is extremely conspicuous, being of a cream colour with orange and black markings. Although it belongs to the group of well-concealed 'stick-caterpillars' (*Geometræ*), of which several instances have been considered in Chapter III., it makes no attempt to hold itself in any of the attitudes characteristic of its group (compare fig. 43 with figs. 1, 2, 3, 4, 6, 8, and 9). All observers agree that birds, lizards, frogs, and spiders either refuse this species altogether, or exhibit signs of the most intense disgust after tasting it.

FIG. 43.—The larva of Magpie Moth (*A. grossulariata*), showing Warning Colouring; full-fed; natural size.

FIG. 44.—The larva of Buff-tip Moth (*P. Bucephala*), showing Warning Colouring; full-fed; natural size; from Curtis.

FIG. 45.—The larva of Cinnabar Moth (*E. Jacobœœ*), showing Warning Colouring; full-fed; natural size; from Curtis.

The caterpillar of the Buff-tip Moth (*Pygæra bucephala*), fig. 44, and the Cinnabar Moth (*Euchelia jacobææ*), fig. 45, are also extremely abundant, and are good examples of the association of Warning Colours with a nauseous taste. Both of them are gregarious, living in large companies, so that their conspicuous appearance is greatly intensified. The colours of the first-named larva are black, yellow, and orange. It feeds on oak, elm, lime, birch, hazel, &c., and the large bare branches which attest its appetite are very familiar sights in autumn. The second caterpillar is coloured by alternate black and yellow rings ; it feeds upon ragwort in the summer. There is plenty of experimental evidence for the unpleasant taste of both caterpillars.

The conspicuous gregarious caterpillars of the Large Garden White Butterfly (*Pieris brassicæ*), which are only too well known in cabbage gardens in the autumn, are also protected in the same manner. Many other instances will be found in the papers already referred to.

A caterpillar may be freely exposed rather than conspicuous

In some cases the warning of an unpleasant quality is conveyed by the caterpillar being freely exposed, while its colours, although sober, do not harmonise with those of the food-plant. This may be true of gregarious species, such as the dark larvæ of the Peacock or Small Tortoiseshell butterflies, which feed freely exposed on the tops of nettles, and which are known to be refused by some insect-eating animals.[1]

The various unpleasant qualities possessed by caterpillars with Warning Colours

Other unpleasant attributes, as well as that of a nauseous taste, may be associated with Warning Colours. A strongly smelling or irritant fluid may be discharged from special glands on the approach of an enemy. Glands of this kind occur on the back of many common caterpillars, such as the brilliantly coloured 'Palmer worm' (larva of *Porthesia auriflua*), or the onspicuous 'Hop-dog' (larva of *Orgyia pudibunda*). The larvæ of some common gregarious saw-flies (*Hymenoptera*), such as *Crœsus septentrionalis*, which completely denudes the branches of birch trees, have a number of odoriferous glands along the middle of the ventral surface. When disturbed, the body is turned forward over the head, and the glands are everted so that their secretion escapes into the air. The meaning of the gregarious habit is very

[1] The gregarious habit may render an insect so conspicuous that it is unnecessary for it to acquire bright colours. The 'warning' significance of the gregarious habit was first suggested by Fritz Müller (*Kosmos*, Dec. 1877). An abstract of this paper has been published by Professor Meldola (*Proc. Ent. Soc. Lond.* 1878, pp. vi. and vii.)

clear in this and parallel cases ; for when many individuals combine to discharge an unpleasant odour, they become surrounded by an atmosphere which acts as a most effective barrier.

Irritating hairs possessed by certain larvæ

Again, caterpillars may be protected by possessing irritating hairs. This is the case with the ' Palmer worms ' mentioned above, which are thus doubly protected. Many people have discovered this fact to their cost after handling these pretty black, red, and white caterpillars, which are so abundant and freely exposed on our hawthorn hedges in early summer. When the face or neck is touched by the hands, which are covered with minute barbed hairs shed by the caterpillar, an intensely irritating rash soon makes its appearance. The same effect is produced, as I shall always remember, if an old cocoon, in which the hairs are interwoven, be pulled to pieces with the fingers. These caterpillars were nearly always refused, but Mr. Butler records that they were in one case eaten without hesitation by a young sky-lark, which soon afterwards died with symptoms which may have been due to the irritating hairs. · One of my lizards also seized a larva, but relinquished it after biting it for some time. The lizard was evidently greatly irritated by the hairs in its mouth. Many other hairy caterpillars also produce a rash : thus, the larvæ of the Fox Moth

(*Lasiocampa rubi*), Oak Eggar (*L. quercus*), and Drinker (*Odonestis potatoria*), have this effect on the skin of the hands if they are held for a long time, and they would certainly act rapidly upon the delicate skin of the mouth. All three caterpillars are fairly conspicuous, and there is experimental evidence that the two latter are disliked.

It will be shown that the hairs are sometimes arranged in tempting tufts, which invite an enemy to seize the caterpillar at a point which does not injure the latter, while it causes the former the greatest discomfort.

The hairs of nearly all caterpillars are probably more or less unpleasant in the mouth. Delicate and sensitive animals, such as the marmoset, although excessively fond of insects, cannot be induced to touch *any* hairy larva. Birds appear to eat them more readily than other animals, but they have peculiar advantages in their power of rubbing off the hairs.

The association of hairs with a conspicuous appearance

Sir John Lubbock[1] has tabulated the appearance of the larvæ of all British butterflies and the larger moths, and he thus shows in a most convincing manner the general association of hairs or spines with conspicuous warning colours. His conclusion is as follows: 'Thus summing up the caterpillars, both of

[1] *Trans. Ent. Soc.* 1878, pp. 239, *et seq.*

9

the butterflies and moths, out of the eighty-eight spiny and hairy species tabulated only one is green (*L. sybilla*), and even this may not be protectively coloured, since it has yellow warts and white lateral lines.   On the other hand, a very great majority of the black and brown caterpillars, as well as those more or less marked with blue and red, are either hairy or spiny, or have some special protection.'

Sir John Lubbock, however, fully recognises that hairs may contribute towards the Protective Resemblance of certain species, examples of which have been already given (see page 35).   Professor Meldola suggests that a probable original meaning of the hairy covering was protection from injury after falling from the food-plant.

Warning Colours in other stages of metamorphosis in Lepidoptera

Lepidoptera of many species are protected by Warning Colours and unpleasant attributes, in other stages in addition to that of the larva; and the same method of defence is also adopted in other orders of insects.   The chrysalis of the Magpie Moth, which is black with yellow bands, and exposed to view in a very slight cocoon, is nauseous like the larva, and the slow-flying moth itself, with white wings rendered conspicuous by yellow markings and black spots, is defended in the same manner.   When captured it makes no attempt to escape, but ' feigns death.' The conspicuous and sluggish day-flying black and red Burnet Moths (*Zygœna*) and Cinnabar Moth (*Euchelia Jacobœœ*) are also nauseous, and so is the gaudy Garden Tiger Moth (*Arctia caja*). Many white moths, or black and white moths, have also been refused by insect-eating animals with every sign of disgust.

Consideration of the later stages of species with unpalatable larvæ

A comparison of the means of defence and palatability in the three stages of metamorphosis, in species of which the larvæ are known to be nauseous, proved to be extremely interesting, and much more work is needed in the same direction. In the first place the comparison showed that when the later stages are nauseous the larva was also nauseous in all cases. The Tiger Moth is probably an exception, for the caterpillar may be defended by its hairs instead of by taste, and the chrysalis seems to be palatable. The Leopard Moth (*Zeuzera œsculi*) is another exception. Such cases are probably very rare, and it is clear that this method of defence, among Lepidoptera, nearly always arose in the larval stage. The larval stage is exposed to more danger and is more helpless than any other: the imago can escape by flight, and the pupa, if exposed, may render its Protective Resemblance complete by entire quiescence, and it is usually effectually protected in other ways.   But the larva must feed, and at the same time is sluggish in its movements, defenceless, and when palatable is more relished than any other stage, for it does not possess the hard investment of the one or the scaly covering of the other.   Hence it is that the great needs of the larva have been so frequently met in this way; but as soon as the unpleasant quality has appeared it will tend to pass on by simple continuity into the other stages.   If these latter are hard pressed, there is always the possibility that such qualities may be made the starting-point of a similar method of defence for them also.   But the disagreeable properties may also pass on into stages which hold their own successfully by elaborate and perfect Protective Resemblances, and then such qualities, unattended by Warning Colours, are entirely useless to the stage, but may be important as a latent possibility for the future.   It must be remembered that an unpleasant attribute must always appear in advance of the warning colouring.   An example is afforded by the Buff-tip Moth (*Pygæra bucephala*), which is beautifully protected, during rest, by resembling a piece of rotten lichen-covered stick (see page 57), but which nevertheless retains something of the unpleasant taste by which its caterpillar is effectually protected.

The metallic appearance of certain pupæ may be of value as a warning

At this point it is of interest to consider the cases in which the metallic appearance of a chrysalis may act as a warning. Dr. Fritz Müller tells me that the brilliant metallic pupæ of the South American butterfly, *Mechanitis lysimnia*, hang in groups from the leaves of their food-plant (*Solanum*). The butterfly of this species is certainly distasteful, for the genus is mimicked by butterflies of other families. This fact, and the gregarious habit of the pupæ, render it nearly certain that the glittering appearance has a warning significance. The same is probably true of the pupa of the abundant Indian butterfly (*Euplœa core*), which Mr. E. A. Minchin tells me possesses a brilliant silvery appearance, and is so conspicuous that it can be seen from a great distance. This butterfly also belongs to a group protected by an unpleasant taste or smell, and there is little doubt that the metallic appearance of the pupa has a warning meaning.

Warning Colours in other orders of Insects

Passing now to the other orders of insects, highly conspicuous and abundant beetles (Coleoptera), such as the black and red 'soldiers and sailors' (*Telephorus*), the red and-black ladybirds (*Coccinella*), and the red and blue-black *Chrysomela populi*, have been shown to be extremely nauseous, and the two latter emit a very unpleasant smell.

The sting possessed by the females of so many Hymenoptera is obviously an unpleasant attribute, rendering the insect disagreeable or even dangerous to eat. We find accordingly that stinging insects are often rendered conspicuous by warning colours, of which the contrasted dark and yellow bands of the Common Wasp, the Hornet, and of many Humble Bees, furnish examples.

Warning Colours are also to be found in other orders, but it is unnecessary to give further examples. They will be recognised in numbers in any country walk during the summer, although the experimental proof of the co-existence of some unpleasant attribute is still wanting in a large proportion of the cases.

Warning Colours can only be safely adopted by a small proportion of the Insects in any country

The acquisition of an unpleasant taste or smell, together with a conspicuous appearance, is so simple a mode of protection, and yet apparently so absolutely complete, that it seems remarkable that more species have not availed themselves of it. What can be the principle which works in antagonism to such a mode of protection? Thinking over this subject, as the result of a lecture upon the facts and conclusions already described,[1] it appeared probable that such an

---

[1] Delivered at the Royal Institution in the spring of 1886.

antagonistic principle would be found in the too complete success of the method itself. If a very common insect, forming the chief food of some animal, gained protection in this way, the latter might be forced to devour the unpalatable food in order to avoid starvation. And the same result might readily be brought about if a scarce and hard-pressed form adopted the same line, and became dominant, after ousting many species which were important as food. If once an insect-eating species were driven to eat any such insect in spite of the unpleasant taste, it would gradually come to devour it with relish, and the insect would be in great danger of extermination, because of its conspicuous appearance.

If this reasoning be correct, it is clear that the mode of defence is by no means perfect, and that it depends for its success upon the existence of relatively abundant palatable forms ; in other words, its employment must be strictly limited.

Absence of Warning Colours in the seasons when Insect life is scarce

A very interesting fact in support of this argument is the entire disappearance of all insects with Warning Colours during the seasons when insect life is scarce, and when insect-eating animals are hard pressed for food. And yet, if it were safe to rely on such a mode of defence, the Warning Colours would be especially conspicuous at these times, when all the tints of nature are sombre and form a background against which the Warning Colours would stand out in startling contrast. Certain species, which are defended in this way, pass the winter in the brightly coloured stage of metamorphosis ; but they conceal themselves as completely as possible under loose bark or among dead leaves, &c. This is true of the common ladybird, and I have noticed that they begin to hide comparatively early in the autumn, when the insects are rapidly diminishing in numbers, but before the beginning of the cold weather. It is therefore probable that they hide in order to conceal their bright colours and not to escape the cold. It is also known that ladybirds are eaten by the Green Tree frog in winter, when other insect food is scarce, and also by hungry birds, although they are intensely disliked and are refused (at any rate by the frogs) if other food can be obtained.

Experimental proof that Insect-eating animals, if hungry, will eat unpalatable species

This conclusion was tested as completely as possible by offering conspicuous unpalatable insects of many species to animals from which all other food was withheld. Under these circumstances the insects were eaten, although often after many attempts, and evidently with the most intense disgust.

Natural selection has enabled certain animals to eat unpalatable Insects with apparent relish

Naturalists have always recognised that an insect may be distasteful to one animal, but palatable to another. It is, however, very probable that these differences have been acquired comparatively recently, and have arisen out of the competition for food. In most cases the change of habit has not become so far confirmed that the previously distasteful food is eaten with avidity and pleasure. Again, when we find that the taste of an insect is recognised as nauseous by a standard wide enough to include mites and spiders as well as birds, lizards, and frogs, it appears probable that any difference of opinion is due to an altogether exceptional immunity conferred upon certain species by natural selection.

Nauseous qualities probably do not affect Insect parasites

It is probable, however, that this argument does not apply to insect parasites, which are not in the position to gratify their tastes, but must make the best of the larva in which the parent has deposited her eggs. It is clear that even the most nauseous forms must suffer greatly from the attacks of enemies, for the average number of individuals in each species appears to remain constant. It is likely that the

numbers are kept down by special liability to the
attacks of insect parasites, in one or more stages.
Thus the larva of the Large Garden White (*Pieris
brassicæ*) is known to be nauseous, but the immunity from attack which it enjoys by no means
extends to its insect foes. In the autumn of 1888 I
collected some hundreds of these larvæ in order to
experiment upon the colours of their pupæ. I obtained 109 pupæ, while 424 mature larvæ died from
the presence of the parasitic grubs of Ichneumon flies

The likes and dislikes of Insect-eating animals are purely relative

It may be taken as proved that the continued
spread of some distasteful form and the corresponding diminution of edible species would lead to the
former becoming the prey of insect-eating animals ;
for a point would ultimately be reached, as it was
reached in many of my experiments, when hunger
would become a stronger stimulus than those lesser
prejudices in which a species can very well afford to
indulge while palatable food is abundant. These prejudices having been overcome in confinement, there is
nothing in the conditions of natural life which could
prevent the same result from being reached, as doubtless it has been reached again and again. The comparison of all experiments of this kind ever made with
insects will show that the likes and dislikes of insect-

eating animals are purely relative, and are manifested to a marked extent when they are offered a variety of insects, and when obviously nauseous species are excluded from the list.

Butterflies and moths are freely eaten by lizards, but they are not enjoyed like houseflies or many caterpillars. This is probably because the former are such dusty and unsatisfactory things to eat, with such a small proportion of body in which the nutriment and taste is contained, and so large an expanse of dry membranous wings with their scaly covering. In this respect butterflies contrast unfavourably with moths, and the latter are certainly greatly preferred by lizards and especially birds. The latter have special advantages in being able to pick off the wings before eating the body.

In the excessive abundance of insect-eating animals and the keen competition for food which takes place, we see the conditions which must render the acquisition of an unpleasant taste together with Warning Colours an exceedingly hazardous mode of defence, if assumed by more than a small proportion of the insects of a country. For in so great a press of competition among the innumerable insect-eaters, we may feel sure that some at least would be sufficiently enterprising to make the best of food which at least has the advantage of being easily seen and caught.

The great principle of Warning Colours has deservedly taken a most important place among the

principles which deal with the infinitely complex and
ever-changing relations which obtain between the
most widely separated, no less than between the most
closely allied, members of the organic kingdom.   But,
nevertheless, this principle carries with it its own
compensating principle, which will come into operation precisely as the former advances to the possession
of undue influence.

**The education of enemies assisted by the fact that
Warning Colours and patterns often resemble each other**

It is probably unnecessary for the young insect-
eating animal actually to make trial of every species
of nauseous insect in its locality, in order to be
equipped with an efficient stock of experiences with
which to conduct its later life.   Such an education
would be somewhat dearly bought; it would be unpleasant to the insect-eater and destructive to the
insect.   Since, however, the same colours are employed again and again by unpalatable or dangerous
insects of very different groups, and since the patterns
are also frequently repeated, it is obvious that a comparatively few unpleasant experiences would be sufficient to create a prejudice against any insect with a
colour or pattern at all resembling the nauseous forms
which had already produced so deep an impression
upon the memory.
This conclusion was drawn from the careful comparison of the colours and patterns of all insects which

have been experimentally shown to be distasteful. The colours which produce the greatest contrast, and therefore the greatest effect, upon the eye of an insect-eating Vertebrate, are black and white, and next to this black (or some very dark colour) and yellow, orange, or red; and it was found that nearly all unpalatable or dangerous insects were coloured with these tints. The advantage gained by the acquisition of such colours is twofold : they afford the combinations which are most conspicuous to an enemy, and their number being small, while nauseous forms are numerous, the continual repetition of the same combination becomes a necessity, and this also facilitates the education of enemies.

There are similarly a few eminently conspicuous and simple patterns. These are—alternating *rings* of different colours, and alternating longitudinal *stripes*, both especially suited to the cylindrical body-form, such as that of caterpillars, &c. ; *spots* upon a background with a contrasted colour, especially suited to a wide expanse such as the wings of Lepidoptera. Every insect which has been proved to be distasteful was found to possess one or other of the above patterns or some combination of them. Here also the frequent similarity of the patterns of nauseous insects is primarily due to the fact that there is only a limited number of appropriate patterns, but also because the repetition is in itself advantageous and has therefore been encouraged by natural selection.

Some of the advantages of true mimicry (to be more fully described below) also follow, when a group of insects is rendered conspicuous by the same colours and patterns, and when certain members of the group are noted for the possession of especially unpleasant attributes. Thus it is more than probable that the species marked by alternate rings of black and yellow (including the chrysalis of the Magpie Moth and the caterpillar of the Cinnabar Moth), gain considerable advantages from the justly respected appearance of Hornets and Wasps. It must not be forgotten, however, that the latter also are probably benefited, although to a much smaller extent, by the greater publicity which follows from the resemblance.

The causes which have determined the resemblance between Warning Colours in different Insects

Hence the causes which determine the frequent repetition of the same colours and markings in distasteful forms are as follows: (1) The fact that a limited number of colours and patterns are especially efficient in attracting the attention of enemies, and in thus facilitating their education; (2) the fact that the education of enemies is also rendered easy by requiring them to learn only a small number of patterns and colours; (3) the great additional advantage conferred by trading upon the reputation of a well-known and much-feared or much-disliked insect.

The warning appearance acquired by any insect is also largely determined by the character of its previous appearance, which formed the material upon which at any rate the first steps of the change were built.

In some cases we can successfully read the history of past changes, and can point to certain parts of a warning appearance which are remnants of a previous mode of defence by means of Protective Resemblance.

Thus the orange rings of the caterpillar of the Cinnabar Moth harmonise well with the flowers of its food - plant, ragwort.[1] The acquisition, or perhaps only the greater prominence, of the strongly contrasted black bands, and above all, the gregarious habits, are the later developments which have followed the acquisition of an unpleasant taste. Again, the caterpillars of the Mullein Moth (*Cucullia verbasci*), which are so abundant and conspicuous on various species of Mullein (*Verbascum*), are even now difficult to detect when resting among the dark and yellow sessile flowers studded upon the surface of the

FIG. 46.—Two larvæ of Mullein Moth (*Cucullia verbasci*) on the spike of the Mullein; small in last stage; natural size.

[1] First noticed by T. W. Wood: *Insects in Disguise*, Student. 1868.

thick green spike (see fig. 46).[1] The conspicuous appearance chiefly depends upon the gregarious habits, and upon the fact that the larvæ commonly rest on the upper surface of the large leaves, which form a background against which the larval

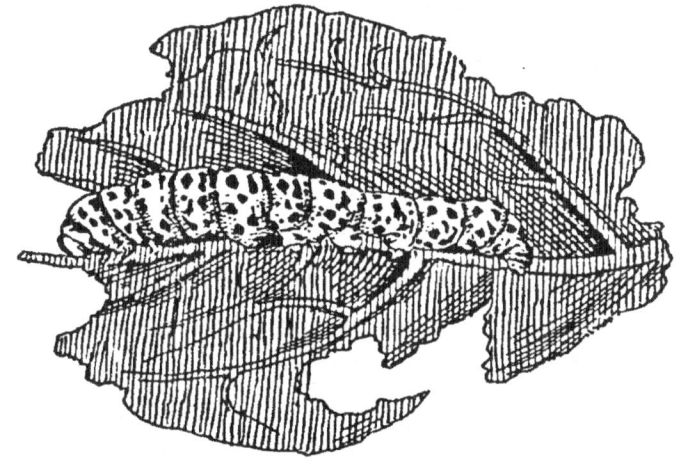

FIG. 47.—Larva of Mullein Moth on leaf of Mullein ; full-fed ; natural size.

colours stand out with startling distinctness (see fig. 47). It has been proved that these larvæ possess an unpleasant although not an extremely nauseous taste, so that here also we have evidence that the change from a palatable well-concealed form is only recent and is as yet incomplete.

[1] This observation was communicated to Professor Meldola by Mr. Thomas Eedle.

CHAPTER XI

WARNING COLOURS (continued)

Sexual colouring may be made use of for warning purposes

In addition to the modes of producing a warning appearance which we have hitherto considered, and which are almost universal in this country, there is another method which is very conspicuous in the tropics. In certain groups of mature insects, and especially in butterflies, the beautiful colours and patterns which have been produced by courtship, appear to have been made use of as an indication of some unpleasant quality.

The differences between Sexual and Warning Colours

The tints used in and produced by courtship are as a rule easily distinguished from Warning Colours, even when both occur in sexually mature insects. The former rarely usurp the whole surface of an insect, and they are carefully concealed during repose. Thus the upper sides of the upper wings of most moths, and the under sides of both wings in butterflies, are generally protectively coloured, and hide the bright colours of other parts when the insect is at rest. If the parts exposed during rest are conspicuously coloured it is clear that they chiefly possess a warning significance. I say 'chiefly,' because it is probable that the appearance of the mature individuals of any species, however much it may be specialised for other ends, possesses a sexual significance, and appeals as an adornment to the modified taste of the individuals of the same species. We have a rough criterion of the extent to which the taste has been modified when we compare the appearances which have other additional meanings with those which possess a sexual value alone, and which are concealed except during flight and are especially displayed in courtship. Warning Colours are also displayed during the sluggish flight of a nauseous species, but the insects with purely ornamental colours are swift and wary when upon the wing.

But quite apart from these considerations, the Warning Colours can be distinguished by the subordination of every other feature to that of conspicuousness. Crude patterns and startling strongly contrasted colours are eminently characteristic of a warning appearance, while the colours and patterns produced by courtship include everything that is most beautiful in insects. The two kinds of appearance differ as an advertisement differs from a beautiful picture: the one attracts attention, the other excites admiration.

The transition from Sexual to Warning Colours

The two groups nevertheless run into each other, and a beautiful transition is afforded by the insects in which sexually produced colours and patterns are made use of for warning purposes. When this is the case the colours spread on to the parts which are exposed during rest, and the flight becomes sluggish, so that they are displayed as completely as possible. These are the insects which are the principal models of mimicry in tropical countries, and Bates's classical paper, in which an intelligible theory of mimicry was first brought forward, deals with the groups which are found in the Amazon valley, and with the forms which resemble them and share the advantages conferred by their well-known and nauseous qualities. The evidence for the existence of such qualities is better considered under the next heading, viz. Mimicry.

Resemblance between such Warning Colours in different species

The members of each of these groups resemble one another to a marked extent; far more so than the species of other groups without Warning Colours. Thus the advantage of facilitating the education of enemies is gained by them, although it has arisen in a manner different from that already described in other unpalatable insects (see pp. 184–86).

The similarity has arisen from the fact that the species in each group are closely related, so that natural selection has maintained an initial resemblance, instead of causing convergence, as it has done with more distantly related species. Hence repetition of the same appearance may be produced by a prevented divergence, as in these cases, or by the actual convergence of forms originally unlike, as in the former cases.

The convergent forms are more perfectly conspicuous, more ideally warning, because they have been further modified from their original appearance; while the forms in which divergence has been arrested have merely adopted, with comparatively slight modification, an appearance which was produced by the operation of other principles, but which is sufficiently well known for the purpose.

These interesting conclusions have gradually grown out of the observations of many naturalists.

The arrested divergence, sometimes aided by actual convergence, has produced such remarkable resemblances between certain species of unpalatable insects, that Bates speaks of the wonderful fact that such species mimic each other. Wallace at first looked upon these mysterious resemblances as due to some unknown cause connected with locality, for the similar species are nearly always found together.

The difficulty was at length explained by Fritz

Müller.[1] This eminent naturalist suggested that both species were benefited by the resemblance, because the number of individuals which must be sacrificed to the inexperience of young birds and other enemies would be made up by both of them instead of by each independently. This fruitful suggestion was at once accepted by Wallace.[2] The mathematical aspects of the subject were accurately worked out by Mr. Blakiston and Mr. Alexander, of Tokio, Japan.[3]

The next step was taken by Professor Meldola,[4] who extended Fritz Müller's explanation of these comparatively rare cases of close resemblance, to the general similarity which obtains throughout whole groups of unpalatable and conspicuous species. ' The prevalence of one type of marking and colouring throughout immense numbers of species in protected groups, such as the tawny species of *Danais*, the barred *Heliconias*, the blue-black *Euplœas*, and the fibrous *Acrœas*, is perfectly intelligible in the light of the new hypothesis.'

This list comprises the whole of the large groups of butterflies alluded to in the last few pages. The species belonging to them are very familiar in every collection of tropical butterflies, while some of them are even abundant in temperate climates. Until re-

[1] *Ituna* and *Thyridia, Kosmos*, May 1879, p. 100, translated by Meldola, *Proc. Ent. Soc. Lond.* 1879, p. xx.

[2] *Nature*, vol. xxvi. p. 86.

[3] *Ibid.*, vol. xxix. p. 405.

[4] *Ann. and Mag. Nat. Hist.* December 1882.

cently, the British butterflies did not include an example, but a large and handsome American Danaid (*Danais archippus*) seems to be gradually extending its range into every country where the food-plants (Asclepiads) of its larva are to be found. Several individuals have been caught in this country of late

FIG. 48.—The North American *Danais arch'ppus*, which has now spread into this country ; upper side ; half natural size.

FIG. 49.—*Danais archippus*, showing the conspicuous colours on the under sides of the wings.

years, and there is no doubt that it will thoroughly establish itself if it can meet with a sufficient supply of larval food, and can withstand the ceaseless energy of collectors. It is far larger than any of our native butterflies. It is shown half the natural size in fig. 48, while fig. 49 gives the appearance of the under side. The latter figure shows that the insect must be as conspicuous at rest as it is on the wing, a fact which is characteristic of those groups of butterflies which are specially defended by being unpalatable. In North America *Danais archippus* is mimicked by *Limenitis misippus*, a butterfly belonging to a very different group.

Although the general resemblance between the species in each of these groups is doubtless due to arrested divergence, there is one very interesting case which is probably to be explained by convergence of groups which were formerly unlike. The *Danaids*, which are found in the same localities as the *Heliconias* of tropical America, have taken the peculiar appearance of the latter, in the arrangement of the colours, and in the long narrow form of the wings. These *Heliconoid Danaids* are therefore distinguished from all the other members of the group. It is quite obvious that both *Heliconias* and *Danaids* are benefited by the fact that the insect-eating animals of the region they inhabit have to learn but a single mode of flight, shape of wing, and general arrangement of colours.

Although these resemblances, produced by convergence or by arrested divergence, are transitional into and often contain an element of true Mimicry, they must be distinguished from the latter. In true Mimicry, the mimicking species are without unpleasant attributes, and are sheltered under the reputation of abundant and well-known forms in which such attributes are strongly marked. In the resemblances considered here, all the similar forms possess unpleasant attributes although they may possess them in different degrees.

The remarkable likeness between many of the species of Burnet Moths (Zygænidæ) is probably due to arrested divergence. They are all conspicuous black and red moths, and some of them are known to be nauseous.

The unpleasant qualities may be concentrated in special parts, which are so placed and coloured as to attract the attention of enemies

In certain cases the warning appearance is of a different kind. The organism possesses a highly conspicuous feature to which the attention of an enemy is directed; if seized, the structure breaks off without harm to the animal, but with very unpleasant results to the enemy. It is probable that this method of defence will be found to be wide-spread.

The defensive value of 'tussocks'

Only recently, in the summer of 1887, this explanation of the beautiful flat-topped tufts of fine hairs, called 'tussocks,' which occur on certain caterpillars, was shown to me by the results of an experiment.[1] The tufts are often light-coloured, and are

[1] *Trans. Ent. Soc. Lond.* 1888, pp. 589-91.

generally placed on an intensely black ground colour, which shows them up and makes them appear to project more than is actually the case. In the well-known 'Hop-dog' or 'Tussock' caterpillar (*Orgyia pudibunda*) there are four 'tussocks,' each upon a separate ring, and the furrows between these rings are of the most intense velvety black. They are concealed until the caterpillar is irritated, when the body is curved in a vertical direction, so that the 'tussocks' diverge, and the furrows appear as black semilunar areas separating them and rendering them conspicuous. The hairs of the 'tussocks' are so fine and so closely packed that the tuft does not appear to be made up of hairs at all, but to be rather a fleshy projection from the back of the caterpillar, and a most convenient part for an enemy to seize. Fine as the hairs are, they nevertheless bristle with minute lateral branches, and would certainly be most unpleasant if brought into contact with the skin of the mouth. If seized by an enemy, the fine hairs come out in immense numbers, and produce such an effect upon the skin of the mouth that the caterpillar escapes unhurt.

The following experiment suggested the explanation which has just been given. A caterpillar of the Common Vapourer Moth (*Orgyia antiqua*) was introduced into a lizard's cage, and when attacked, instantly assumed the defensive attitude, with the head tucked in and the 'tussocks' separated and rendered as

10

prominent as possible. An unwary lizard seized the apparently convenient projection; most of the 'tussock' came out in its mouth, and the caterpillar was not troubled further. The lizard spent a long and evidently most uncomfortable time in trying to get rid of its mouthful of hairs.

On another occasion a full-grown 'Hop-dog' was offered to a hungry adult *Lacerta viridis*, but the lizard knew the danger, and kept trying to find some part of the body which could be safely seized. The caterpillar remained motionless in the defensive attitude during the whole attack, which lasted several minutes. In this attitude the 'tussocks' were held in the most tempting manner, while all other parts of the body bristled with sharp stiff spines. This experienced lizard finally seized the back of the larva a long way behind the 'tussocks,' evidently looking upon the bristles as the lesser evil. Although killed the caterpillar was not swallowed, and it had only been seized after many attempts and the closest examination. It is quite clear that the hairy covering would have saved it from any except a very hungry enemy.

Evidence that Insect-eating Animals learn by experience

When we compare the behaviour of these two lizards we find strong evidence for the opinion that insect-eating animals learn by experience. I have, however, come across more direct and convincing proofs of this conclusion. Thus, the chamæleon which has been previously referred to had just been imported into this country when I received it, and it had probably never seen a common hive-bee in its life. I put a living bee in the cage, and the lizard immediately began to watch it, and, as soon as it had settled, captured it with a dexterous shot of its long tongue. As the tongue was being withdrawn with the bee adhering to the sticky pad at its extremity, the chamæleon was stung and immediately showed signs of discomfort, throwing its head from side to side, and thus jerking the bee off. For many months after this I put bees into the cage at irregular intervals; but the chamæleon's education in this direction was complete, the single experience was sufficient, and no other bee was touched.

Similar highly-coloured and specially defended features occur in certain Marine Animals

A very similar example from an entirely different group of animals has been recently brought forward independently by Professor W. A. Herdman [1] and Mr. Garstang. These naturalists suggest that the brightly-coloured dorsal papillæ of Eolids (Nudibranchiate gastropods) have the same meaning as the 'tussocks' of *Orgyia*, being far more conspicuous than the rest of the body, easily detached, and often reproduced by

[1] *Report of British Association at Newcastle*, 1889.

growth in two or three days. The nematocysts at the tips of the papillæ would convey a lesson to the enemy similar to that taught by the fine hairs of the 'tussocks.'

Mr. Garstang has now tested this suggestion by experiment, and he finds that fish will not attack the Eolids under normal conditions. He therefore threw one of them (the orange variety of *Cavolina Farrani*) into the tank containing young pollack (*Gadus pollachius*), which generally swallow any object while it is descending to the bottom. The Eolid was swallowed and rejected after a second or two by two fish, which then shook their heads as if experiencing discomfort. Similar movements were made when the fish were induced to seize the specially defended tentacles of sea-anemones, and when they attempted to swallow the *Polycirrus*, described on p. 201. Mr. Garstang then found that the Eolid causes a distinct, though faint, tingling sensation when placed on the tongue; while larger species (*Facelina coronata* and *Eolis Alderi*) produce much more marked effects.

The protectively coloured Opisthobranch, *Hermæa* (see p. 70), has well-developed defensive papillæ, and Mr. Garstang finds that whenever a shadow passes over it, the head is at once retracted, and the papillæ rendered very prominent. This behaviour is exactly similar to that described in the larvæ of *Orgyia* (see pp. 197–98). The reaction under the stimulus of light is associated with the unusually large eyes of the genus.

Mr. Garstang has still more recently come across an instance of the same kind in a bright red marine worm, one of the *Terebellidæ* (*Polycirrus aurantiacus*), which, unlike the rest of its family, has dispensed with the protection of a tube, and creeps about in the crevices of stones and among the roots of *Laminaria*. It has an immense number of long, slender·tentacles, and when touched, coils itself up in the middle of them. The tentacles break off very easily, and evidently possess some unpleasant attribute. When the animal is irritated the tentacles become brilliantly phosphorescent, so that they are conspicuous by night as well as day. Mr. Garstang obtained experimental evidence of the validity of this interpretation. He placed a specimen in one of the fish-tanks in the Plymouth Laboratory: only one pollack ventured to seize the worm, but ejected it immediately, and would not touch it again. Another fish made three vigorous attempts to swallow it, but finally left it. Another, a very voracious rock-fish, actually swallowed it, but immediately afterwards began to work its jaws about as if experiencing discomfort. Mr. Garstang then cut the head and tentacles away from the body and threw both pieces into the pollack tank: the tentacles were untouched, but a fight took place over the body, which was torn into several pieces and swallowed with great relish. Mr. Garstang has kindly allowed me to describe these interesting experiments, which have only just been made, and have not, as yet, been published elsewhere.

Adventitious warning colours

Under this head we may include a few very interesting cases in which palatable animals make use of others which are specially defended and conspicuous in order to gain protection. Such a method of defence bears the same relation to Warning Colours as the examples of Adventitious Protection and Colouring bear to true Protective Resemblance (see pp. 76–80).

A mollusc which encourages a dense growth of algæ upon its shell is defended by Adventitious Protective Resemblance; if, however, the algæ were brilliantly coloured and nauseous or poisonous, the example would fall under Adventitious Warning Colouration.

Professor Romanes [1] brings forward examples of a most interesting association of crabs with sea-anemones. He quotes from Möbius [2] the remarkable case of ' two crabs belonging to different genera which have the habit of firmly grasping a sea-anemone in each claw, and carrying them about ; ' also from P. H. Gosse [3] the fact that when the sea-anemone (*Adamsia palliata*) is removed from its position upon the shell of the hermit crab (*Pagurus Prideauxii*), which invariably carries it, the crab ' always took it up in

---

[1] *Animal Intelligence*, International Science Series, pp. 233–34.
[2] *Beiträge zur Meeresfauna der Insel Mauritius.*
[3] *Zoologist*, June 1859, pp. 6580–6584.

its claws and held it against the shell "for the space of ten minutes at a time, until fairly attached by a good strong base." ' This fact seems to indicate that the crab detaches and refixes its anemone when it changes its shell in the course of growth. Romanes, however, quotes from Dr. R. Ball [1] the statement 'that when the common *Sagartia parasitica* is attached to a stone, and a hermit crab is placed in its vicinity, the anemone will leave the stone and attach itself to the hermit's shell.'

Mr. Garstang tells me that at Plymouth there are two species of hermit crab associated with two distinct species of anemone: the *Pagurus* and Actinia mentioned on p. 202, and *P. bernhardus*, which bears *Adamsia Rondeletii*. He finds that hermit crabs are eaten with great relish by fish; they are, in fact, much used as bait by fishermen. Hence the association with the inedible Actinians must be of great service. When the hermit crabs are young and small they are obliged to live in shells without anemones, and Mr. Garstang has often found them, shells and all, in the stomachs of gurnards and other fish. He has never found the larger crabs with shells suited for Actinians in the stomachs of fish.

Another hermit crab at Plymouth (*Pagurus cuanensis*) is always found in shells covered with a bright orange-red sponge (*Suberites domuncula*). Mr. Garstang finds that sponges are intensely disliked by fish;

[1] *Critic*, March 24, 1860.

the smell alone is generally sufficient to repel them. Many Crustacea are known to live in the canal systems of sponges, and are thus protected. The significance of this association is to be found in the fact that Crustacea are the animals most relished and sought after by fishes, and that sponges are extremely repugnant to the latter.

Such cases as these are some indication of the severity of the struggle for existence among marine forms of life. Very interesting evidence of this is to be found in Bateson's notes on the protective habits of shrimps and prawns.[1] He states that the wrasse will find a shrimp if the least bit be exposed, in spite of its protective colouration. If, however, ' the sand be fine, a shrimp will bury itself absolutely.' We can well understand the immense advantage which would be gained by a much persecuted crustacean if it associated with some animal repugnant to its foes.

Colours and markings which direct the attention of an enemy to some non-vital part, but which are not attended by unpleasant qualities

From cases such as those which have been just described we pass, by a very natural transition, to colours and markings which attract the attention of an enemy to some non-vital part after the animal

---

[1] *Journ. Mar. Biol. Ass.*, New Series, vol. i. no. 2, Oct. 1889, pp. 211 *et seq.*

has been discovered. The part seized by the enemy breaks away, and thus gives the animal another chance of escape. The cases differ, however, from the preceding ones in that the enemy is in no way injured by its mistake. In correspondence with this difference such features are associated with Protective Resemblances leading to concealment, and are not themselves highly conspicuous, or are only conspicuous when the animal is thoroughly on the alert. The object of these characters is to direct attack to some unimportant part after all other methods of defence have failed, after disguise has been penetrated or speed surpassed.

This is probably one of the meanings of the brightly-coloured wings of butterflies, in addition to their more obvious use in courtship. When the insect is flying they form a conspicuous mark easily seized by an enemy, and yet readily tearing without much injury to the insect. On this account we generally find the wings torn and notched when an insect has been long on the wing.

In the spring of 1888 I caught a large number of Clouded Yellow Butterflies (*Colias edusa*) in Madeira. The limited number of species in the island (there are only about a dozen), and the abundance of small omnivorous lizards and of insect-eating birds, lead to the keenest pursuit of the butterflies, and I noticed that the hind wings of a considerable proportion of the Clouded Yellows were notched just behind the body. The notches generally corresponded on both hind wings, the insect having been seized at the instant when the wings came together in flight, or during one of its short pauses upon a flower. From the position of the injury it is clear that the enemies were aware of the situation of the body and attempted to seize it, but that they had been frustrated by the swift and wary butterfly with its bright yellow wings extending behind the short body, and offering an apparently convenient point for seizure.[1]

The bright yellow black-bordered under wings of the moths of the genus *Tryphœna* (Yellow Underwings) also possess this among their other meanings, as Mr. Jenner Weir has pointed out: they are exposed during flight, and their colours are far brighter than any other part of the insect. It is also very common to find the margin of these wings notched in captured specimens, and this is often the case when all other parts are fresh and perfect. The red and black under wings of the genus *Catocala* (including the Red and Crimson Underwings) are perhaps useful in the same way.

A still more interesting and obvious character of this kind is to be found in markings which actually suggest the presence of a vital part, such as an enemy would be likely to seize. On one occasion I intro-

---

[1] Skertchly has found such mutilations not uncommon among Bornean butterflies: he also notices the correspondence of the injury on the two sides. The wings are not torn in this way by flying through thick branches ; Skertchly states that even the most fragile butterflies can pass unharmed through dense undergrowth.

duced a Small Heath Butterfly (*Cœnonympha pamphilus*) into a lizard's cage. It was at once obvious that the lizard was greatly interested in the large eye-like mark on the under side of the fore wing: it examined this mark intently, and several times attempted to seize the butterfly at this spot. The observation seems to point to, at any rate, one use of the eye-like markings which are common on the under sides of the wings of butterflies.

A very perfect and elaborate example of the same kind is witnessed in the Hairstreak Butterflies (*Thecla*). Each hind wing in these butterflies is furnished with a 'tail,' which in certain species is long, thin, and apparently knobbed at the end. When the butterfly is resting on a flower the wings are closed and the hind wings are kept in constant motion, so that the 'tails' continually pass and re-pass each other. This movement, together with their appearance, causes the 'tails' to bear the strongest likeness to the antennæ of a butterfly; the real antennæ being held so as not to attract attention. Close to the base of the supposed antennæ an eye-like mark, in the most appropriate position, exists in many species. The effect of the marking and movement is to produce the deceptive appearance of a head *at the wrong end of the body.* The body is short and does not extend as far as the supposed head, so that the insect is uninjured when it is seized.

This interesting fact of the resemblance of the

tails and adjacent parts to a head in *Thecla* has been long known : it was first observed by Dr. Arnold in the case of a foreign species (*Thecla Iarbas*), and was confirmed by Dr. Forsströna in other species. The fact is quoted by Kirby and Spence under ' Means of Defence of Insects,' but the interpretation offered, that the insects 'perhaps thus perplex or alarm their assailants,' hardly expresses the true significance of the character.[1]

The same fact was independently discovered by Mr. R. C. L. Perkins in 1888, and this keen naturalist at once perceived the meaning of the character—to divert the attention of an enemy towards a non-vital part. The discovery is of especial interest because it was made upon an English species (*Thecla W-album*), and because Mr. Perkins tested his explanation by finding that this part had been torn in a considerable proportion of the butterflies.

The observation renders it extremely probable that the slender ' tails ' which occur in the same position in many ' Blues ' (*Polyommatus*), and the bright colours and eye-like spots which are often associated with them, have a similar meaning. The ' Blues,' when resting on a flower, have the same habit of moving the hind wings, as I have often observed in our common English species which are without ' tails.' The movement is such as would render the ' tails ' prominent and antenna-like if

[1] *Kirby and Spence*, People's Edition, 1867, p. 423.

they were present ; and it may, therefore, have persisted from a time when the butterflies possessed these
appendages. .

Similar features in Reptiles

A similar interpretation applies to the tails of
lizards, which break off the instant an attempt is
made to capture the animal by seizing this part. The
tail is, of course, the first part which the pursuer has
the chance of seizing. The great length of the tail,
and the rapidity with which it is renewed after being
shed, also support this interpretation.

Similar features in Mammals

It is very possible that the well-known peculiarity
of the tail of the dormouse is to be explained in the
same manner. The large bushy tail of the squirrel
may possess a similar meaning (among others), for an
enemy in pursuit would be liable to get only a mouthful
of fur. In the north of Europe the squirrels which
frequent the birches are black, while those on the
pines are brown : both varieties, which are probably
protective, become greyish in winter, and thus harmonise with the frosted bark. But the tails of both
retain their summer colour, and would be thus more
conspicuous. This fact was pointed out to me by my
friend Mr. H. Balfour.[1]

[1] On the other hand a seasonal change in the colour of the tail

Similar features in Mollusca

Semper [1] has shown that certain freely exposed and active snails in the Philippines (*Helicarion*) have the same power of readily parting with their tails, and this is also true of a snail in the West Indies (*Stenopus*). The tail, or rather hinder part of the foot, which the animal sheds when it is seized and afterwards renews, is more conspicuous than the rest of the body. Semper found that the tails had been shed in about ten per cent. of the individuals of a species (*Helicarion gutta*) very common in the north-east of Luzon.

Recognition Markings

A special kind of marking is often of great value in attracting the attention of individuals of the same species, instead of attracting the attention of enemies. From its obvious relation to the latter form of marking it is best included under the division of Warning Colours. Mr. A. R. Wallace has directed attention to the importance of Recognition Markings, and an account of them will be found in his recently published

seems to be not uncommon in certain localities in this country. The tail becomes cream-coloured at the end of summer, but resumes its ordinary appearance at the beginning of winter. Smaller differences appear to be general, the summer fur on the tail being coarser and more uniformly red than the winter fur.—Bell's *British Quadrupeds*, 2nd edition, p. 279.

[1] Semper: *Animal Life*, International Scientific Series, pp. 395 *et seq.*

volume, 'Darwinism' (pp. 217–27).[1] Such characters may be of use in aiding a species to escape from its enemies. Thus gregarious mammals, ' while they keep together, are generally safe from attack, but a solitary straggler becomes an easy prey to the enemy; it is therefore of the highest importance that in such a case the wanderer should have every facility for discovering its companions with certainty at any distance within the range of vision' (*loc. cit.* p. 217). Recognition Markings would be especially useful ' at a distance or during rapid motion in the dusk of twilight, or in partial cover.'

Recognition Markings in Mammals

A very beautiful and familiar illustration is given by Mr. Wallace—the white upturned tail of the rabbit, by which the young and inexperienced, or the least wary individuals, are shown the way to the burrow by those in front. It is very interesting to compare this marking with that of the skunk, which has been already described as possessing a very conspicuous white tail. In the latter case the tail is held so that the slow-moving animal is always conspicuous, and appeals to the imagination and memory of its enemies ; the tail of the rabbit only becomes conspicuous when it is needed by other individuals of the same species, and

---

[1] The principle of Recognition Markings is set forth in a work by the late Alfred Tylor, *Colouration in Animals and Plants*, 1886, p. 30.

when the animal is already alarmed and in full retreat for a place of security.

In this way Mr. Wallace explains the conspicuous markings often present on gregarious ruminants, which are nevertheless protectively coloured in other respects. The remarkable differences in the length and form of the horns of different species are explained in a similar manner.

Recognition Markings in Birds

Mr. Wallace also shows that such characters are especially numerous and suggestive among birds. ' Recognition Marks during flight are very important for all birds which congregate in flocks or which migrate together ; and it is essential that, while being as conspicuous as possible, the marks shall not interfere with the general protective tints of the species when at rest. Hence they usually consist of well-contrasted markings on the wings and tail, which are concealed during repose, but become fully visible when the bird takes flight ' (*loc. cit.* p. 222).

Recognition of Birds' eggs may be aided by variation in certain species

It is very probable that the great variation in the colours and markings of birds' eggs, which are laid close together in immense numbers, may possess this

significance, enabling each bird to know its own eggs.
I owe this suggestive interpretation to my friend
Mr. Francis Gotch : it is greatly to be hoped that
experimental confirmation may be forthcoming. The
suggestion could be easily tested by altering the
positions of the eggs and modifying their appearance
by painting. Mr. Gotch's hypothesis was framed
after seeing a large number of the eggs of the guillemot
in their natural surroundings. It appears to be a
more feasible explanation than that offered by Mr.
Wallace. 'The wonderful range of colour and marking
in the eggs of the guillemot may be imputed to the
inaccessible rocks on which it breeds, giving it complete protection from enemies ' (*loc. cit.* p. 214).

Recognition Markings in Insects

Turning to insects, I do not believe with Mr.
Wallace that colours and markings generally are to
be explained in this way, although many instances
of undoubted recognition characters will probably be
found among them. In fact, a very interesting
example only recently came before me.

It has been already mentioned that Lepidopterous
larvæ are especially subject to the attacks of parasitic
insects (Hymenoptera and Diptera), which lay their
eggs in or upon them. It is of the highest importance
for a parasite to know whether a larva is already
' occupied,' and also to ensure that other parasites

shall recognise and avoid the larvæ in which it has laid its eggs. When the eggs are laid within the body of a caterpillar the skin is pierced, and a small amount of blood exudes and generally forms a black clot. These black spots are probably recognised by other parasites, and the larva is consequently avoided. Although the spots would disappear after a change of skin, the parasites generally lay their eggs at about the same period of larval growth, and would be warned over a considerable part of this period. Although these are not, properly speaking, Recognition Markings, we shall see that they form the foundation on which such characters have arisen.

Other parasites (among the Hymenoptera), such as those of the genus *Paniscus*, lay eggs upon the body of their prey. The eggs are pear-shaped, and are firmly fixed by the stalk, which is knobbed at the end. So tightly do the eggs adhere that the caterpillar can change its skin without removing them (see pp. 275–77). Several eggs are fixed upon a large caterpillar, two or three upon a small one, although the number varies greatly in different individuals.

These external eggs are black and shining, and they are very conspicuous against the colour of the caterpillar, which is generally green. When Professor Weismann was staying with me in the summer of 1887, I showed him a larva of the Puss Moth (*Cerura vinula*) to which several eggs were attached. This led to a discussion as to the meaning of the colour, in

the course of which we both independently arrived at
the opinion that it is adapted to serve as a warning
to other parasites that the larva is already ' occupied.'
The eggs, being black, somewhat resemble the scars
caused by the introduction of internal eggs, so that
the species which deposit such eggs may be warned
off, as well as those of the genus *Paniscus.*

CHAPTER XII

PROTECTIVE MIMICRY

WE now approach one of the most interesting aspects of our subject, and one that has played an important part in the history of evolution and of natural selection.

History of the subject

The fact that certain butterflies belonging to widely separate groups, but inhabiting the same localities, possess the most remarkable superficial resemblance, has been known for a very long time. An interesting quotation from Boisduval's ' Species Général des Lépidoptères ' (pp. 372, 373) is given by Mr. Roland Trimen at the head of his paper on Mimicry among African butterflies.[1] Boisduval's sentence, written in 1836, refers to an African Swallowtailed Butterfly, which still remains the most remarkable instance of Mimicry known in the world: ' C'est une chose bien remarquable que de voir la nature créer à côté les uns des autres l' *Euplœa Niavius*, le

[1] *Linn. Soc. Trans.* xxvi. p. 497.

Diadema dubia, et le *Papilio Westermanni,* trois Lépidoptères qui se ressemblent presque complétement par le port, le dessin, et la couleur, quoique appartenant à des genres fort éloignés et de tribus différentes.'

From 1836, and the even earlier dates at which these remarkable resemblances had been noticed, until 1862, no attempt at explanation had been made ; but in that year Mr. Bates's classical paper appeared.[1] In this admirable essay the author showed the advantage which must necessarily be gained by a palatable form, hard pressed by enemies, if it sheltered itself under the reputation of some conspicuous species well known to be inedible.

Only three years before, Darwin, writing to Asa Gray, had said : ' I cannot possibly believe that a false theory would explain so many classes of facts as I think it certainly does explain. On these grounds I drop my anchor, and believe that the difficulties will slowly disappear.'[2] One great difficulty which had so long been a puzzle to naturalists was therefore satisfactorily explained by the new theory, within a few years of Darwin's prediction.

It is most delightful to read of the interest and enthusiasm with which Bates's paper was received by Darwin. ' In my opinion it is one of the most remarkable and admirable papers I ever read in my

[1] *Contributions to an Insect Fauna of the Amazons Valley. Linn. Soc. Trans.* vol. xxiii.
[2] *Life and Letters,* vol. ii. p. 217.

life,' he writes. 'I am rejoiced that I passed over the whole subject in the " Origin," for I should have made a precious mess of it. You have most clearly stated and solved a most wonderful problem. Your paper is too good to be largely appreciated by the mob of naturalists without souls; but rely on it that it will have *lasting* value, and I cordially congratulate you on your first great work.'[1] This was Darwin's opinion of a theory which is often lightly criticised or even condemned by many biologists who offer nothing in its place.

The relation of the theory of Mimicry to Evolution

Mr. Bates's paper afforded a twofold support to the arguments in the 'Origin of Species,' at a very critical time in the history of these opinions. In the first place it showed that an important class of facts was unintelligible upon any theory except that of evolution. The proof of this is best given in Darwin's own words, also quoted by Mr. Francis Darwin.[2] 'By what means, it may be asked, have so many butterflies of the Amazonian region acquired their deceptive dress? Most naturalists will answer that they were thus clothed from the hour of their creation —an answer which will generally be so far triumphant that it can be met only by long-drawn arguments; but it is made at the expense of putting an

---

[1] *Life and Letters*, vol. ii. pp. 391–93.
[2] *Ibid.*, vol ii. pp. 391–92.

effectual bar to all further inquiry. In this particular case, moreover, the creationist will meet with special difficulties; for many of the mimicking forms of *Leptalis* can be shown by a graduated series to be merely varieties of one species; other mimickers are undoubtedly distinct species, or even distinct genera. So again, some of the mimicked forms can be shown to be merely varieties, but the greater number must be ranked as distinct species. Hence the creationist will have to admit that some of these forms have become imitatory by means of the laws of variation, whilst others he must look at as separately created under their present guise; he will further have to admit that some have been created in imitation of forms not themselves created as we now see them, but due to the laws of variation! Professor Agassiz, indeed, would think nothing of this difficulty; for he believes that not only each species and each variety, but that groups of individuals, though identically the same, when inhabiting distinct countries, have been all separately created in due proportional numbers to the wants of each land. Not many naturalists will be content thus to believe that varieties and individuals have been turned out all ready made, almost as a manufacturer turns out toys, according to the temporary demand of the market.' [1]

But Mr. Bates's theory was equally important in

[1] From a review of Bates's paper by Charles Darwin.—*Natural History Review*, 1863, p. 219.

another respect. It not only supported the doctrine of evolution, but it afforded strong confirmation of the theory of natural selection, by which Darwin explained how it was that evolution took place. Every step in the gradually increasing change of the mimicking in the direction of specially protected form, would have been an advantage in the struggle for existence, while the elements out of which the resemblance was built exist in the individual variability of the species, a variability which is hereditary.

The transition from Warning to Mimetic appearances

It will have been observed that Mimicry has already been mentioned in the pages on Warning Colours, and that a gradual transition may be traced from the one principle to the other. And yet Mimicry itself was explained long before many of the conclusions concerning Warning Colours which have been described. In this, as in so many other cases, the steps by which the subject is best approached are almost exactly opposite to the historical steps by which it was gradually understood.

The transition from warning to mimetic forms may be shortly recapitulated.

1. The existence of Warning colours, attitudes, &c. in species which possess some quality unpleasant to the enemies of their class : recognised by Bates in butterflies which are mimicked by others (*loc. cit.* 1862) ; the

principle especially supported and extended by Wallace; also greatly supported by Trimen, Belt, and many others.

2. The tendency for the species in each specially protected group of butterflies to resemble each other (by convergence or arrested divergence) more closely than those in other groups not similarly protected, thus suffering a smaller amount of destruction while their enemies are being educated to avoid them; suggested by Meldola ('Ann. and Mag. Nat. Hist.' Dec. 1882) as an extension of the principle discovered by Fritz Müller and described in the next paragraph.

3. The tendency for the members of distantly related groups of specially protected butterflies to resemble each other, thus gaining the advantages described above: discovered by Fritz Müller ('Proc. Ent. Soc. Lond.' 1879, p. xx.). The fact of the resemblance was first observed by Bates (loc. cit.).

4. An extension of the same principle to all the groups of such specially protected animals: in these the same colours and patterns occur again and again, and advantage is gained by the fact that the types of appearance are those which produce most effect upon the sight of an enemy, as well as by the fact that only a few different types have to be learnt. Certain types of colour and pattern are eminently advantageous for animals in which the special protection is imperfect, because they are so thoroughly advertised by other animals in which the protection is complete and

11

inspires great dread (Poulton, 'Proc. Zool. Soc.' March 1887).

5. The latter cases naturally lead to those of true Mimicry, in which a group of animals in the same habitat, characterised by a certain type of colour and pattern, are in part specially protected to an eminent degree (the mimicked), and in part entirely without the special protection (the mimickers), so that the latter live entirely upon the reputation of the former.   Discovered by Bates in Tropical America, (*loc. cit.* 1862), then by Wallace in Tropical Asia and Malaya (*loc. cit.* 1866), and by Trimen in South Africa (*loc. cit.* 1870).

Cases to which the term Mimicry is best applied

The term Protective Mimicry is best applied to the deceptive appearance of the unprotected forms in the last class only.   Instances of such true Mimicry, in which the resemblance deceptively suggests the presence of some positively unpleasant quality, are so common and striking that we need some name for them; and it is in every way best to retain the historic term.   An additional advantage is that the word Mimicry implies the deception and unreality which is so obvious in the last class of cases described above.   For this reason it is best to include all the other classes and the protected forms in the fifth class, under Warning Colours; for their object is to warn an enemy, as effectually as possible, of real danger or unpleasantness ; while the object of the unprotected forms in the fifth class is to suggest the presence of some unpleasant attribute which has no existence in fact.

The transition from Warning to Mimetic colours which occurs in the fourth class is no objection to this arrangement ; for we cannot escape transition in any classification of the uses of colour in animals. Some authorities have failed to make any distinction between Mimicry and the other forms of Protective and Aggressive Resemblance ; but such an arrangement would confound together cases in which appearance is used for concealment, and those in which it is made use of in order to attract attention.[1]

---

[1] S. B. J. Skertchly has recently (*Ann. and Mag. Nat. Hist.*, Series vi. vol. iii. pp. 477 *et seq.*) urged (*a*) that 'protective resemblance copies stationary objects, mimicry simulates moving ones.' He accordingly maintains that the former is a defence against enemies which attack butterflies at rest, the latter against those which attack them on the wing. He further argues that the attacks of birds constitute the only real danger to an insect on the wing ; (*b*) that certain observers (Skertchly, Pryer, Scudder) agree in considering these attacks to be of very little importance ; and (*c*) that therefore Mimicry, together with the shyness of moving objects exhibited by all butterflies on the wing, 'are habits acquired long since, which have survived the necessity that gave them birth.' He maintains that this argument is supported by (*d*) the 'law that the amount of apprehended danger is measurable by the efforts taken to avoid it,' inasmuch as examples of Mimicry are far rarer than examples of Protective Resemblance.

To this we may reply: (*a*) the alleged contrast between Protective Resemblance and Mimicry is only a usual consequence of the real difference between them (see pp. 222–23, also p. 71). Further-

Convenience of the term Mimicry

Mr. Bates's term has been criticised because it is generally used to describe voluntary actions, whereas the Mimicry alluded to in these pages is of course unconscious, and has been gradually produced by the operation of natural selection.[1] This use of the word

more, the alleged contrast frequently breaks down; thus, a dead leaf driven by the wind (see p. 56), or a piece of stick swinging by a thread, are not uncommonly resembled; while the conspicuous appearance of Mimetic and Warning Colours are most certainly of value during rest as well as during flight (see pp. 189–95). Against the evidence offered by Skertchly (b) may be put the observations of other naturalists (see pp. 228–30; many other examples might have been recorded). We must also remember that very little of the destruction of life which we know takes place is actually witnessed by us. Against (c) may be urged the fact that characters begin to decline directly they become useless, while certain mimetic resemblances are perhaps more wonderfully elaborate and perfect than anything else in the animal kingdom. Every naturalist will agree with (d), but it is really destructive of the argument based upon it. The danger to most mimetic species must indeed be great if measured by the efforts taken to avoid it. Some of the marvellous results of such 'efforts' are described in this volume. Skertchly's argument only applies to the *numerical ratio* between the examples of Mimicry and Protective Resemblance; and this ratio is readily explicable on other grounds. It has been shown that Warning Colours can only be adopted safely by a small proportion of the insect fauna in any country (see pp. 178–80), and also that mimetic individuals must be far rarer than the nauseous forms they resemble (see pp. 243–44; see also p. 231).

[1] After this sentence had been printed I came across a most extraordinary statement of the theory of Mimicry by Skertchly, *l.c.* This theory 'presupposes (a) that danger is universal; (b) that some butterflies escape danger by secreting a nauseous fluid; (c) that other butterflies *noticed this immunity*; (d) *that they copied it.*' The opinions expressed in the words I have italicised will hardly be accepted by a

is, however, well known, and is not likely to mislead anyone; and in addition to its historical accuracy the word is more convenient than any other, as Mr. Wallace has pointed out. Thus we obtain the convenient series of words — *mimic, mimicry, mimetic, mimicker, mimicked, mimicking.*

Various degrees of affinity between mimicking and mimicked species

The various examples of Mimicry may be divided according to the affinity of the forms which resemble each other. Thus a species may mimic another closely allied species, or one of a widely separated family, of a distinct order, class, or even sub-kingdom. Mr. Bates first explained the Mimicry of butterflies and moths, so that in this case the divergence between the species, although generally very great, is not nearly so large as that of other examples. The former, however, includes some of the most striking examples known, and will be first described.

The Butterflies which afford models for Mimicry

In giving some account of Mimicry among butterflies, it is first necessary to speak of the models which are most generally copied in all the warmer parts of

single naturalist. I imagine that even the American Neo-Lamarckians do not follow their founder so far as to believe that the volition of an animal could account for all the details of mimetic resemblance.

the world. These models almost invariably belong to the two great families *Danaidæ* (including *Euplœa*, *Danais*, and *Hestia*) and *Acræidæ*, while the *Heliconidæ* of Tropical America are also mimicked. It has been already pointed out that the *Danaidæ*, which inhabit the region of which the *Heliconidæ* are characteristic, have adopted the appearance of the latter, and may therefore be called Heliconoid *Danaidæ*.[1]

Proof that the mimicked Butterflies are specially protected by a nauseous taste or smell

It is of the greatest importance to prove that these butterflies are specially protected in some unusual and exceptionally complete manner, so that resemblance to them would be advantageous. All observers speak of their slow flight, gaudy colours, and abundance. Thus Mr. Trimen's descriptions of the *Danaidæ* and *Acræidæ* are equally true of the *Heliconidæ*, and of all other butterflies or moths which are the objects of Mimicry. 'The slow flight, the conspicuous colours, the complete disregard of concealment, no less than the great abundance of individuals, are characteristics indicating unmistakably that these butterflies are favoured races, enjoying advantages and immunities above their fellows.'[2] The colours of the under sides

---

[1] Bates called them 'Danaoid *Heliconidæ*,' but Trimen pointed out that the transposed words more truly express the relationship (*loc. cit.* p. 499).

[2] *Loc. cit.* p. 498.

of the wings are the same as those of the upper sides, or at any rate are equally conspicuous. A peculiar and frequently unpleasant smell has been noticed by all observers who have studied these groups. It is probable that the same means of defence is present in the other stages, and this has been proved in certain cases (e.g. *Acræa horta*, Trimen). The unpleasant smell frequently resides in a clear yellow fluid which exudes on the slightest pressure.

Mr. Trimen [1] has also called attention to the fact that the conspicuous butterflies and moths which possess such qualities have a remarkably elastic structure, and can endure very severe pressure without injury. The wings are so flexible that they can be bent and distorted without breaking the nervures. The insects can in this way often recover from the mistaken attacks of insect-eating animals. Skertchly also maintains, from his experience in Borneo, that nauseous properties are accompanied by strong vitality.

There is, unfortunately, too little direct experimental proof of the unpalatability of the specially protected groups which are the chief models of Mimicry. When, however, all the observations are brought together they constitute a fair amount of evidence, and there can be no doubt about the results of future experiments.

Mr. Bates mentions the glands near the anus

[1] *Loc. cit.* pp. 498, 499.

of certain *Heliconidæ*, and he noticed that they all possess a peculiar smell. Neither Bates nor Wallace saw them attacked by birds, dragon-flies, lizards, or predaceous flies (*Asilidæ*), although all these devour other butterflies, and the *Heliconidæ*, from their abundant flocks and slow flight, would be a particularly easy prey.[1]

In Brazil and in Nicaragua some important observations upon the *Heliconidæ* (probably including the *Danaidæ*) were made by Mr. Belt. He says : ' I have seen even spiders drop them out of their webs again ; and small monkeys, which are extremely fond of insects, will not eat them, as I have proved over and over again.'[2] 'I observed a pair of birds that were bringing butterflies and dragon-flies to their young, and although the Heliconii swarmed in the neighbourhood, and are of weak flight so as to be easily caught, the birds never brought one to their nest.' A tame white-faced monkey ' would greedily munch up beetle or butterfly given to him, and I used to bring to him any insects that I found imitated by others, to see whether they were distasteful or not. I found he would never eat the Heliconii. He was too polite not to take them when they were offered to him, and would sometimes smell them, but invariably rolled them up in his hand and dropped them quietly again after a few moments. There could be no doubt, however,

---

[1] *Loc. cit.* p. 510 ; *Darwinism*, p. 234.
[2] *Naturalist in Nicaragua*, p. 109.

from the monkey's actions, that they were distasteful to him.' [1]

Mr. Belt, however, observed that a yellow and black wasp caught these butterflies to store up in its nest, and that the *Heliconidæ* were very wary when the wasp was near, although quite fearless in the presence of other enemies. They were also attacked by a flower-haunting spider. These exceptions are very interesting, because the unpleasant qualities of such specially defended groups generally appeal with success to the taste of animals from the most widely-separated places in the animal kingdom. When certain enemies are thus careless of the qualities which inspire such general respect, it is probable that we witness a result brought about in the first instance by the excessive competition for food. In times of scarcity, any individuals of a species which were able to disregard the unpleasant taste, would be likely to predominate over those with more delicate gustatory susceptibilities.

From Africa, Mr. Trimen quotes an observation of Mr. Bowker upon a small Kaffrarian lizard which pursues a peculiarly wary butterfly with the greatest energy and persistence, while it neglects the inert and abundant *Acræidæ*. Mr. Trimen has made similar observations with regard to dragon-flies and *Mantidæ*, both of which feed largely on butterflies, but were never seen to touch an *Acræa* or *Danais*.[2]

[1] *Loc. cit.* pp. 316, 317.   [2] *Loc. cit.* p. 500.

In India, on the other hand, M. de Nicéville found that *Acræa violæ* was the only butterfly refused by all the species of *Mantis* with which he experimented. Mr. Wallace quotes an observation by the Hon. Justice Newton, upon the bulbul, which chases and greedily devours a swift but palatable butterfly, but could only be induced to touch a *Danais* by repeated persecution.[1]

Some very interesting observations prove that the unpleasant qualities are retained in the dried specimens long after death. ' Mr. Bates observed that, when set out to dry, specimens of *Heliconidæ* were less subject to the attacks of vermin ; '[2] while Professor Meldola even found that ' in an old collection which had been destroyed by mites, the least mutilated specimens were species of *Danais* and *Euplœa.*'[3] This observation has been confirmed by Mr. J. Jenner Weir.

Conclusion warranted by the evidence

I have brought together all the available evidence on this subject, because there has been of late years a rather wide-spread tendency to reject the explanation offered by Mr. Bates. The evidence, however, certainly warrants the conviction that experiment would prove *all (protectively) mimicked species to be in some way disagreeable or even dangerous to the enemies of their class;* and if this be so, the probability that

---

[1] *Darwinism*, p. 235.　　　　[2] *Darwinism*, p. 234.
[3] *Proc. Ent. Soc. Lond.* 1877, p. xii.

all mimetic resemblances are due to natural selection contrasts in the strongest manner with the entire absence of any alternative theory on the part of Mr. Bates's critics.

Conditions under which Protective Mimicry occurs

The conditions under which Mimicry occurs also strongly confirm the view that these resemblances have been produced by the operation of natural selection. These conditions have been found to be very nearly constant by every naturalist who has published any observations on the subject. They have recently been very concisely stated by Mr. Wallace as follows.[1]

‘ 1. That the imitative species occur in the same area and occupy the same station as the imitated.

‘ 2. That the imitators are always the more defenceless.

‘ 3. That the imitators are always less numerous in individuals.

‘ 4. That the imitators differ from the bulk of their allies.

‘ 5. That the imitation, however minute, is *external* and *visible* only, never extending to internal characters or to such as do not affect the external appearance.’

[1] *Darwinism.* pp. 264. 265.

Mimicry in the Butterflies of Tropical America

The *Heliconidæ*, and *Danaidæ* which resemble them, in Tropical America, are chiefly mimicked by *Pieridæ* —the family of 'Whites' to which our common Cabbage Butterflies or Garden Whites belong. Mr. Bates figures one non-mimetic species of the family, and the resemblance to our familiar butterflies, together with the immense difference between it and the mimetic *Pieridæ* in the same country, are very striking.   He also figures many beautiful examples of Mimicry, and the two plates should be studied by anyone who can obtain access to Vol. xxiii. of the 'Transactions of the Linnean Society' (pp. 495–566).   One of the most striking instances is reproduced in Mr. Wallace's recent work.[1]

Mr. Bates found that two different *Heliconidæ* in two adjacent areas were in certain cases mimicked by two varieties of the same species of Pierid, a fact which points to the comparatively recent origin of the resemblance ; for otherwise the two varieties would have had time to become distinct species.   A similar fact was observed by Mr. Wallace in the Malay Archipelago.

The specially protected forms were not only mimicked by *Pieridæ* but by Swallow-tails (*Papilio*) and other butterflies, and in many cases by day-flying moths also.

[1] *Loc. cit.* p. 241.

I have recently heard the objection raised to the theory of Mimicry, that non-mimetic *Pieridæ*, with the typical appearance of their group, are among the commonest butterflies in South America. It is therefore argued that the *Pieridæ* are quite able to take care of themselves, and, if any of them resemble other forms, it cannot be in order to shelter themselves under the reputation of the latter. There does not seem to be much force in this objection ; the forces which tend to the extermination of a species are so nicely balanced against the forces by which its existence is maintained, that a very minute and often quite inappreciable difference may lead to predominance or to scarcity, perhaps ending in extermination. Because the typical *Pieridæ* in South America appear to be predominant, it by no means follows that all the species of this group have always been so. Furthermore, the fact that all mimicking *Pieridæ* are scarce, and that they invariably resemble the butterflies of specially protected groups which are also mimicked by other butterflies and by moths, is a practical and complete answer to the objection.

Mimicry in Asiatic Butterflies

In the Malayan islands and in India Mr. Wallace[1] found that the *Danaidæ* are the chief models for Mimicry, although certain *Morphidæ* and one section

[1] *Linn. Soc. Trans.* vol. xxv. pp. 19–22.

of Swallow-tailed Butterflies (*Papilio*) were also resembled. He gives a list of eighteen examples of mimetic resemblances from among the Swallow-tails alone. Among these was an interesting case in which the males of a Malayan species (*Papilio paradoxa*) mimicked the males of one *Euplœa* (*E. Midamus*), while the females mimicked the females of another *Euplœa* (*E. Rhadamanthus*). A special section of Swallow-tails are also the objects of Mimicry in South America.

The African Papilio merope as an example of Mimicry

By far the most remarkable example of Mimicry is that alluded to in the passage quoted from Boisduval, and which has been worked out, together with many other cases of Mimicry, by Mr. Roland Trimen in South Africa. This wonderful example does not appear to be sufficiently well known, although it is excellently described and illustrated in Mr. Trimen's paper,[1] from which this account and the figures upon the coloured plate are taken. Each of the figures has been reduced to half the natural size.

[2] Fig. 1 closely resembles the male, while fig. 2 represents the female, of a beautiful pale yellow and black Swallow-tailed Butterfly (*Papilio meriones*) which is found in Madagascar. The only marked difference in colour between the sexes is the larger amount of

[1] *Linn. Soc. Trans.* vol. xxvi. pp. 497–522.
[2] See the coloured plate at the beginning of the volume.

black in the female. In Africa a Swallow-tailed Butterfly (*Papilio merope*) occurs, of which the male is represented in fig. 1; the female, on the other hand, is without the 'tails' on the hind wings, and presents a totally different appearance from the male; it occurs in three different varieties, each of which mimics a different species of *Danais* prevalent in its district.

Fig. 3ᴀ represents *Danais echeria*, a specially protected butterfly, common in South Africa, and rendered conspicuous by light brown and white patches and spots upon a black ground. The appearance of the female *P. merope* (the *P. cenea* form) in the same locality is shown in fig. 3. It is very interesting to find that *D. echeria* is also mimicked by two other species of Swallow-tail and by another butterfly (*Diadema mima*). In Natal the ordinary form of the *Danais* is replaced by a variety in which the spots on the fore wings are white instead of ochreous. In Natal the female *P. merope* undergoes a corresponding change, and intermediate varieties of both mimic and mimicked are also found.

The appearance of another unpalatable butterfly, *Danais niavius*, is shown in fig. 4ᴀ. This conspicuous black and white butterfly is abundant in tropical Western Africa, and it is very faithfully imitated by two other butterflies in the same locality, a *Diadema* and a form of the female of *Papilio merope* (the *P. hippocoon* form), shown in fig. 4. This is the example of Mimicry alluded to by Boisduval, although he uses different names for the butterflies. The Natal form of *Danais niavius* is rather different, having broader white markings, especially on the hind wings, and both its mimics have undergone a corresponding change in the same locality. The Natal varieties are represented in figs. 4A and 4. It is very interesting to learn that the two varieties of *P. merope* which mimic the two species of *Danais*, although so widely different in appearance, are still connected by intermediate forms.

A third species of *Danais*, the conspicuous black, reddish-brown, and white *D. chrysippus*, is extremely abundant and has a very wide range, occurring throughout Africa, in Southern Europe, Southern Asia, the Malay Archipelago, &c. This butterfly, represented in fig. 5A, is almost everywhere attended by its mimic, *Diadema bolina*, which occurs in two forms exactly resembling the two forms of the *Danais*. A third variety of the female *P. merope* (the *P. trophonius* form), shown in fig. 5, occurs in Cape Colony, and mimics *Danais chrysippus*.

The female of *P. merope* also occurs as a fourth variety, unlike the others, but connected with the second of them by an intermediate form. Mr. Trimen considers that this variety ' is probably modified, or in course of modification, in mimicry of some other protected butterfly, possibly not a *Danais*.'

To recapitulate this marvellous instance of the relations which may obtain between the organisms inhabiting the same land :—Three well-known species of *Danais* occur in Africa, each of which is mimicked by a special variety of the female of *Papilio merope*; two of the *Danaidæ* present two varieties in the range over which they are accompanied by the *P. merope*, and some females of the latter undergo corresponding changes; intermediate varieties occur and also connect one of these forms with a fourth variety of the female. Furthermore, in Madagascar, which in so many other instances furnishes us with a glimpse of what the ancestral African fauna must have been, a *Papilio* is still living with a male like that of *P. merope*, and having a female only differing in the rather greater predominance of dark markings, a predominance which is thus entirely in the direction of the far darker African females.

It requires a very slight exercise of the imagination to picture the steps by which these marvellous changes have been produced ; for here the new forms have arisen at so recent a date that many of the intermediate stages can still be seen, while the parent form has been preserved unchanged in a friendly land, where the keener struggle of continental areas is unknown.[1]

[1] Since the appearance of Mr. Trimen's important paper, the interest and intricacy of the case have much increased. Mr. Mansel Weale (*Trans. Ent. Soc. Lond.* 1874, pp. 131 *et seq.*) found a number of the larvæ feeding together in one locality, near King William's Town. From these he bred seven males, four females of the *Cenea* form, one of the *Trophonius*, and one of the *Hippocoon* form, thus confirming Mr. Trimen's original suggestion, that all these belong to the same species. The butterflies have furthermore been taken *in coitu* more

Protective Mimicry more often found in female Butterflies than in males

This example enforces a conclusion arrived at by the study of mimetic butterflies in all parts of the

than once. Mr. Mansel Weale also points out that the sexes are remarkably different in their manner of flight.

It is now admitted that the West African forms must be separated from the Southern as a distinct species. The western species is now called *P. merope*, while the name *P. cenea* is extended to cover all the varieties of the southern species. The males of the two species are very similar, but *P. cenea* has somewhat shorter wings, shorter tails, &c. The female *P. cenea* presents all three varieties described above. The western females lack the *Cenea* form which mimics *D. echeria*; and the *Hippocoon* form differs in its larger size and smaller extent of the white markings, especially on the hind wing, in these respects agreeing with the western form of *D. niavius*, which it mimics. It is interesting to note that the western *Trophonius* form, mimicking the small *D. chrysippus*, is little if at all larger than the corresponding form of the southern species. A third variety of the western female, the *P. dionysos* form, is of extreme interest, in that it combines the features of *Hippocoon* and *Trophonius*, and also indicates a transition towards the female *P. meriones* of Madagascar. Mr. Trimen also describes many varieties transitional between the three forms of the southern female. For further details and a thorough discussion of the whole question, consult Mr. Roland Trimen's *South African Butterflies*, vol. iii. 1889, pp. 243–55 ; also the same author in *Trans. Ent. Soc. Lond.* 1874, pp. 137 *et seq.*

Two new species have also been added to the *P. merope* group. In the island of Grand Comoro, adjacent to Madagascar, another species, *P. Humbloti*, has been discovered. *P. Humbloti* somewhat resembles *P. meriones*, but the sexes are even more alike. The other species, *P antinorii*, has been found in Abyssinia, and is of extreme interest, in that the sexes are nearly alike, as in the island forms. It is much to be hoped that further research will bring to light the causes which have favoured the persistence of the ancient unmodified form in this one locality on the mainland of Africa.

I wish to express my sincere thanks to Mr. Roland Trimen for kindly looking through the proofs and suggesting references.

world—that the females are far more liable to assume this method of defence than the males. Thus Mr. Wallace found that the eastern *Morphidæ* and the special group of Swallow-tails were only mimicked by the females of other Swallow-tails ; and similar facts have been observed in America.

Mr. Wallace, in his paper on the Malayan Swallow-tails, explains the commoner mimetic resemblances of females, because ' their slower flight, when laden with eggs, and their exposure to attack while in the act of depositing their eggs upon the leaves, render it especially advantageous for them to have some additional protection.'

Mr. Belt adopts the same explanation, and also makes the very ingenious suggestion that, when the males have not been similarly modified, it is because of the preference of the more conservative sex for consorts which retain the ancestral colour of the group to which they belong. He points out that the males of many of the mimetic ' Whites ' (*Pieridæ*) ' have the upper half of the lower wing of a pure white, whilst all the rest of the wings is barred and spotted with black, red, and yellow, like the species they mimic. The females have not this white patch, and the males usually conceal it by covering it with the upper wing, so that I cannot imagine its being of any other use to them excepting as an attraction in courtship, to exhibit to the females, and thus gratify a deep-seated preference for the normal colour of the order to which ' these mimetic forms belong.[1] Ingenious as this suggestion is, it needs confirmation by a careful observation of the habits displayed during the courtship of these species.

Protective Mimicry in Moths

Certain conspicuous moths are also mimicked by other moths only distantly related to them. A good example was discovered at Amboyna by the naturalists of the ' Challenger ' expedition ; the figures are reproduced by Mr. Wallace.[2]

Protective Mimicry in British Moths .

The only examples of mimicked species known in the British Lepidoptera occur among the moths. Mr. Wallace first called attention to the resemblance of the female of the Muslin Moth (*Diaphora mendica*) to the far more abundant White Ermine Moth (*Spilosoma menthastri*), both species being white with black spots, and occurring at the same time of the year. The mimicked species has been proved to be unpalatable, while the fact that the male of the mimicker is dark coloured and well-concealed is evidence that the latter is palatable. The conclusion should, however, be confirmed experimentally, for, until the test has been applied, we cannot be sure that the case is one of true Mimicry rather than one of

[1] *Loc. cit.* pp. 384–85. [2] *Darwinism*, p. 247.

resemblance between unpalatable forms, described under Warning Colours (see pp. 191–96). The close affinity between the two species, and their similarity to other closely related species, probably indicate that the resemblance is due to arrested divergence rather than convergence; if so, the case before us is not a good and typical example of Mimicry.

A similar objection holds against an example in which I have experimentally proved that the benefits of true Protective Mimicry are certainly conferred. I refer to the unpalatable and abundant white Satin Moth (*Stilpnotia salicis*), which is resembled by its near relative, the common white Gold Tail Moth (*Porthesia auriflua*). The abundance of the latter, and the affinity between the two species, make this instance a very bad one, but the experiments were most instructive, and indicate the benefits derived from Mimicry in a most suggestive manner.

Experimental evidence of the protection afforded by mimetic resemblance

I offered a Satin Moth to a marmoset which was excessively fond of insects, and which had not gratified this appetite for some days. He seized the moth, and ate it with the strongest expressions of disgust, well known to all who are acquainted with him; in fact, had not the attempt been made to take the moth away, I believe that he would have rejected it. As

soon as he had finished this nauseous morsel, I offered
him a Gold Tail Moth, but he shrank from the sight of
it, and had evidently had quite enough of white moths
for the time being. And yet he eagerly seized and
devoured many other inconspicuous insects which I

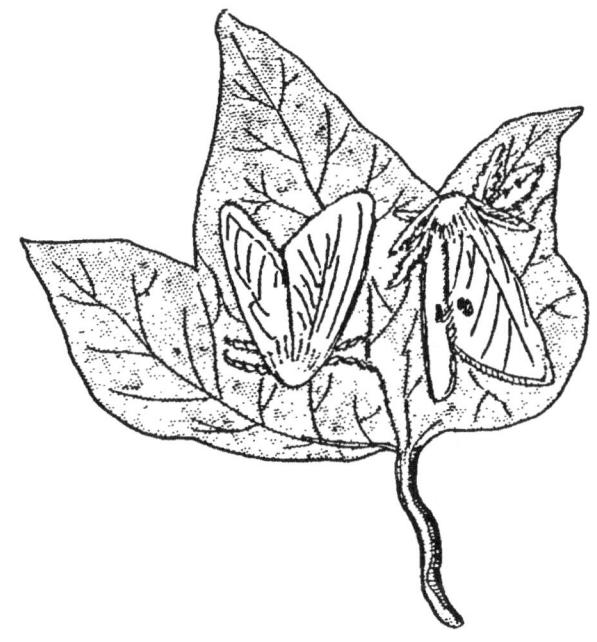

Fig. 50.—Satin Moth (to the left) and Gold Tail Moth on an ivy leaf;
natural size. Although the moths are often of the same size, the
Gold Tail is generally the smaller.

offered to him. It was merely the resemblance to the
moth which had so disgusted him that saved the Gold
Tail, for on another occasion he ate four of these
moths one after the other with the greatest relish.
The marmoset has a far more delicate taste than any

other insect-eating animal with which I am acquainted, and it appears therefore to be certain that the Gold Tail Moth is palatable. I have also confirmatory evidence as to both these species, from the behaviour of other animals. The great abundance of the Gold Tail, in spite of its agreeable taste, must be in part explained by the fact that the caterpillar is specially protected in different ways (see pp. 171–72), but it must also follow from the fact that white and conspicuous moths are generally unpalatable. The strong superficial resemblance between the two moths is shown in fig. 50.

Mimicry may be a source of danger to the mimicked species

While the experiment with the marmoset illustrates the benefits conferred on the mimicker by the well-deserved reputation of the form it imitates, an experiment made by Professor Weismann proves that the safety of both may be endangered when the mimicker becomes relatively abundant. Professor Weismann found that the black and yellow caterpillars of the Cinnabar Moth (*Euchelia jacobææ*) were refused by the Green Lizard (*Lacerta viridis*); he then introduced some young caterpillars of the Fox Moth (*Lasiocampa rubi*), which are very similar in appearance. The lizards first cautiously examined these larvæ, and then ate them. After this they were seen to taste the Cinnabar caterpillars, in order to test whether they were really as unpalatable as they appeared to be.[1]

Further examples from the British Moths

Professor Meldola has also suggested that three abundant species of *Geometræ* (*Asthena candidata, Cabera pusaria*, and *C. exanthemaria*) may be unpalatable, for they are all white and very conspicuous when flying at dusk. If this be- the case it is very probable that the resemblance of two much scarcer Geometers to some of these may be an example of true Mimicry (viz. *Acidalia subsericeata* and the first mentioned ; *Corycia temerata* and the second, or both second and third). It is much to be hoped that the experimental evidence will soon be forthcoming.

I have given many instances of Mimicry in Lepidoptera because the subject has been more fully investigated within the limits of this order, and because of the beauty and interest of the examples themselves. But the same principles are of very wide application, as I shall be able to show in the next chapter, although limited space will prevent me from giving many examples.

---

[1] For these and other experiments on unpalatable insects see *Studies in the Theory of Descent*, Part ii. pp. 336 40; English translation by Professor Meldola.

CHAPTER XIII

PROTECTIVE AND AGGRESSIVE MIMICRY

WE have seen that a Lepidopterous insect occasionally mimics another closely related to it, although the resemblance is almost invariably between distantly connected species ; while in many cases the relationship is very far removed, as when a moth imitates the appearance of a butterfly. Corresponding cases occur in other orders of insects, but we must now pass on to consider some of the numerous instances in which the mimetic species is separated from the form which it deceptively resembles by the wide interval which removes one order of insects from another.

Hymenoptera mimicked by other orders of Insects

The Hymenoptera, including the formidable hornets, wasps, bees, and ants, are more frequently mimicked than any other order. In several of the British moths the wings have lost their scales and have become transparent, while the other parts have

12

also been modified, so as to produce a more or less
perfect resemblance to some stinging Hymenopterous
insect.

Mimicry of Hymenoptera by Lepidoptera

This is the case with two of the hawk-moths, called
Bee Hawks (*Sesia fuciformis* and *S. bombyliformis*),
which in some degree suggest the appearance of
humble-bees. The habits are, however, entirely different, and the resemblance very imperfect—so much
so that a lizard (*Lacerta muralis*), to which I offered a
living specimen, was not imposed upon in the least,
but devoured the insect without hesitation or caution.
Although humble-bees are eaten by lizards, they are
always seized cautiously, and disabled before being
swallowed.

In one respect these Bee Hawks are extremely interesting, for they provide a conclusive answer to those
who believe that such mimetic forms have not been
modified from a condition which is more characteristic
of the group to which they belong. When the Bee
Hawk emerges from the chrysalis its wings are even
now thinly clothed with scales, which are shaken off
in its first flight. The history of the change is still
recapitulated, as in so many other cases, in the history
of the individual.

The two Hornet Clear-wing Moths (*Sphecia api-
formis* and *S. bembeciformis*) afford far more perfect

examples of Mimicry, the resemblance to a hornet or large wasp being so strong that the great majority of people would shrink from them in fear. The insect carries out the imitation to the end, and when seized moves its body as if it were about to sting.

Experimental proof that Protective Mimicry at first deceives an enemy

The protective effect of the resemblance was well seen when I offered one of these moths (*S. bembeciformis*) to *Lacerta muralis*. The lizard was evidently highly suspicious, and yet afraid. It examined the insect very keenly from a distance, approached cautiously, and touched it with its tongue. The effect of this investigation was evidently reassuring, as we might expect ; for the soft scaly body of the moth is very different from the hard polished surface of a wasp or hornet. And yet the lizard seized the moth with the greatest care, by the head and thorax, and began to thoroughly crush these parts, behaving exactly as it would have done with a wasp or bee. The texture, and perhaps the taste, of the insect, however, soon revealed the deception, and the lizard then treated the moth as unscrupulously as any other harmless insect. A few days afterwards I offered another moth of the same kind to the same lizard ; but the lesson had been learnt, and the insect was seized without special examination or caution, and devoured directly it was seen.

This experiment supports the conclusion previously arrived at, that insect-eating animals do not start with an instinctive knowledge, but learn by experience. It also proves that the mimetic resemblance may deceive a peculiarly sharp and clever enemy, and certainly acts as a protection to the insect. In this case the moth was brought within a few inches of the lizard : in nature it would be seen from a much greater distance, and would, doubtless, be at once avoided, unless the enemy was impelled by excessive hunger.

Mimicry of Hymenoptera by Diptera

Other orders of insects also commonly mimic the Hymenoptera. A very common British insect belonging to the Diptera (the order including flies, gnats, daddy-longlegs, &c.) is known as the Drone-fly (*Eristalis*), although it is often wrongly called a Drone. It very frequently flies into houses, and may be seen walking, in a very bee-like manner, on the window-panes. In addition to the striking resemblance to a bee (see fig. 51) it buzzes in a most alarming manner when captured, and moves its body in a way that is too suggestive for the nerves of most people. And yet its anatomical structure is entirely different from that of a bee, and a superficial examination will show that it has only two wings, instead of the four possessed by the Hymenoptera and most of the other orders.

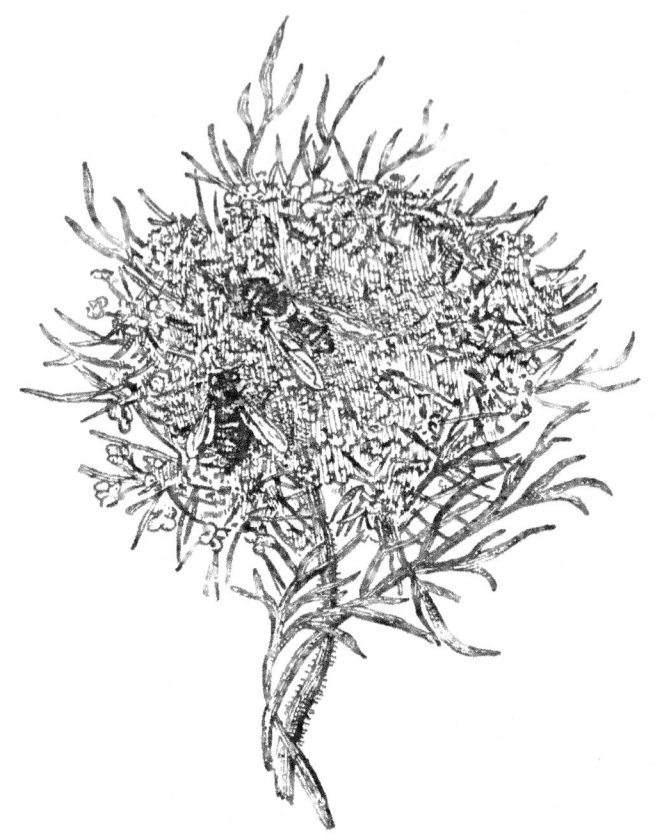

FIG. 51.—Drone-fly (*Eristalis*), to the right, and bee on a carrot-blossom ; natural size.

Mimicry of Hymenoptera by Coleoptera

Among the Coleoptera (beetles) a common English beetle (*Clytus arietis*) resembles a wasp in a very striking manner (see fig. 52). The slender waist, the shape of the head and antennæ, and the black, yellow-banded body are all most suggestive; and although the transparent wings are concealed except during

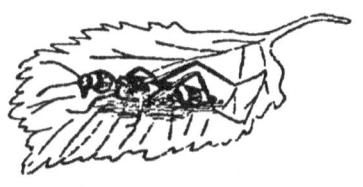

flight, it will be remembered that the wings of a wasp attract very little attention under the same circumstances.

But the most remarkable point in the resemblance can only be appreciated by observ-

FIG. 52.—A common British beetle (*Clytus arietis*) which resembles a wasp; natural size.

ing the living insect. When walking, the slender wasp-like legs are moved in a rapid somewhat jerky manner, very different from the usual stolid Coleopterous stride, but remarkably like the active movements of a wasp, which always seem to imply the perfection of training. Wallace, Belt, and Semper also give many instances of beetles and other insects imitating the appearance of ants, which are extremely abundant, and seem to be very free from attack, in the tropics.

I have chiefly selected a few common British insects as examples of Mimicry, but the number might be multiplied indefinitely from the insect fauna of other countries. The examples are, of course, most remarkable when the appearance of the order to which the mimetic form belongs diverges most widely from that which includes the imitated species.

Mimicry of Hymenoptera by Hemiptera

The flattened bodies of the common plant-bugs (Hemiptera) are peculiarly characteristic, and they are in many ways very unlike other insects. In spite of the immense structural difference which separates them from the Hymenoptera, Mr. Belt describes and figures a Nicaraguan bug which mimics a hornet so closely that he caught it in his net, fully believing that it was a hornet.

So common are mimetic resemblances in tropical countries, although, doubtless, unobserved by any except the keenest naturalists, that Mr. Belt writes : ' Whenever I found any insect provided with special means of defence I looked for imitative forms, and was never disappointed in finding them.' Many examples will be found in his most interesting book, from which I have already often quoted.

Mimicry of Coleoptera by Orthoptera

Many examples are also given by Wallace [1] and Semper.[2] One of the most remarkable is a grass-hopper (Orthoptera) from the Philippine Islands, which mimics a ladybird,[3] and has acquired the rounded convex shape which is characteristic of these

[1] *Darwinism*, pp. 257–61.
[2] *Animal Life*, International Scientific Series, pp. 889–91.
[3] Semper, *loc. cit.* p. 890.

nauseous little beetles, and is so totally different from the usual appearance of a grasshopper. There are also many instances, from this and other localities, of insects resembling specially protected beetles. Sometimes the peculiar defence of the mimicked species takes the form of a hardness so extreme that insect-eating animals are unable to make any way against it. Such uneatable beetles are generally imitated by other, and often distantly related, beetles; but there is a cricket (Orthoptera) which defends itself in this way. The active and predaceous tiger-beetles are also mimicked by other beetles and insects of different orders. Thus in the Philippines a harmless cricket mimics one of these dreaded insects in the closest manner.

A wonderfully detailed example of Mimicry from Tropical America

One of the most interesting cases I have yet met with was found by my friend Mr. W. L. Sclater in Tropical America. In this part of the world leaf-cutting ants are only too well known, being most destructive of the introduced trees. They are seen in countless numbers passing along their well-worn roads to the formicarium, and every homeward-bound ant carries a piece of leaf, about the size of a sixpence, held vertically in its jaws.[1] Mr. Sclater found an insect of an entirely different kind, and, I believe, belonging to

---

[1] An interesting account of these ants, from which I have taken this short description, is given by Mr. Belt, *loc. cit.* pp. 71 *et seq.*

a different order,[1] which mimicked the ant, *together with its leafy burden*. The piece of leaf was imitated by a thin, flat expansion, and the resemblance was so striking that Mr. Sclater's servant, who was a keen observer, actually believed that he was looking at an ant carrying its piece of leaf.

Such cases can be explained by the operation of natural selection

This last example is, as far as I am aware, unique in the detail with which the original is reproduced ; not only is the specially protected species copied, but it is depicted at its usual occupation, and the material upon which it labours is also included in the picture. I quote below a passage from Mr. Belt's work, because it expresses in the clearest and simplest way what I believe to be a complete reply to those who would urge the incompetence of natural selection to produce so faithful and detailed a likeness.

' The extraordinary perfection of these mimetic resemblances is most wonderful. I have heard this urged as a reason for believing that they could not have been produced by natural selection, because a much less degree of resemblance would have protected the mimetic species. To this it may be answered that natural selection not only tends to pick out and preserve the forms that have Protective Resemblances,

---

[1] Professor Westwood and Mr. W. F. Kirby believe that the insect was one of the *Membracidæ* (Homoptera).

but to increase the perceptions of the predatory species of insects and birds, so that there is a continual progression towards a perfectly mimetic form. This progressive improvement in means of defence and of attack may be illustrated in this way. Suppose a number of not very swift hares and a number of slow-running dogs were placed on an island where there was plenty of food for the hares, but none for the dogs except the hares they could catch ; the slowest of the hares would be first killed, the swifter preserved. Then the slowest-running dogs would suffer, and, having less food than the fleeter ones, would have least chance of living, and the swiftest dogs would be preserved ; thus the fleetness of both dogs and hares would be gradually but surely perfected by natural selection, until the greatest speed was reached that it was possible for them to attain. I have in this supposed example confined myself to the question of speed alone, but, in reality, other means of pursuit and of escape would come into play and be improved. The dogs might increase in cunning, or combine together to work in couples or in packs by the same selective process ; and the hares, on their part, might acquire means of concealment or stratagem to elude their enemies ; but, on both sides, the improvement would be progressive until the highest form of excellence was reached. Viewed in this light, the wonderful perfection of mimetic forms is a natural consequence of the selection of the individuals that, on the one side, were more and more mimetic, and, on the other (that of their enemies), more and more able to penetrate through the assumed disguises.' [1]   This argument is of course equally applicable to the wonderful cases of Protective Resemblance for the sake of concealment.

Insects mimicked by animals belonging to a different class

We must now pass on to cases in which there is a still wider interval between the mimicker and the species which shelters it from attack.   The Insecta form one important class of the sub-kingdom Arthropoda, while the Arachnida (including the spiders and scorpions) constitute another of its classes.   Very important anatomical differences separate these two classes, and yet members of the latter are known to mimic species belonging to the former.   Thus, spiders which mimic ants are known in both the Old and the New World.   One such mimetic spider was believed by Mr. Belt to be an ant until he had killed it.   The antennæ of the ant were represented by the two fore legs of the spider, and they were held and moved about in the characteristic manner.   This resemblance has been explained as Aggressive rather than Protective Mimicry, enabling the spiders to approach the ants upon which they are supposed to prey.   Mr. Belt, however, points out that the ants, being free from

[1] *Loc. cit.* **pp. 383, 384.**

attack, are very bold and fearless, so that no disguise is necessary in order to approach them. The spiders, on the other hand, are eagerly sought for by insectivorous birds; hence there is little doubt that the mimicry is protective.[1]

E. G. Peckham also describes two ant-like spiders in North America. *Synageles picata* (see fig. 53) is

FIG. 53.—*Synageles picata*; an ant-like spider (from Peckham).

like an ant in form and colour; but 'by far the most deceptive thing about it is the way in which it moves. It does not jump like the other *Attidæ*, nor does it walk in a straight line, but zigzags continually from side to side, exactly like an ant which is out in search of booty. . . . The ant only moves in this way when it is hunting, at other times it goes in a straight line; but its little imitator zigzags always.' Unlike Mr. Belt's spider, *S. picata* holds up its second pair of legs to represent antennæ. 'Spiders commonly remain nearly motionless while they are eating; *picata*, on the other hand, acts like an ant which is engaged in pulling some treasure-trove into pieces convenient for carrying. I have noticed a female *picata* which, after getting possession of a gnat, kept beating it with her front legs as she ate, pulling it about in different directions, and all the time twitching her ant-like abdomen.' This spider certainly does not molest the

[1] *Loc. cit.* pp. 314, 315.

ants it resembles, so that the Mimicry is probably protective. *Synemosyna formica* (see fig. 54) is even more

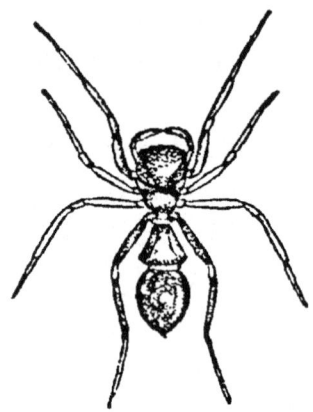

FIG. 54.—*Synemosyna formica,* an ant-like spider (from Peckham).

like an ant than *S. picata* ; it also holds up its second pair of legs as antennæ, and its walk is described as very different from that of closely allied spiders.[1]

Insects which mimic Vertebrate animals

We finally reach the most remarkable cases of Protective Mimicry, in which the defenceless form lives upon the reputation of some dangerous animal belonging to another sub-kingdom.

Mr. Bates describes a South American caterpillar which startled him, and everyone to whom he showed it, by its strong resemblance to a snake, and it even possessed the features which are characteristic of a poisonous serpent.[2]

[1] *Loc. cit.* pp. 110–12.　　　　　　[2] *Loc. cit.* p. 509.

Equally interesting examples are to be found among our British caterpillars. The brown (or occasionally green) mature larva of the Large Elephant Hawk Moth (*Chærocampa elpenor*) generally hides among the dead brown leaves on the older parts of the stem of its food-plant, the Great Willow-herb (*Epilobium hirsutum*). In this position it is difficult to see, for it harmonises well with the colour of its

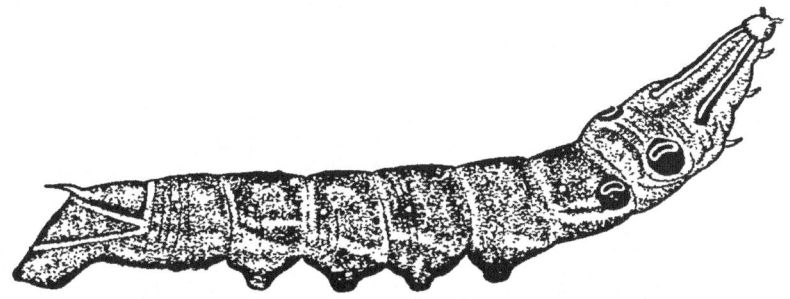

FIG. 55.—The caterpillar of the Large Elephant Hawk Moth (*Chærocampa elpenor*) when undisturbed; full-fed; natural size (from Weismann).

surroundings. It possesses an eye-like mark on each side of two of the body-rings (the first and second abdominal segments); but these markings do not attract special attention when the animal is undisturbed. The appearance of the caterpillar is shown in fig. 55.

As soon, however, as the leaves are rustled by an approaching enemy, the caterpillar swiftly draws its head and the three first body-rings into the two next rings, bearing the eye-like marks. These two rings are thus swollen, and look like the head of the animal, upon which four enormous, terrible-looking eyes are prominent. The effect is greatly heightened by the suddenness of the transformation, which endows an innocent-looking and inconspicuous animal with a terrifying and serpent-like appearance. I well remember the start with which I drew back my hand as I was going to take the first specimen of this caterpillar that I had ever seen. The appearance of the closely allied *C. porcellus* in the alarming attitude is shown in fig. 56. The posterior ' eyes ' are insignificant in this species.

FIG. 56.—The caterpillar of the Small Elephant Hawk Moth (*Chærocampa porcellus*) in its terrifying attitude after being disturbed (from Weismann); stage iv.; about twice natural size.

Such caterpillars terrify their enemies by the suggestion of a cobra-like serpent; for the head of a snake is not large, while its eyes are small and not specially conspicuous. The cobra, however, inspires alarm by the large eye-like ' spectacles ' upon the dilated hood, and thus offers an appropriate model for the swollen anterior end of the caterpillar with its terrifying markings. It is extremely interesting that the caterpillar should thus mimic a feature which is only deceptive in the snake itself.

Experimental proofs of the protection afforded by resemblance to serpents

The success of this method of defence depends upon an elaborate system of intimidation. An obvious criticism suggests that this interpretation is too fanciful, and that the appearance must have some other meaning. It is therefore of the highest importance to bring forward direct evidence proving that insect-eating animals are actually terrified by such caterpillars.

Professor Weismann offered a Large Elephant caterpillar to a tame Jay, which immediately killed and devoured it. His fowls were, however, much awed by the appearance of a larva, although after great deliberation one of them ventured to attack it, when the imposition was of course instantly revealed, and the caterpillar devoured. He then placed one in the seed-trough, and found that the sparrows and chaffinches were effectually kept off by it. One sparrow flew down obliquely, so that the caterpillar was hidden by the side of the trough until the bird was close upon it; the instant the caterpillar was seen, the bird clearly showed its alarm by the sudden manner in which it altered its course.[1] Lady Verney also found that small birds would not come near a tray containing breadcrumbs when one of these caterpillars was placed upon it.[2]

[1] *Loc. cit.* pp. 330-33.   [2] *Good Words*, 1877, p. 833.

I offered a mature larva of the same kind to a full-sized Green Lizard (*Lacerta viridis*), and closely watched the encounter: The lizard was evidently suspicious, and yet afraid to attack the caterpillar, which maintained the terrifying attitude in the most complete manner throughout. The lizard kept boldly advancing and then retreating in fright; but at each advance it approached rather nearer to the caterpillar. After this had taken place many times and nothing had happened, the lizard grew bolder and ventured to gently bite what appeared to be the head of the caterpillar; it then swiftly retired, but finding that there was no retaliation, it again advanced and gave a rather harder bite. After a few bites had been given in this cautious manner, the lizard appeared satisfied that the whole thing was a fraud, and devoured the caterpillar in the ordinary manner. There could be no doubt whatever that the lizard was intimidated at first, and that its alarm was due to the appearance of the caterpillar. I had often given the same lizard equally large hawk moth caterpillars of other species, and they were invariably attacked and devoured without any ceremony. I have never seen a lizard behave with such caution as on the occasion I have just described.

Lizards have good reason for such an instinctive dread, for the appearance suggests that of one of their most terrible foes. Mr. Belt graphically describes the pursuit of a lizard by a snake. 'I was once standing near a large tree, the trunk of which rose fully fifty feet before it threw off a branch, when a green *Anolis* dropped past my face to the ground, followed by a long green snake that had been pursuing it amongst the foliage above, and had not hesitated to precipitate itself after its prey. The lizard alighted on its feet and hurried away; the snake fell like a coiled-up watch-spring, and opened out directly to continue the pursuit; but, on the spur of the moment, I struck at it with a switch and prevented it. I regretted afterwards not having allowed the chase to continue, and watched the issue, but I doubt not that the lizard, active as it was, would have been caught by the swift-gliding snake, as several specimens of the latter that I opened contained lizards.'[1]

It is almost certain that these terrifying appearances in the larvæ of our temperate latitudes first arose in warmer countries, where the danger deceptively suggested by the Mimicry is real and obvious. The success which attends this method of defence, in countries where the reptilian fauna cannot be said to constitute a source of alarm, is similarly due to the inheritance of instincts which arose in the tropics, and which live on, as that unconquerable dread of anything snake-like, which is so commonly exhibited by the land vertebrates, including ourselves.

[1] *Loc. cit.* pp. 339, 340.

Similar mimetic resemblance in tropical larvæ

Lord Walsingham has shown me some beautiful specimens of an Indian caterpillar in which the terrifying ' eyes ' are placed further back than in the Elephant Hawks ; in fact, so far back that the appearance of a head cannot be produced by telescoping the front part into that which bears the marks.   The larva, however, achieves the same end by doubling the front part of its body beneath the rest, the bend being made at the spot where the eye-like marks are placed, so that the

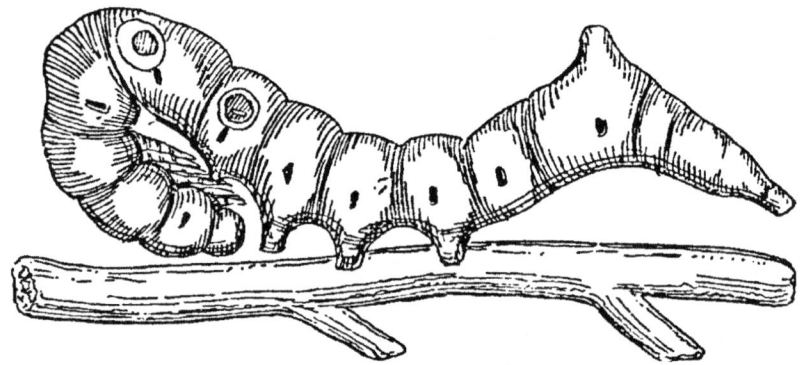

FIG. 57.—Indian larva (*Ophideres*) in the terrifying attitude ; full-fed ; natural size.

latter are brought into an appropriate position at the anterior end, while the real head is of course concealed under the body (see fig. 57).   The effect is not equal to that produced by *Chærocampa*, but it must be very striking when the larva is partially concealed among the leaves of its food-plant.

- The larva of the European Tau Emperor (*Aglia*

Tau) has an eye-like mark which it can expose when attacked, but which is otherwise concealed. The appearance of the larva in its terrifying attitude is shown in fig. 58.

FIG. 58.—The larva of *Aglia Tau* in its terrifying attitude with the eye-like mark exposed ; full-fed ; natural size.

It is obvious that this kind of intimidation requires a caterpillar of a considerable size in order to carry it off; and as a matter of fact we never find it attempted by small caterpillars. A full-grown Large Elephant Hawk is quite as thick as a small snake, and when partly hidden among leaves its length might be safely left to the imagination.

Some reasons why Mimicry is so frequent and perfect in Insects

Although mimetic resemblances are far commoner and more perfect among insects than any other group of animals, the phenomena will probably be found to occur very widely when attention is directed to the subject. It is, however, very unlikely that any one group of animals employs this method of defence to an extent which at all approaches the insects. The defenceless character of the group as a whole, the extent to which they are preyed upon by the higher animals, their enormous fertility, and the rapidity with which the generations succeed each other, are reasons why natural selection operates more quickly and more perfectly than in other animals, producing mimetic resemblances or other forms of Protective Resemblance in number and fidelity of detail unequalled throughout organic nature.

Protective Mimicry in Vertebrata

Mimicry is by no means unknown among the Vertebrate animals. Thus the brightly coloured snakes of the genus *Elaps*, already alluded to, are closely resembled by harmless snakes belonging to different families. The names of several mimetic species, and further instances of the same kind among African snakes, will be found in Mr. Wallace's ' Darwinism.' The same writer also gives many instances of Mimicry in birds. Thus the powerful and aggressive friar-birds in the Malay Archipelago are exactly mimicked by weak and timid orioles, representative species of both friar-bird and oriole occurring in several of the islands.[1]

Two classes of Protective Mimicry .

Two classes may be distinguished among the preceding examples. In the vast majority of cases the

[1] *Loc. cit.* pp. 261-64.

mimicking species is defended against the enemies which are afraid of or dislike the mimicked form. In a relatively few cases, however, it seems to be defended from the attacks of the mimicked form itself. Thus Bates describes a genus of South American crickets (*Scaphura*) which closely resemble 'different sand wasps of large size, which are constantly on the search for crickets to provision their nests with.' Another cricket resembled a predaceous tiger-beetle, and was 'always found on trees frequented by the beetles.'[1] A few other examples will be found in the preceding pages.

Aggressive Mimicry

In most cases of Aggressive Mimicry one species resembles another in order to be able to approach it without exciting suspicion. The former is thus able to injure the latter in some one of the ways which will be described below. Aggressive Mimicry is far less common than Protective Mimicry.

Trimen has shown that hunting spiders are sometimes very like the flies on which they prey. The general resemblance in size, form, and colouring is greatly aided by the movements of the spiders, which evidently mimic 'the well-known movements so characteristic of flies.' Bates has described a *Mantis* which closely resembles the white ants on which it feeds.

In some cases the Mimicry enables the aggressive

[1] *Loc. cit.* p. 509.

form to lay eggs in the nest of that which it resembles, so that its larvæ live upon the food stored up by the latter or even upon the larvæ themselves. The boldness of these enemies sometimes depends upon the perfection of their disguise. Thus the larvæ of flies of the genus *Volucella* live upon the larvæ of bees and wasps. *Volucella bombylans* occurs in two varieties, which prey upon the humble-bees, *Bombus muscorum* and *B. lapidarius,* and are respectively like these Hymenoptera. The resemblance is very perfect, and the flies enter the nests to lay their eggs. *Volucella inanis* is less like the common wasp (*Vespa vulgaris*), and only dares to lay its eggs in the evening at the entrance of the nest, so that the larvæ may crawl in, or they or the eggs may be accidentally carried in by the wasps. It is said that the resemblance often fails to conceal the fly, which is then killed by the wasps.[1] Some Hymenoptera also live upon the labours of other species of the same order, and often resemble the species they delude. Thus, bees of the genus *Psithyrus* closely resemble humble-bees (*Bombi*) : they lay their eggs in the nests of the latter, and their larvæ are developed among those of the *Bombi*.[2]

[1] Mr. C. R. L. Perkins attributes the cautious habits and frequent failure of *V. inanis* to the acuteness and ferocity which distinguish the wasps from humble-bees.

[2] Mr. Perkins considers that the Mimicry is intended to enable the *Psithyri* to leave the nests after emerging from the pupa, rather than to enable the mature females to deposit their eggs in it.

The mimicking form may prey upon some animal which accompanies the species mimicked

In certain cases the Aggressive Mimicry is of a different kind: the mimicking species preys upon some animal which is not afraid of the mimicked species, or which even lives in company with the latter. Thus E. G. Peckham thinks it possible that the ant-like spider, *Synageles picata* (see fig. 53, page 256), may prey upon beetles which accompany ants.[1] As this does not appear to be sufficiently proved, I have retained the spider as an example of Protective Mimicry. Professor Meldola has suggested [2] that certain ant-like spiders from Africa, described by Mansel Weale, are enabled to approach the flies on which they prey, because the latter are not afraid of ants; for ants and flies may be seen feeding together upon the sweet secretion of the same tree.

The clear distinction of both Protective and Aggressive Mimicry into two classes I owe to E. G. Peckham. [3]

[1] *Loc. cit.* p. 111.
[2] *Proc. Ent. Soc. Lond.* 1878, p. xix.
[3] *Loc. cit.* p. 103.

.

CHAPTER XIV

THE COMBINATION OF MANY METHODS OF DEFENCE

IT has already been shown by repeated examples that, although the various uses of colour are quite distinct from one another, they are frequently combined in a single animal. Thus the larvæ of the Elephant Hawk Moths (*Chærocampa elpenor* and *C. porcellus*) were shown to be well concealed among brown leaves; but they assume a terrifying attitude when detected and attacked. I will now bring forward two striking examples of the different lines of defence which are successively adopted by certain caterpillars.

The larva of Puss Moth well concealed by General Protective Resemblance

The larva of the Puss Moth (*Cerura vinula*) is very common upon poplar and willow. The circular dome-like eggs are laid, either singly or in little groups of two or three, upon the upper side of the leaf, and being of a reddish colour strongly suggest the appearance of little galls or the results of some other injury.

13

The youngest larvæ are black, and also rest upon the upper surface of the leaf, resembling the dark patches which are commonly seen in this position. As the larva grows, the apparent black patch would cover too large a space, and would lead to detection if it still occupied the whole surface of the body. The latter gains a green ground-colour which harmonises with the leaf, while the dark marking is chiefly confined to the back. As growth proceeds the relative amount of green increases, and the dark mark is thus prevented from attaining a size which would render it too con-

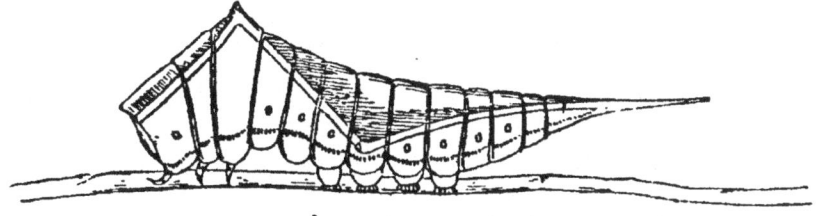

FIG. 59.—The larva of Puss Moth (*C. vinula*) when undisturbed ; full-fed ; natural size.

spicuous. In the last stage of growth the green larva becomes very large, and usually rests on the twigs of its food-plant (see fig. 59). The dark colour is still present on the back but is softened to a purplish tint, which tends to be replaced by a combination of white and green in many of the largest larvæ. Such a larva is well concealed by General Protective Resemblance, and one may search a long time before finding it, although assured of its presence from the stripped branches of the food-plant and the fæces on the ground beneath.

The same larva assumes a terrifying attitude (mimetic of a vertebrate appearance) when disturbed

As soon as a large larva is discovered and disturbed it withdraws its head into the first body-ring, inflating the margin, which is of a bright red colour. There are two intensely black spots on this margin in the appropriate position for eyes, and the whole appearance is that of a large flat face extending to the outer edge of the red margin (see fig. 60). The effect is an intensely exaggerated caricature of a vertebrate face, which is probably alarming to the vertebrate enemies of the caterpillar. The terrify-

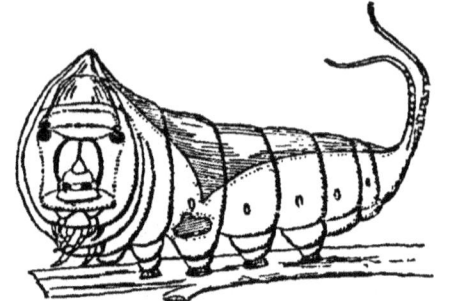

FIG. 60.—The larva of Puss Moth in its terrifying attitude after being disturbed; full-fed; natural size.

ing effect is therefore mimetic. The movements entirely depend on tactile impressions : when touched ever so lightly a healthy larva immediately assumes the terrifying attitude, and turns so as to present its full face towards the enemy; if touched on the other side or on the back it instantly turns its face in the appropriate direction.

Effect heightened by two pink whips

The effect is also greatly strengthened by two pink whips which are swiftly protruded from the prongs of the fork in which the body terminates (see fig. 61). These prongs represent the last pair of larval legs, which have been greatly modified from their ordinary shape and use. The end of the body is at the same time curved forward over the back (generally much

FIG. 61.—One of the pink whips of larva of Puss Moth, completely protruded from the conical receptacle; × 4.

farther than in fig. 60), so that the pink filaments are brandished above the head. Although the filaments are no thicker than a rather coarse cotton thread, they are hollow, and contain a delicate muscle which runs through their whole length and is attached at the top. When the muscle contracts the filament is withdrawn, being turned outside in : protrusion is brought about by the pressure of the blood, which drives the filament before it. The process could be almost exactly imitated by fastening a string to the tip of the finger of a glove and letting the string pass down inside the finger and out at the wrist.

The finger could then be withdrawn by pulling the string, and protruded by blowing into the glove. The filaments are especially used in young and half-grown larvæ; the larger caterpillars often lose the power of protruding them.

The appearance of the caterpillar is sufficiently alarming to human beings, and most people believe that the black marks are really eyes. Rösel was afraid to touch the larva when it assumed its terrifying attitude. Izaak Walton speaks of the black marks as 'his eyes black as jet,' in a description which, by the way, is a translation of the Latin account given by Muffett (or Moufet),[1] or more probably slightly modified from the account in Topsell's 'History of Serpents' (!) which is borrowed from Muffett.[2]

The care necessary if we are to obtain experimental proof of the protective value of such terrifying appearances

I have found that the marmoset was certainly terrified by a large Puss caterpillar, and although it is said to be greedily devoured by birds, I do not expect that the experiment was carried out in a manner at all fair to the larva. When a larva is unscrupulously flung into a cage by some one from

[1] *Insectorum sive minimorum Animalium Theatrum.* London, 1634, p. 183.
[2] London, 1658, p. 666.

whom the birds expect to be fed, it is almost certain to be attacked before it has a chance of assuming its terrifying attitude. In conducting such an experiment a healthy vigorous larva should be chosen and carefully introduced, so that it may have the same opportunities of defence which it would possess in a wild state.

The larva of Puss Moth can further defend itself by ejecting an irritant fluid

All the defensive measures hitherto described are of a passive nature, but if further attacked the caterpillar can defend itself in a very effective manner. The lower part of the red margin below the real head of the animal is perforated by a slit-like opening (see fig. 60), leading into a gland which secretes a clear fluid. This fluid is stored up in considerable quantity and is ejected with great force when the caterpillar is irritated. The ' face' being turned towards any point at which the larva is touched, the stream is sent in the direction of the enemy. It has been long known that this fluid causes acute pain if it enters the eye.

In working out the chemistry of this secretion I have been very kindly helped by many eminent chemists. My thanks are especially due to Professor R. Meldola and Mr. A. G. Vernon Harcourt. The secretion proved to be a mixture of formic acid and water: in a mature larva the proportion of acid is as high as forty per cent., and a twentieth of a gramme can be ejected if the caterpillar has not been irritated for some days.   Half grown individuals eject nearly as much, but the fluid is weaker, containing about thirty-three to thirty-five per cent. of acid.   The rate of secretion is slow ; two days and a half after the fluid had been collected from two large caterpillars they only yielded a fortieth of a gramme between them.[1]   So far as we know at present, no other animal secretes a fluid containing anything which approaches this percentage of strong acid.

The value of this strongly irritant liquid is sufficiently obvious.   I have seen a marmoset and a lizard affected by it, and have myself twice experienced sharp pain as the result of receiving a very small quantity in the eye.   Although the secretion is therefore useful as a defence against vertebrate enemies, it is probably chiefly directed against ichneumons.

The most deadly enemy of the larva of the Puss Moth

The caterpillar of the Puss Moth is especially attacked by an ichneumon (*Paniscus cephalotes*), which attaches its shining black eggs to the surface of the skin. These eggs are always fixed in such a position behind the head that the caterpillar cannot bite them or the maggots which hatch from them, and on a spot where

[1] For further details of this investigation see *Report of British Association at Manchester*, 1887, pp. 765–66.

the ichneumon would probably escape the shower of formic acid. I have never witnessed the attack, but I imagine that the ichneumon swoops down upon the back of the larva just behind the head, and holds on so tightly with its sharp claws that it cannot be dislodged by the violent struggles of the caterpillar. Probably many fail and are struck by the acid shower, which has a very fatal effect upon them.

I have enclosed ichneumons of the genus *Paniscus* in a glass cylinder containing the larvæ. The latter showed not the slightest sign of any knowledge of the presence of their deadly foes, until accidentally touched by the ichneumons as they were hurrying up and down in their endeavours to escape. The instant the larvæ were touched they assumed the terrifying attitude and turned towards the spot, the lips of the opening of the gland swollen by pressure from within, in readiness for an immediate discharge. When an ichneumon was held in the forceps and thus made to touch the caterpillar several times, the fluid was ejected almost instantly, while the larva also made vigorous efforts to bite its enemy with its powerful mandibles. A little of the secretion was collected in a tube and placed on the ichneumons, which collapsed at once, and either died or took many hours to recover.

When once the eggs are fixed the larva is doomed ; the maggots begin sucking its juices as soon as their heads emerge from the egg-shell, while the tail remains firmly adherent in the latter. They are thus tightly fixed to the larva by both ends. The caterpillar is nearly always allowed to become full grown and spin a cocoon before the maggots have become large. In this way the latter secure a safe retreat and more abundant food. When they have grown large and their prey is shrivelled and almost dead, they lose the attachment to the egg-shell and devour from all points, until nothing but a dry and empty skin is left. They then spin their own cocoons within that of the caterpillar. The latter is also attacked by other parasites and probably often by vertebrate insect-eaters.

A well-protected larva is often especially liable to attack

Thus, in spite of the fact that the caterpillar possesses so many defensive appliances, it is especially liable to attack, far more so than many other larvæ which are less protected. Mr. G. C. Bignell enumerated seven species of parasites which attack it. At first sight this seems to be a difficulty, but we must remember that we are probably dealing with an animal which has been especially attacked for a long period of time, and which has been saved from extermination by the repeated acquisition of new defensive measures. But any improvement in the means of defence has been met by the greater ingenuity or boldness of foes; and so it has come about that many of the best pro-

tected larvæ are often those which die in the largest
numbers from the attacks of enemies. The exceptional standard of defence has been only reached
through the pressure of an exceptional need.

The larva of Lobster Moth well concealed by Special Protective Resemblance

The caterpillar which I select as a second example
of the way in which various modes of defence may be
combined, is that of the Lobster Moth (*Stauropus
fagi*), which is rare in this country. Its usual food-
plant is beech, and when at rest it is well concealed
by resembling a withered leaf irregularly curled up.
The stalk is represented by two long thin appendages,
which, like the fork of the Puss caterpillar, have been
modified from the last pair of claspers. At rest, these
appendages are held together and appear to be one.
The second and third pairs of true legs are extraordinarily long, but the length of each is halved by
doubling in the middle, and all four doubled-up legs
hang down in a bunch. They thus resemble in the
most remarkable manner the bunches of brown scales
(the stipules of the foliage leaves) which enclose the
buds of the beech, and hang down after the latter are
unfolded. The colour, length, and shape of each
folded leg, and the number of legs which thus hang
down together, are all such as strongly to suggest the
appearance of the scales.

The same larva assumes a terrifying attitude (mimetic of a spider) when disturbed

As soon as the larva is disturbed it holds the anterior part erect, and assumes a terrifying position which mimics that of a large spider. All the points in a spider's attitude and appearance which impress the imagination are seized upon by the larva and exaggerated for the sake of effect, while quite novel touches are added with the same object. The first pair of legs, which are not unusually long, are held so as to suggest the jaws of a spider, but they are larger and more widely gaping than any actual jaws. The four elongated legs are held widely apart and are made to quiver in the most terrific manner, as if the animal was preparing to seize its prey. The hind part of the body is turned so far over the head that the two appendages project over it, and they are at the same time made to diverge. In this position they strongly suggest the appearance of a pair of antennæ, and add an ideal finish to the apparent monster, which is, indeed, exactly like nothing upon earth, but which is, nevertheless, most effective in its appeal to the imagination. When the hind part is thus turned forward, its ventral surface of course becomes the dorsal surface of the abdomen of the supposed spider, and it is appropriately coloured and has an appearance of plumpness which greatly adds to the resemblance. When the larva is much irritated, it gently moves this hinder part from side to side, and with it the antenna-like appendages. . This movement also adds to the general effect.

When the larva is slightly irritated, the position is often imperfectly assumed at first, but as the irritation is repeated and increased, the animal adds the various details which go to make up the terrifying attitude in its most perfect and elaborate form.

Experimental proof of the protective value of the terrifying attitude in the Lobster caterpillar

I offered two of these larvæ to the marmoset, and the results proved the importance of conducting such experiments with the greatest care, if reliable conclusions are to be obtained. The marmoset knew that my boxes contained insects, and was always very keen and excited at the sight of them. When the box containing one of the ' Lobsters ' was opened, the caterpillar was seized and devoured before it had time to alter its position, and before the marmoset could have had the chance of being intimidated. The second caterpillar was placed on the table and made to assume its terrifying attitude, and then the marmoset was allowed to approach it. Although a caterpillar of the same size had just been eaten without the slightest hesitation, the marmoset was much impressed by the alarming sight, and only ventured to attack after the most careful examination, and even then in the most

cautious manner. However, as no resistance was met
with, the larva was soon devoured and greatly relished.
I then tried a similar experiment with a lizard, which
only attacked the larva after a cautious examination.

The interpretation of the attitude assumed by
the irritated caterpillar was originally offered by H.
Müller, and it may be now said to rest upon a basis
of experimental proof. It is also very likely that the
spider-like appearance is a defence against the insect
enemies of *S. fagi*. This is rendered very probable by
H. Müller's observation, that ichneumons keep out of
the way of spiders and are rarely seen in their webs.

The Lobster caterpillar also deceptively suggests that it has been already stung by an insect parasite

But the caterpillar possesses another method of
defence, if hard pressed by an insect foe. On the side
of each of the fourth and fifth
body-rings there is an intensely black patch sunk below
the general surface and concealed by a triangular flap.
When irritated, the flap is
lowered and the black patches
become very conspicuous (see
fig. 62). It is probable, as H.
Müller has suggested, that
these marks serve to imitate the appearance of

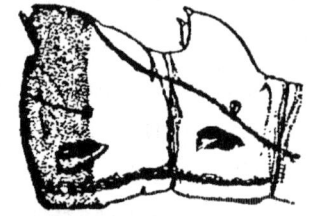

FIG. 62.—The 4th and 5th body-
rings (1st and 2nd abdominal)
of the larva of *Stauropus fagi* as
seen from the right side when
the irritated larva has exposed
the black marks by lowering the
flaps; last stage; × 2¼. The
details of the surface are only
indicated in the posterior part
of the 5th body-ring.

ichneumon stings, or perhaps the result of a struggle with some insect enemy, in which the larva has been wounded. The blood of caterpillars forms a black clot, so that wounds are nearly always black until after the next change of skin.

This is another form of mimetic resemblance—the deceptive appearance of the traces left by an enemy suggesting that the larva is already 'occupied.'

The larva of *Stauropus fagi* therefore bristles with defensive structures and methods. At rest, it is concealed by a combination of the most beautiful Protective Resemblances to some of the commonest objects which are characteristic of its food-plant. Attacked, it defends itself by a terrifying posture, made up of many distinct and highly elaborate features, all contributing to this one end. Further attacked, it reveals marks which suggest that it can be of no interest to an insect enemy, for another parasite is already in possession.

The failure of this combination of defensive methods

The caterpillar is so rare in this country that we know but little of the enemies which attack it. Two parasites are, however, mentioned in Mr. Bignell's list. Its very rarity, however, proves the constant failure of all defensive measures. There is little doubt that the larva is in the same position as that of the Puss Moth, but has not been equally successful.   The means of defence have been the response on the part of the organism to the increasing attacks of enemies, and the latter on their part have met the response by increased vigilance, activity or boldness.   Mr. Belt's metaphor of the mutual selective action between dogs and hares exactly explains the relation between these highly-protected larvæ and their enemies, and serves to show why it is that less attacked larvæ are also less defended (see pp. 253–55).

When we compare the elaborate defence of these two much-persecuted larvæ, with the far simpler and less effective protection of many caterpillars which are less subject to attack, we are made to realise the pre-eminence of natural selection in moulding the forms of life around us for their ceaseless mutual strife.

CHAPTER XV

COLOURS PRODUCED BY COURTSHIP

In addition to the colours and patterns which assist an animal to evade or warn off its enemies or to secure its prey, there are also colours and appendages which must have some very different meaning. These appearances are seen in mature animals, and frequently undergo periodical development at times which correspond to the breeding season; and when the two sexes differ, the males are almost invariably the more brilliant. Although far less important and wide-spread than the protective or aggressive colours, they are more generally known and appreciated, because they are conspicuous as well as beautiful, and are freely displayed by the animals which possess them.

The theory of Sexual Selection

However these colours may have arisen, every observer must admit that they are in some way connected with sex. Darwin accounted for them by his celebrated theory of ' Sexual Selection.' [1]   He supposed that

----

[1] *The Descent of Man*, Part ii. *Sexual Selection*.

the æsthetic sense is widely distributed among the higher animals (vertebrates and some of the most specialised invertebrates), and that the colours which certainly appeal to this sense in man, are not without effect in causing gratification to the animals themselves. Among the other forms of rivalry between the males for the possession of the females, there is rivalry in beauty and its appropriate display; and the choice of the females being largely determined by their æsthetic preferences, the beauty and agility of the males has been gradually increased. The females may share in the growing adornment, for the qualities of the male will tend to pass over by degrees into the female offspring, although such tendencies will be often checked by the operation of natural selection, as Mr. Wallace has shown us in a most convincing manner.[1]

This explanation of the origin and meaning of sexual colouring is not accepted by Mr. Wallace, Darwin's great compeer in the discovery of the fruitful principle of natural selection, and he brings forward many difficulties, and suggests alternative explanations in his recent work on ' Darwinism.'

It is of course quite impossible to discuss this most interesting and difficult subject in any adequate manner within the limits of the present work. This volume would, however, be incomplete without some

[1] *Darwinism*, 1st edit. chap. x. pp. 268-300. Further allusions to Mr. Wallace's views on the subject refer to this chapter of his work.

account of the subject; and furthermore there are certain recent observations which seem to me to yield strong support to Darwin's theory.

Insufficient evidence for existence of æsthetic preferences

Mr. Wallace's chief objection is the lack of evidence that the female has any æsthetic preferences at all in the selection of her mate. When, however, he admits that display of their decorative plumage by male birds is 'demonstrated,' and that the females are in all probability 'pleased or excited by the display,' he certainly admits ·the possession of an æsthetic sense; while the insufficient evidence that the final choice of the female is frequently determined by the gratification of this sense, may, I think, be chiefly due to want of patient or discriminating observations upon wild animals in their natural conditions.

Reasons for the lack of evidence

It is a very remarkable fact that the great impetus given to biological inquiry by the teachings of Darwin has chiefly manifested itself in the domain of Comparative Anatomy, and especially in that of Embryology, rather than in questions which concern the living animal as a whole and its relations to the organic world. And yet these were the questions in which Darwin himself was principally interested.

Sexual Selection is still to some extent *sub judice*, simply because the vast majority of those interested in nature are either anatomists, microscopists, systematists, or collectors.   There are comparatively few true naturalists—men who would devote much time and the closest study to watching living animals amid their natural surroundings, and who would value a fresh observation more than a beautiful dissection or a rare specimen.   I trust that it may not be supposed that I in any way undervalue the immense importance of these other subjects ; but there are certain problems which they can never solve, and Sexual Selection is one of these.

The only reliable evidence on this subject can be obtained frcm the study of wild animals in their natural surroundings

Some of the most beautiful sexual colours are found among the butterflies, and the males are frequently far more brightly coloured than the females. Mr. Wallace has pointed out that the only direct evidence is opposed to the theory that any choice is exercised by the females.   The evidence depends upon the observations of several entomologists upon moths, and especially those of Dr. Alexander Wallace, of Colchester, upon *Bombyx cynthia*.   The strength of this evidence is much shaken by the fact that the moths were bred in captivity, and I think that the question can only be settled by careful observation under the most natural conditions. This conclusion is rendered probable by the following considerations.

The female of the Emperor Moth (*Saturnia carpini*) is so eagerly sought by the males, that when a virgin female is taken into a favourable locality the collector is soon surrounded by troops of males which have been guided by a marvellously delicate sense of smell residing in their branching antennæ. So delicate is the sense that the female is recognised perhaps miles away, and recognised as a virgin. Directly mating takes place the other males disappear. In this case selection chiefly, if not entirely, tends to improve the sense of smell in the males and the mode and rapidity of their flight. The mode of flight is probably important in enabling the insect to cover as wide a volume of air as possible while it advances, and thus to stand a greater chance of crossing some thin stratum or current of air in which the odoriferous particles are contained. To such a selective process we must ascribe the wonderful antennæ of these males and their peculiar and rapid flight. Since, however, both males and females are very beautiful, the males possessing the brighter colours, this example seems at first sight to support Mr. Wallace's views. I shall endeavour to show that the facts are capable of an opposite interpretation. I have here called attention to the habits of the species, because it is nearly allied to *Bombyx cynthia*, and because the keenness of the males in pursuing the females is so well known and remarkable.

In spite of this very exceptional keenness in the wild state, my friend Dr. Dixey found in two successive years that it is by no means easy to pair them, when both males and females are bred in captivity. I have had exactly the same experience with the continental Tau Emperor (*Aglia tau*), although the wonderful antennæ of the male show that the powers of this species are even more intense than those of our own Emperor Moth. If there is such a marvellous change in the disposition of these species, it is at least probable that similar changes occur in other species with more phlegmatic males. The difficulty with which the great majority of butterflies and moths can be induced to pair when bred in captivity (although captured females, already fertilised, will generally lay eggs), and the fact that an increased chance of success is afforded by imitating the natural conditions as far as possible, point in the same direction.

The argument applies with even greater force to many of the higher animals. The effect of domestication upon the brain of the domestic duck has been proved in the most striking manner by Sir James Crichton Browne.[1] The comparison between twenty

[1] The interesting facts and conclusions summarised on p. 290 were contained in a paper read at the meeting of the British Association at Sheffield in 1879. The paper has never been published, but Sir James Crichton Browne has kindly allowed me to use the manu-script.

wild and twenty domestic ducks showed that the brain of the former is, in proportion to the weight of the body, nearly twice as heavy as that of the latter. The average weights were as follows :—

	Domestic duck	.	.	1816·768	grammes
Brain of	„ „	.	.	5·370	„
	Wild duck	.	.	1155·813	„
Brain of	„ „	.	.	6·433	„
Brain weight to body weight as 1 to 338·318 in domestic duck					
„ „ „ 1 to 179·669 in wild duck.					

These results were confirmed by the examination of over sixty individuals, in addition to the forty alluded to above.

The effects of this degeneration are seen in the fact that the ‘ wild duck is, from first to last, a superior being, mentally considered, and exhibits an amount of intellectual and instinctive acuteness, and force and independence of character, to which the barn-door variety can make no pretension.’ A careful comparison of the habits and instincts of the type with those of the domestic race, shows that ‘ altogether there is a mental sprightliness and momentum in the wild duck that have no counterparts in its domestic congener.’ The domestic duck, ever since its first subjugation by man, ‘ for eighteen centuries, and notwithstanding occasional infusions of wild blood, has been sinking into imbecility.’

These facts are also true of many other domesticated animals, and they serve to indicate that Sexual Selection can only be tested fairly by the observation of wild forms. This is even the case with the few races which have, perhaps, been raised by domestication to a higher intellectual level; for the mental development which has been induced by artificial selection has reference to the requirements or fancies of man, rather than to the necessities of the species.

The 'Assembling' of male Moths

In many species of moths the males 'assemble' round the freshly emerged female, but no special advantage appears to attend an early arrival. The female sits apparently motionless while the little crowd of suitors buzz around her for several minutes. Suddenly, and, as far as one can see, without any sign from the female, one of the males pairs with her and all the others immediately disappear.

In these cases the males do not fight or struggle in any way, and as one watches the ceremony the wonder arises as to how the moment is determined, and why the pairing did not take place before. All the males are evidently most eager to pair, and yet when pairing takes place no opposition is offered by the other males to the successful suitor. Proximity does not decide the point, for long beforehand the males often alight close to the female and brush against her with fluttering wings.

In watching this wonderful and complicated courtship, one is driven to the conclusion that the female must signify her intention in some way unknown to us, and that it is a point of honour with the males to abide by her decision.

I have watched the process exactly as I have described it in a common northern Noctua, the Antler Moth (*Charæas graminis*), and I have seen the same thing among beetles. The fact is well known to entomologists, and, as far as the evidence goes, it supports Darwin's theory.

The females of certain Butterflies more beautiful than the males

Another class of facts quoted by Darwin is barely alluded to by Wallace; but I think that it will be of the utmost importance in deciding this question when further and more detailed observations are made.

The females of many butterflies are more beautiful than the males, and then ' the plainer males closely resemble each other, showing that here the females have been modified; whereas in those cases where the males are the more ornate, it is those which have been modified, the females remaining closely alike.' [1] Many examples are found among our British butterflies, *e.g.* the Meadow Brown, the Clouded Yellow, and the Whites. The females of such species support the males during the marriage flight, while the opposite is known to occur in many other butterflies. It

---

[1] Darwin *loc. cit.* 1874, p. 318.

is therefore probable that the females take the more active share in the wooing, and that the males have exercised their æsthetic preferences, and have thus caused their mates to be more beautiful than themselves. These striking facts were brought before Mr. Darwin by Professor Meldola, who informs me that he has confirmed the facts by his own observation in the field.

During the past summer (1889) I have seized every available opportunity of watching the wooing of our common white butterflies (*Pieris brassicæ*, *P. rapæ*, and *P. napi*), and I can quite confirm Professor Meldola's prediction. The females were far more ardent than the males, and when the courtship came to an abrupt termination, as it generally did, it was invariably due to the coyness of the males. These facts strongly support the opinion that the beauty of the females has been gradually produced by the preferences of the males.[1]

---

[1] S. B. J. Skertchly has recently (*Ann. and Mag. Nat. Hist.* Sept. 1889, pp. 209 *et seq.*) described a case in which the rare female of *Ornithoptera brookeana* eagerly and persistently courted a male, although males are more abundant and far more brilliantly coloured. Professor Moseley, on the other hand, describes the courtship of *Ornithoptera poseidon* in the following words:—'I once . . . was lucky enough to find a flock of about a dozen males, fluttering round and mobbing a single female. They were then hovering slowly, quite close to the ground, and were easily caught. The female had thus a large body of gaudy admirers from which to make her choice.' (*A Naturalist on the ' Challenger,'* p. 373.) The wide difference between these two accounts of courtship in closely allied species, proves the importance of making *many* observations before we can hope to

Disappearance of the beauty of males when the females become degenerate

I will now return to the Emperor Moth, and attempt to show how its bright colours can be explained by the theory of Sexual Selection. In its present condition the female is certainly passive, and probably always accepts the attention of the first male to arrive. The antennæ, which are so wonderfully complex in the males, are simple and rudimentary in the female, and probably valueless as sense organs. We must therefore believe that the conditions which produced the bright colours and patterns are now at an end, and that their disappearance is only a question of time. And there is evidence for both these conclusions.

If we examine the female chrysalis, the antennæ are seen to be large and well-formed, and altogether out of proportion to the slender thread-like organs which are formed within them. The antennæ have dwindled in the moth, but so recently that the pupal organs within which they are formed have undergone but slight diminution, if any at all. This most interesting fact was brought before my notice by Professor Moseley. Here then we have the clearest evidence

reach a safe conclusion. Professor Moseley's account is, however supported by a large number of observations upon other species, in which the relation between the sexes resembles that obtaining in *Ornithoptera.*

that the female Emperor was very different from the inert creature I have described. In the full possession of her faculties, she doubtless took that intelligent interest in courtship which is to be expected of every properly endowed female.

I have also maintained that under these circumstances the colours are likely to disappear. Such a conclusion can be tested by examining other species in which the degeneration of the female is more complete, and has doubtless occupied a far longer time.

In another genus of Bombyces (*Orgyia*), some of the females (of which the common Vapourer Moth is an example) are far more degenerate. They never leave the cocoon, but lay their eggs all over it ; their antennæ and wings are rudimentary. The male, on the other hand, flies actively about and has enormously developed antennæ. Success in courtship is almost certainly a mere question of speed and keen scent.[1] In this case the male is very plainly coloured in various shades of brown, but he still retains a trace of his vanished beauty in a white spot in the centre of each fore wing. An examination of the pupa shows us that the female once possessed larger wings and more perfect sense organs.

In *Psyche* and allied genera the change has pro-

---

[1] Mr. E. B. Titchener tells me that this is not always the case ; for a female in his possession refused the first male which arrived. The usual experience with the Emperor Moth, &c., seems to indicate that such an exception is very rare.

ceeded much farther in the same direction. In the most degenerate species the female is a mere bag of eggs, without limbs or sense organs; she does not even leave the pupa-case, but thrusts out the end of her body that fertilisation may take place. In the pupa-case of the most degenerate forms, no distinct trace of former organs can be made out, but in that of certain closely allied species they can still be recognised, although in a very rudimentary condition; in others again, still more distinctly. In the extreme forms the degeneration of the female has proceeded as far as it is possible to go, and in all it must be excessively ancient. The males of nearly all *Psychidæ* are characterised by a uniform sombre colour of a brown or grey tint; all bright colours and all traces of pattern are almost invariably absent.

The successive degrees of degeneration and attendant loss of colour by the males have been traced in species all of which belong to the Bombyces; the males are in all cases day-flying. The day-flying Bombyces, in which the females retain full possession of their faculties, are remarkable for the brightness and beauty of their colours, and this is true of species which are probably without any special protection by a disagreeable taste or smell.

The condition presented by the *Psychidæ* was suggested to me by my friend Mr. W. White. I could give many details which seem to explain the cause of the degeneration, but this is unnecessary for the present purpose. The comparison, which is, I believe, now made public for the first time, appears to yield a very strong support to the views of Mr. Darwin on this question.

Sexual Selection tested by the courtship of Spiders

Mr. Wallace quotes an opinion against Sexual Selection which is certainly of the greatest weight, that of our eminent authority on spiders, the Rev. O. Pickard-Cambridge.[1] I am therefore especially pleased to be able to refer to an American paper which has appeared in the present year (1889), describing the most careful observations upon the courtship of spiders.[2] As the result of their investigations, especially directed towards the solution of this very question of the existence of Sexual Selection, the authors come to a conclusion which is the opposite of that drawn by Mr. Pickard-Cambridge.

The spiders of the family *Attidæ*, which were the subjects of investigation, appear to be very suitable for the purpose, because courtship does not appear to be checked or modified by confinement, as it is in so many Lepidoptera. The amount of labour spent in this admirable piece of work may be gathered from

---

[1] *Darwinism*, pp. 296–97.

[2] *Occasional Papers of the Natural History Society of Wisconsin*, vol. i. 1889, Milwaukee. *Observations on Sexual Selection in Spiders of the Family Attidæ*, by George W. and Elizabeth G. Peckham.

the fact that the authors 'often worked four or five hours a day, for a week, in getting a fair idea of the habits of a single species.'

The courtship of *Saitis pulex* appears to be a most elaborate affair. A male was placed in a box containing a mature female. 'He saw her as she stood perfectly still, twelve inches away; the glance seemed to excite him and he moved toward her; when some four inches from her he stood still, and then began the most remarkable performances

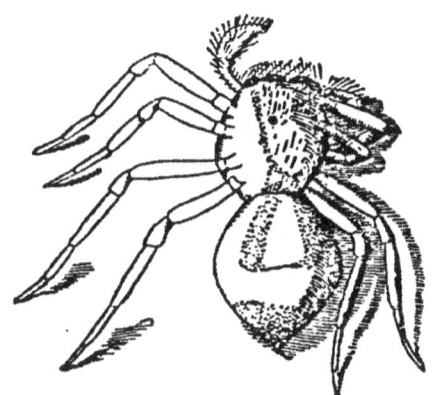

that an amorous male could offer to an admiring female. She eyed him, eagerly, changing her position from time to time so that he might be always in view. He, raising his whole body on one side by straightening out the legs, and lowering it on the other

FIG. 63.—*Saitis pulex.* Male dancing before female (from Peckham).

by folding the first two pairs of legs up and under, leans so far over as to be in danger of losing his balance, which he only maintained by sidling rapidly towards the lowered side. The palpus, too, on this side was turned back to correspond to the direction of the legs nearest it (see fig. 63). He moved in a semicircle for about two inches, and then instantly reversed the position of the legs and circled in the opposite direction, gradually approaching nearer and nearer to the female. Now she dashes towards him, while he, raising his first pair of legs, extends them upward and forward as if to hold her off, but withal slowly retreats. Again and again he circles from side to side, she gazing towards him in a softer mood, evidently admiring the grace of his antics. This is repeated until we have counted 111 circles made by the ardent little male. Now he approaches nearer and nearer, and when almost within reach, whirls madly around and around her, she joining and whirling with him in a giddy maze. Again he falls back and resumes his semicircular motions, with his body tilted over ; she, all excitement, lowers her head and raises her body so that it is almost vertical ; both draw nearer ; she moves slowly under him, he crawling over her head, and the mating is accomplished. After they have paired once the preliminary courtship is not so long.' On one occasion a female was the more eager of the two, but this is evidently very exceptional. The female always watches the antics of the male intently, but often refuses him in the end, ' even after dancing before her for a long time.' Such observations strongly point towards the existence of female preference based on æsthetic considerations.

In *Epiblemum scenicum* ' the females seemed to have some difficulty in choosing from among the males, but after a decision had been reached, and a male accepted, there appeared to be complete agreement.' *Icius sp.* was watched for hours under natural conditions as well as in confinement. ' A dozen or more males and about half as many females were assembled together within the length of one of the rails. The males were rushing hither and thither, dancing opposite now one female and now another; often two males met each other, when a short passage of arms followed. They waved their first legs, sidled back and forth, and then rushed together and clinched, but quickly separated, neither being hurt, only to run off in search of fairer foes.'

The dangers of courtship were also often witnessed. A male of *Hasarius Hoyi* continued to advance after the female had shown signs of impatience, ' when she seized him and seemed to hold him by the head for a minute, he struggling. At last he freed himself and ran away. This same male after a time courted her successfully.' The male of *Phidippus rufus* was caught and eaten when he insisted upon showing off his fine points too persistently. The single female of *Phidippus morsitans* under observation ' was a savage monster. The two males that we provided for her had offered her only the merest civilities, when she leaped upon them and killed them.' The first pair of legs are long and covered with white hairs in the male : ' it was while one of the males was waving these handsome legs over his head that he was seized by his mate and devoured.'

When the males possess any special adornments they make a point of displaying them as fully as possible. The male of *Synageles picata* (see fig. 53, page 256) has the first pair of legs especially thickened : ' these are flattened on the anterior surface, and are of a brightly iridescent steel-blue colour.' As he is approaching the female he pauses ' every few moments to rock from side to side, and to bend his brilliant legs so that she may look full at them; . . . he could not

FIG. 64.—*Habrocestum splendens*; position of male approaching female (from Peckham); × about 8 or 9 times.

have chosen a better position than the one he took to make a display.' In fact, his attitude appears to have first directed the attention of the authors to his peculiar beauty. The male of *Dendryphantes capitatus* has a bronze-brown face, rendered conspicuous by snow-white bands, and, whether intentionally or not, he assumes an attitude which serves admirably to expose this feature to the attentive female. This, however, is by no means his only charm, and his ' antics are repeated for a very long time, often for hours, when at last the female, either won by his beauty or worn out by his persistence, accepts his addresses.' In the male of *Habrocestum splendens* the abdomen is of a magnificent purplish red, and he assumes an attitude which displays this beauty very completely (see fig. 64).

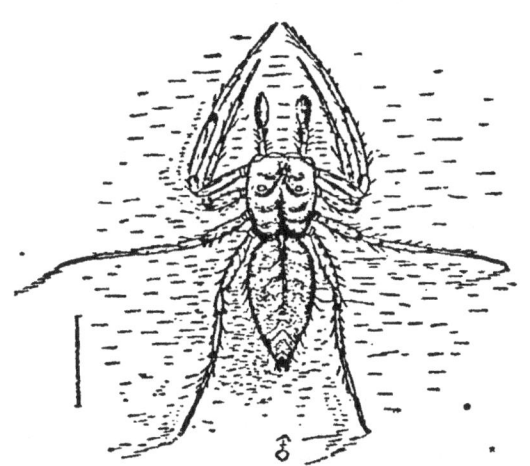

FIG. 65.—*Astia vittata* ; position of red variety of male approaching female (from Peckham).

The case of *Astia vittata* is especially interesting, because there are two well marked varieties of male, one red like the female, and the other black, with three tufts of hair on the cephalothorax. The two forms pass into each other, although the tufts only occur in

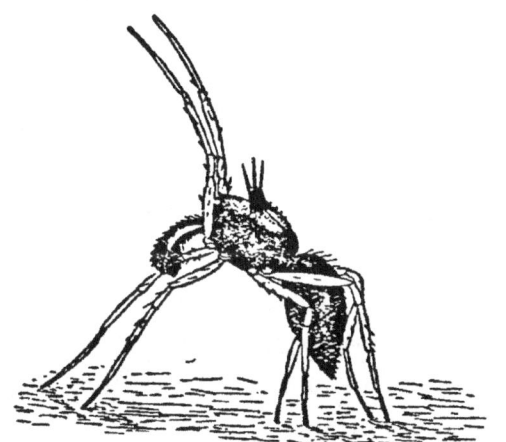

FIG. 66.—*Astia vittata*, var. *niger* ; position of black variety of male approaching female (from Peckham).

the fully developed *niger* form. The attitudes and movements of courtship are entirely different in the two varieties (compare figs. 65 and 66) : ' the *niger* form, evidently a later development, is much the more lively of the two, and whenever the two varieties were seen to compete for a female, the black one was successful.' It must be admitted that these facts afford the *strongest support* to the theory of Sexual Selection.

I have quoted much from this important paper because, as far as I am aware, it is the only attempt to solve the question by the systematic observation of courtship in a single group of animals. Many other equally interesting and significant cases are also recorded, and the paper is profusely illustrated with representations of the most characteristic attitudes. As the result of the whole body of observations the authors are of the opinion that ' in the *Attidæ* we have conclusive evidence that the females pay close attention to the love dances of the males, and also that they have not only the power, but the will, to exercise a choice among the suitors for their favour.' Remembering that this conclusion has only been reached in the *Attidæ* by the closest study, I think we may safely explain the smaller confidence with which we can speak of other animals by the want of sufficiently careful and systematic investigation.

Display in courtship occurs in plainly coloured as well as in ornamental species

In speaking of the display of decorative plumage, Mr. Wallace remarks : ' It is very suggestive that similar strange movements are performed by many birds which have no ornamental plumage to display.' The same facts are probably true of all groups of animals in which the males of certain species are specially adorned. It was certainly the case with spiders, and the ' assembling ' of the males of the sombre Antler Moth has been already described.

The great beauty of many appearances which are, nevertheless, of extreme importance as Protective Resemblances, is doubtless explicable in the same manner. It is likely that all visible parts of the organism, even those with a definite physiological meaning, appeal to the æsthetic sense of the opposite sex. The harsh contrasts and gaudy colours of warning appearances, and the sombre tints which bring perfect concealment, must alike possess a meaning in courtship, but the tendency towards the development of higher forms of beauty is rigorously kept in check by natural selection. Remove the check or render it less exacting, and the tendency at once manifests itself (see pp. 311–13).

Such facts point towards the existence of a wide-spread æsthetic sense in the higher animals

All such facts taken together seem to me to support the opinion that an æsthetic sense exists in the females of all groups in which courtship is accompanied by display of any kind, and that the males vie in gratifying this sense as far as possible with whatever endowments they may possess. I believe that more extended observations like those upon spiders will prove that any variation of the male in the direction of greater adornment will, if not disadvantageous to the species, increase the chances of success in courtship. As such new points arise the attitudes and movements will be modified in order to show them off to the greatest perfection.

Mr. Wallace, while admitting the display and the pleasure given by it to the females, considers that it by no means follows that slight differences of shape, pattern, or colour would lead a female to prefer one male to another, 'still less that all the females of a species, or the great majority of them, over a wide area of country, and for many successive generations, prefer exactly the same modification of the colour or ornament.'

If, however, we consider a hypothetical case in the light of ascertained facts, the probabilities do not seem to favour Mr. Wallace's opinion. Let us suppose that the ancestor of *Synageles picata* only differed from this species in having the first pair of legs coloured like the others. The whole body of facts brought together by G. W. and E. G. Peckham strongly support the opinion that any variation of the male with rather more brilliant first legs would be preferred by the great majority of females, and that the character and its display would be improved during successive generations by their continued preference.

The courtship of the Argus Pheasant

Mr. Wallace says that it was the case of the Argus Pheasant, ' as fully discussed by Mr. Darwin, which first shook my belief in " sexual " or more properly " female " selection.' [1]

Since Darwin's description and Wallace's objection, Mr. Forbes has given us an account of the habits of this bird in its native country ; and the elaborate display of the plumage by the males and the evident attention of the females, render it at least probable that the latter have decided opinions as to the relative beauty of their suitors, and that their preferences have led to the gradual evolution of the wonderful markings, shaded so as to represent ' balls lying loosely within sockets.' [2]

Mr. Forbes tells us that the bird makes ' a large

[1] *Tropical Nature*, pp. 205–206.
[2] The Duke of Argyll in *The Reign of Law*, 1867, p. 203.

circus, some ten to twelve feet in diameter, in the forest, which it clears of every leaf and twig and branch, till the ground is perfectly swept and garnished. On the margin of this circus there is invariably a projecting branch or high-arched root, at a few feet elevation above the ground, on which the female bird takes its place, while in the ring the male —the male birds alone possess great decoration— shows off all his magnificence for the gratification and pleasure of his consort, and to exalt himself in her eyes. When the male bird has been caught . . . the female invariably returns to the same circus with a new mate, even if two or three times in succession her lord should be caught.' [1]

Although the head of the male is completely shielded by the immense fan-like expansion which he unfurls before the female, he can judge of the impression he is making by pushing his head between two of the feathers, or by peeping round the edge of the fan.[2]

The complete subordination of Sexual to Natural Selection

Every one will admit that such a process as this has been rigorously checked by the far more important process of Natural Selection. But it does not there-

---

[1] H. O. Forbes, *A Naturalist's Wanderings in the Eastern Archipelago*, p. 131.
[2] Darwin, *The Descent of Man*, 1874, p. 398, *et seq.*

fore follow, as Mr. Wallace argues, that ' the effect of
female preference will be neutralised by Natural Selection.' It must be remembered that such preferences
can only decide between males which have already
successfully run the gauntlet of by far the greatest
dangers which beset the higher animals, the dangers of
youth. Natural Selection has already pronounced a
satisfactory verdict upon the vast majority of animals
which have reached maturity. The male which has
only just passed this test, and is nevertheless accepted
because of some superior attraction, will soon succumb
and will leave far less offspring than one of equal
or perhaps inferior attractions, which is fitted to live
for the natural term of its life. Furthermore, the
offspring of the former will stand a greater chance of
failure than those of the latter. Natural Selection is a
qualifying examination which must be passed by all
candidates for honours : Sexual Selection is an honours
examination, in which many who have passed the previous examination will be rejected. But the conditions
for qualifying are more rigid than in any existing
system ; for the candidates who have barely qualified,
or have qualified by some piece of luck, or have failed
to keep up to the necessary standard in after life,
will in the end be excluded from the advantages of any
honours they may have gained.

Mr. Wallace states that ' the action of Natural
Selection does not indeed disprove the existence
of female selection of ornament as ornament, but

it renders it entirely ineffective.' This opinion can hardly be maintained if we believe that such preference leads to the failure, comparative or complete, of the plainer or less graceful males, although the equal in other respects of their more successful rivals. Each of these two processes will check the other : Natural Selection will ensure that the males which succeed because of their beauty are among the fittest ; Sexual Selection will ensure that the males which succeed on account of their ' fitness ' are among the most beautiful.

When courtship is decided by wager of battle, Sexual Selection is hardly called into play

When the males habitually fight for the possession of the females, and successful courtship is determined by victory, the results are, as Mr. Wallace points out, due to Natural Selection rather than Sexual Selection. It is, I think, in favour of Mr. Darwin's theory, that any remarkable beauty of colour or pattern is generally absent when the possession of the female is determined by wager of battle ; while the special weapons of such warfare are generally wanting when any peculiar beauty exists : there are, however, exceptions to this rule. Mr. Wallace points out that ' almost all male animals fight together, though not specially armed,' but there is no evidence to show that courtship is frequently decided in this way.

Battles between males are often quite unimportant

Referring again to the spiders of the family *Attidæ*, we read, in the paper quoted on p. 297, that battles between the males were extremely common in the breeding season, but nothing seemed to come of them, and they appeared to be supremely unimportant in determining the issue of courtship. Two males of *Zygoballus bettini*, ‘that were displaying before one female, rushed savagely upon each other and fought for twenty-two minutes, during one round remaining clinched for six minutes. . . . The combatants appeared tired at the close of the battle, but after a short rest were perfectly well, and fought a number of times subsequently.’ Eight or ten males of the very quarrelsome *Dendryphantes capitatus* were put in a box : ‘after two weeks of hard fighting we were unable to discover one wounded warrior.’ The weaker males are probably often driven away, but the crucial point in courtship is to win the consent of the female, and this seems to have been obtained by the tactics already described.

Mr. Wallace refers to the battles of butterflies, but such struggles are neither common enough nor fatal enough to be of great importance in courtship. I have never seen any indication of a struggle between ‘ assembling ’ males, and the courtship of butterflies is generally allowed to proceed unmolested in the presence of other males, although interference leading to a mild kind of struggle is by no means uncommon.

The colours displayed in courtship are generally concealed at other times

The ceaseless sway of Natural Selection over all the results of female choice is well seen in the arrangements by which any conspicuous adornment is concealed until it is wanted. The brilliant legs of the male *Synageles* were only observed when they were being specially displayed : the bright colours of the upper sides of the wings of most butterflies are concealed by the sombre and protective tints of the under sides, except during flight and the short pauses between the flights : the bright under wings of many moths are similarly concealed by the upper wings, which harmonise with the surroundings.

The colours displayed in courtship are specially developed and specially conspicuous in species which are best adapted to their conditions

An interesting contrast is afforded by species which are so perfectly adapted to their conditions that free play is given to Sexual Selection : in these, the colours or appendages used in courtship make up the chief part of the male's appearance. Mr. Wallace points to the abundance of birds of paradise in New Guinea, and of peafowls in India, as proofs that these species are especially well equipped in the battle of life, and he believes that scope has thus been given to the causes which have produced the sexual adornment. This argument of course holds good, even if we are compelled to reject the causes suggested by him. A still better example is afforded by the Australian pigeons, which 'are sometimes adorned with colours vying with those of the gayest parrots and chatterers.' Mr. Wallace explains this fact as due to 'the entire absence of monkeys, cats, lemurs, weasels, civets, and other arboreal mammals'; while the green colour of the upper part may be due to the need of concealment from birds of prey. In some small islands of the Pacific, where such foes are very scarce, the pigeons may assume a rich yellow colour.[1] We see the same tendency in those predaceous insects which have little to fear, and which are swift enough to catch their prey without attempt at concealment.

The dangers of bright sexual colouring may be averted by extreme wariness

In many cases the danger incurred by the attainment of sexual colours may be balanced by the special development of some quality such as extreme wariness. I was very much struck by the opposite kinds of colouring exhibited by the fish which were extremely abundant at low water in the rock pools at Orotava, Teneriffe. The colours of some were extremely beauti-

---

[1] Wallace, *Distribution of Animals*, vol. i. p. 395.

ful and bright, but those were always very shy and difficult to catch ; others were protectively coloured and exactly resembled the sand, rock, or sea-weed, and these when detected were easily captured. Professor W. A. Herdman of Liverpool has also observed the same facts in other groups of marine animals.

CHAPTER XVI

OTHER THEORIES OF SEXUAL COLOURING

IT now remains to consider the causes which Mr. Wallace and other writers believe to have been efficient in producing sexual colouring.

A wide extension of the principle of Recognition Markings is believed largely to explain sexual colouring

In the first place, this distinguished naturalist very widely extends the principle of Recognition Markings, and believes that one of the chief meanings of sexual colouring is to enable ' the sexes to recognise their kind, and thus avoid the evils of infertile crosses.' Thus he considers that ' among insects the principle of distinctive colouration for recognition has probably been at work in the production of the wonderful diversity of colour and marking we find everywhere, more especially among the butterflies and moths ; and here its chief function may have been to secure the pairing together of individuals of the same species.'

Recognition between the sexes appears to be complete, and infertile crossing does not occur even when two species closely resemble each other

To this it may be replied that pairing between the individuals of distinct species is extremely rare, and does not seem to be any commoner among species in which this means of recognition would lead to failure. If the resemblance between the white variety of the female Clouded Yellow (*Colias edusa*, var. *helice*) and the female Pale Clouded Yellow (*Colias hyale*) does not lead to infertile pairing; if the practical identity of the Sallow and Poplar Kittens (*Cerura furcula* and *C. bifida*), of the Swallow Prominent and Lesser Swallow Prominent (*Leiocampa dictæa* and *L. dictæoides*), of the Common and Dark Dagger Moths (*Acronycta psi* and *A. tridens*), does not lead to dangers of the kind, we must conclude that wide differences of colour and pattern cannot have been produced by a gradually lessening number of infertile crosses.

In the case of mimetic species, it is a comparatively common thing for the female of one species to be chased by the male of another, and yet, in spite of a wonderful superficial resemblance between the females, it is very improbable that the courtship proceeds beyond its most preliminary stages. The same is true of the Clouded Yellows referred to above, and of Clouded Yellows and Common Whites. These, and many other examples of the kind show that this means of sexual recognition may, and frequently does, fail without injury to the species.

One of the most fundamental instincts provides for an unfailing recognition between the sexes, in which certainty is ensured by the unanimous witness of all the senses, so that even the closest resemblance between distinct species does not appear· to produce any evils of the kind suggested by Mr. Wallace.

The necessity for Recognition can never explain the æsthetic value of the results produced

It may also be urged that the beauty of the colours and patterns displayed in courtship can never be explained by this principle. For the purposes of recognition, beauty is entirely superfluous and indeed undesirable; strongly marked and conspicuous differences are alone necessary. But these, which are so well marked in Warning Colours, are not by any means characteristic of those displayed in courtship.

If an artist, entirely ignorant of natural history, were asked to arrange all the brightly coloured butterflies and moths in England in two divisions, the one containing all the beautiful patterns and combinations of colour, the other including the staring, strongly contrasted colours, and crude patterns, we should find that the latter would contain, with hardly an exception, the species in which independent evidence has shown, or is likely to show, the existence of some unpleasant quality. The former division would contain the colours displayed in courtship and when the insect is on the alert, concealed at other times.

The immense difference between the two divisions, the one most pleasing, the other highly repugnant to our æsthetic susceptibilities, seems to me to be entirely unexplained if we assume that the colours of both are intended for the purposes of recognition. But these great differences are to be expected if we accept Mr. Darwin's views ; for the colours and patterns of the latter division appeal to a vertebrate enemy's sense of what is *conspicuous*, while those of the former appeal to an insect's sense of what is *beautiful*. It is, of course, highly remarkable that our own æsthetic sense should so closely correspond with that of an insect. I believe, however, that it is possible to account for this wonderful unanimity in taste.

Our standards of beauty have been largely created for us by insects

Our standards of beauty are largely derived from the contemplation of the numerous examples around us, which, strange as it may seem, have been created by the æsthetic preferences of the insect world. One of the most fruitful inquiries originated by Darwin has been the renewed investigation of the marvellous relation between insects and flowers, a subject which had been previously attacked by Sprengel in 1798.

15

Darwin's work has been extended by others, and especially by Hermann Müller. As the result of these investigations it is now well known that the fertilisation of flowers has been largely carried on by insect agency, and that insect preferences have decided as to the colours and patterns which prevail among the wild flowers of any country.[1] This is now generally admitted, and as Mr. Wallace himself points out, 'we have abundant evidence that whenever insect agency becomes comparatively ineffective, the colours of the flowers become less bright, their size and beauty diminish, till they are reduced to such small, greenish, inconspicuous flowers as those of the rupture-wort (*Herniaria glabra*).[2]'

But if this conclusion be accepted, if the beauty of flowers has followed so completely from insect selection, are we not compelled to admit that insects possess an æsthetic sense—a sense which could discriminate between the slightly different attractions displayed by suitors, just as we all admit that it has discriminated between the slightly different attractions displayed by flowers?

[1] Consult *The Fertilisation of Flowers*, by Hermann Müller, English translation by D'Arcy W. Thompson : London.   Also *British Wild Flowers in relation to Insects*, by Sir John Lubbock: Nature Series.

[2] *Loc. cit.* p. 332.

The musical value of the song of birds cannot be explained as a means of Recognition between the sexes

Similar objections may be urged against Mr. Wallace's contention that the songs of birds are to be explained as a means of recognition, and that their 'production, intensification, and differentiation are clearly within the power of natural selection.' Recognition between the sexes, and invitation from the male to the female, are most important benefits conferred by song, but these can never account for the marvellous degree of elaboration, and the high musical value of the results attained by many of our singing birds. The beauty of song is something more than its 'clearness, loudness, and individuality,' just as the beauty of appearance is something more than its conspicuousness ; and the fact that these two forms of beauty are complementary, so that the brightest birds do not sing, while song birds are sober in appearance, is quite consistent with the origin of these qualities by the accumulated results of female preference. We know that the excessive cultivation of one taste is inconsistent with the equal cultivation of others, and when the small brain of a bird is constantly directed to appreciating the beauty of song, it may well become comparatively indifferent to beauty of person. Besides, the qualities conferred by this means are always more or less of a danger to the species, and an especially high development in one direction will tend to prevent any great development in other directions.

The habits of Bower-birds as evidence for the existence of an æsthetic sense

The habits of the Australian Bower-birds are further evidence for the existence of a strongly marked æsthetic sense in birds. Just as certain females are gratified by the display of personal adornment on the part of their suitors, others are pleased by the display and arrangement of beautiful or curious objects collected in the bowers. The latter are built on the ground and are intended for courtship alone, the nests being formed in trees. They are often very elaborate structures, and each species decorates its bower in a different manner. The Satin Bower-bird collects brightly coloured feathers, bleached bones, and shells: 'these objects are continually rearranged, and carried about by the birds whilst at play.' The Spotted Bower-bird lines its bower with tall grasses, kept in place by round stones which are brought from great distances, together with shells. The Regent bird makes use of bleached shells, blue, red, and black berries, fresh leaves, and pink shoots; 'the whole showing a decided taste for the beautiful.'[1]

I have mentioned these well-known but most interesting facts, which were considered by Darwin as

[1] The facts are quoted by Darwin from Gould and Ramsay, *Descent of Man*, pp. 413, 414.

'the best evidence . . . of a taste for the beautiful,' because of the confirmation which has been afforded by some more recent observations upon a New Guinea Bower-bird.

All the æsthetic taste of this bird appears to be concentrated on the bower and its surroundings, for the bird itself is, as its name (*Amblyornis inornata*) implies, very plainly coloured. It is called the Gardener Bower-bird, because of its remarkable habits, and its native name also means 'the gardener.' The bower and adjacent 'small meadow enamelled with flowers' were seen by the Italian traveller, Dr. Beccari,[1] on Mount Arfak, in New Guinea. He states that the *Amblyornis* chooses a flat surface at the base of a small tree, against which, as a central pillar, it builds a very regular conical hut, with an opening at one point. The hut, which is nearly three feet in diameter at the base, is formed of the twigs of an orchid, which, being an epiphyte, bears fresh leaves for a very long time, and greatly adds to the beauty of the bower. Within the hut a small cone of moss, about the size of one's hand, is heaped round the base of the tree. 'Before the cottage there is a meadow of moss. This is brought to the spot and kept free from grass, stones, or anything which would offend

---

[1] An abstract of Dr. Beccari's description appeared in *The Gardeners' Chronicle*, March 16, 1878, with a figure of the bower reproduced from a painting made on the spot. This article is quoted in Gould's *Birds of New Guinea*, vol. i., which also contains a coloured plate founded upon the above-mentioned figure.

the eye. On this green turf flowers and fruit of pretty colour are placed, so as to form an elegant little garden. The greater part of the decoration is collected round the entrance to the nest, and it would appear that the husband offers there his daily gifts to his wife.' Among the objects—which were always brightly coloured—Dr. Beccari noticed the fruit of *Garcinia*, like small apples; the fruits of *Gardenias*; the 'beautiful rosy flowers of a splendid new *Vaccinium* (*Agapetes amblyornithis*);' fungi, and mottled insects. 'As soon as the objects are faded they are moved to the back of the hut.' It is not known whether the female assists the male in making the bower, which is believed to last several seasons.

I think it may be safely affirmed that the explanation of sexual colours as a means of recognition can never account for their æsthetic value, while the existence of an æsthetic sense, to which such characters may appeal, appears to be rendered certain by many observations.

The hypothesis that sexual colouring is due to a surplus of vitality or is developed in relation to underlying structures

Mr. Wallace also believes that the appearance of beautiful colours and the growth of plumes and other appendages is due to a surplus of vitality, and may be connected with the vivacity and excitability of the males in the breeding season. He also accepts Mr. Alfred Tylor's theory that colours and patterns are developed in relation to underlying organs and structures. It is convenient to discuss these two views together, for they have much in common.

Mr. Tylor argued that the modification of pattern in the different regions of the body of such an animal as the zebra, is related to the changes in the various parts of the skeleton which are concealed beneath the surface; he even believed that the black marks on the heads of tigers, &c., are related to the chief convolutions on the surface of the brain beneath.

It is quite possible to understand why the pattern should change in the different regions of the animal body, because of the greater protective value or higher æsthetic effect of such an arrangement, so that if Sexual Selection be accepted Mr. Tylor's theory becomes unnecessary. Furthermore, it is difficult to see why such an inert, although important, structure as the skeleton should so greatly affect the appearance of an animal. Why should not the liver, with its vast blood-supply and manifold functions, produce some of the effects believed to be wrought by one of the most passive tissues in the body? Or if the muscles and nerves which follow the skeleton are supposed to be the efficient cause, rather than the bones themselves, it must be pointed out that the structure of such nerve- and muscle-fibres, together with the impulses which pass along the one and the contractions which are evoked in the other, are essentially similar throughout.

The colours of underlying structures may be made use of in many cases

It is perfectly true that the colours of underlying structures may be made use of for ornamental or protective purposes. The red colour of our blood is useless as colour in most parts of the body, but the transparency of the skin has permitted it to be made use of in the acquisition of 'complexion'; and I believe that I am not wrong in supposing that we are still true to the preference which has doubtless encouraged the growth of this attraction.

The same thing is true of many insects in which the white colour of fat, the green colour of the blood, or even of the food lying in the alimentary canal, may be employed in the production of a protective appearance (see p. 39, also pp. 79, 80). Natural Selection has rendered these ready-made colours available by making the superficial parts transparent, and in many cases such stint have been deepened or outlines strengthened by the appearance of true pigment in the skin. But these admitted facts do not support the theory that there is any necessary relationship between superficial pigment and the organs or structures which lie beneath.

The objection to Mr. Wallace's explanation of the immense tufts on Birds of Paradise

Mr. Wallace, however, follows up this idea, and argues that ' the immense tuft of golden plumage in the best known birds of paradise' is related to the proximity of the most powerful muscle in the body (the pectoral), of certain large blood-vessels and nerves, and of certain parts of the skeleton.   The contractions of the muscle mean of course a great expenditure of energy, but the present state of physiology lends no support to the opinion that such expenditure could afford any explanation of the size and special peculiarities of an appendage produced by an adjacent surface.   The nervous and arterial trunks imply that nervous energy and food material are being conveyed in large quantities to the localities where the nerves and arteries are finally distributed ; but their size and importance as they pass beneath the base of the tuft can have no relation to the growth and appearance of the latter.   The travelling facilities and means of communication in any village depend upon the local arrangements of its railway station and telegraph office ; not upon the number of express-trains and telegrams which rush through it on their way to a distant town.

The supposed causes of colouring suggested by Wallace and Tylor bear no true relation to the effects

But even greater difficulties are encountered by those who accept Mr. Wallace's and Mr. Tylor's views upon the subject. If colours and patterns were invariably caused by different kinds of colouring matter or pigment, it might not appear to be very improbable that the kind of pigment, and therefore the kind of colour, might be slightly varied as a result of the causes suggested by these writers: but even then there would not be any foundation for the assumption that the pigments which produce the brightest colours are necessarily more difficult of elaboration than the others, or more likely to be formed by an organism with surplus vitality or upon that portion of the surface beneath which the most important functions are performed. A change of chemical composition will nearly always mean the absorption of different rays of light and therefore a different colour; but the quality of the latter, as measured by our æsthetic sense, will bear no necessary relation to the strain put upon the organism in producing the pigment.

When, however, we remember that a very large proportion of the colours and patterns distinctive of sex are only partially dependent upon pigment, the difficulties become insuperable. Let us first consider the case of *white*, which forms an important part in the patterns of so many birds and mammals.   The whiteness of a hair or feather is produced, just as the whiteness of snow is produced, by the presence of gas entangled in the loose meshes between the component parts of their substance (see pp. 3–6).   We cannot suppose that the surplus vitality which is believed to be efficient in producing some new or especially bright colouring matter on one part, will on another part be equally efficient in withholding it [1] and in causing the substitution of bubbles of gas.

But *white* is not the only difficulty; the most beautiful of all colours in nature, the iridescent tints of many animals, are not due to pigment at all, but frequently to interference of light, the cause which produces the colours of a soap-bubble or that of mother-of-pearl (see pp. 6–10).

The interference colours of animals are similarly due to fine lines on the surface of structures, or more frequently to excessively thin sheets of air or occasionally of fluid, enclosed between layers of denser substance.   The varying tints are caused by excessively minute differences in the width of the chinks in which the air is contained.   But it would be a very rash hypothesis which suggests that a surplus of vitality regulates the width of these chinks to the production of this or that colour.   There is absolutely no reason

[1] When a permanent white patch appears upon a mammal, the pigment is withheld; it is only retained, and masked by the formation of gas-bubbles, in the whitening of *existing* dark hairs (see pp. 98, 99).

for believing that a width which just prevents the appearance of colour is an indication of want of vitality.

We must also remember that these iridescent tints occur in combination with colours produced in other ways. If we take a hypothetical case, the inadequacy of 'surplus vitality' as an explanation becomes at once apparent.

Let us suppose that a male bird becomes more beautiful in appearance, and that the change consists in the addition of white feathers, of new tints or shades in the colours due to pigments, and of those due to interference.[1] We must therefore suppose that a 'surplus of vitality' favours the disappearance of pigment and the substitution of bubbles of gas, in one part, although albinism affords rather strong evidence that such a result is certainly not an indication of strength : we must suppose that the same cause favours slight changes in the chemical constitution of pigments, in other parts, involving the excessively unlikely hypothesis that the æsthetic value of the results is a measure of the difficulty involved in their production : and we must finally suppose that, elsewhere, the same cause is efficient in adjusting with mathematical precision the width of spaces in the tissue, although it is wildly improbable that the minute differences which correspond

---

[1] Admitting, for the sake of argument, that this cause is effective in birds, as it certainly is in insects.

to the production or change of colour bear such a relation to the vital energy expended in their development, that we can judge of the amount of the expenditure by the degree of admiration excited in ourselves.[1]

The effects are only explicable by a theory of selective breeding

We are also required to believe that these heterogeneous elements are combined by the same means into an elaborate and harmonious whole. A process of selective breeding, like that of Sexual Selection,

---

[1] A white peacock in the Zoological Gardens, shown to me by Mr. F. E. Beddard, appears at first sight to support Mr. Wallace's views ; for the 'pigment' colours and 'structural' colours are alike absent (see p. 11). Closer examination reveals the fact that regions in which 'structural' colours usually appear are readily recognisable, the white being of a different quality. The 'eyes' on the train, for example, are quite distinct, coming out like the pattern on a white damask table-cloth.

Dr. Gadow informs me that the same fact is true of white ducks and drakes, the wing coverts, which are blue in normally pigmented individuals, exhibiting a peculiar sheen or gloss, differing from the rest of the plumage. Dr. Gadow states that the structural colours are absent, because the existence of a pigment beneath the superstructure is necessary in order to show them off ; and he points out that the ancestors of birds with such structural colours cannot well have been white, because the *effect* depends in part upon pigment.

Mr. Gotch and I found that the 'eyes' of the white peacock do not regain the normal appearance in any of the colours of the spectrum, nor when examined by monochromatic light.

Inasmuch as we can trace the form and distribution of all structural markings in an albino animal, it is clear that the physical cause of the appearance is not affected by albinism, in the same manner as the cause of pigment colours.

affords an explanation of the gradual growth of such a pattern in spite of its heterogeneous elements, an explanation which I do not think is supplied by any other theory. Mr. Wallace has greatly insisted on the amount of individual variation, and we know that variations in the minutest elements of organs must occur as constantly as in the organs themselves. The presence or absence of bubbles of gas and of pigment, the chemical constitution of pigments, the width of spaces in the tissues, are all subject to constant variation, and afford abundant material for the production of any æsthetic effect, if only subjected to selective breeding. And I have endeavoured to show that selection by female preference is now supported by certain striking facts, which were not available when Darwin first argued that this principle has been efficient in producing the colours displayed in courtship.

The unsatisfactory nature of the phrase ' surplus of vital energy '

I will only briefly allude to the unsatisfactory nature of such vague phrases as ' surplus of vital energy,' when used to explain the appearance of the definite results which have been described above. The only evidence for such surplus vitality is the excitability of the nervous system, which is correlated with the activity of the reproductive organs in the breeding season, and which leads to violent and active movements generally forming part of the display in courtship.

Certain general considerations which support Darwin's theory of Sexual Selection

There are also one or two general facts which seem to me to strongly support the theory of Sexual Selection, and to oppose any theory which is not based on selective breeding.

Sexual Colours only developed in species which court by day or twilight, or have probably done so at no distant date

The appearance of beautiful colours and patterns, which are displayed in courtship, invariably occurs in diurnal or partially diurnal animals.   The colours only appear when the conditions for female preference are present also. If we compare butterflies with moths, or moths which fly by day and twilight with those which fly in darkness, we find that brilliant tints and ornamental patterns are only found when there is light enough for the female to see them.   The consideration of apparent exceptions will be found to support the argument.   The same evidence may be drawn from birds and other animals. If, however, such colours were merely the symptom of vitality, we should not expect to find this invariable relationship between the colours of one sex and the conditions for seeing it in the other.

**Sexual Colours are not developed on parts of the body
which move so rapidly that they become invisible**

Another fact of the same kind has only suggested
itself to me lately. The bright colours of courtship
are especially characteristic of two groups of animals,
birds and insects, and it may not unreasonably be supposed that this fact is related to the convenient frame-
work afforded by the surface of the wings. In each
group we may distinguish two kinds of flight : in one
it is produced by an excessively swift vibration of the
wings, in the other by a relatively slow flapping movement. In the former, including the humming-birds
and the majority of insects, the wings are quite
invisible, owing to their rapid motion ; in the latter,
including the majority of birds and butterflies and
many moths, they can be easily seen. We find, as a
general rule, that the colours distinctive of sex are
displayed on the wings in the latter group, but are
absent from the wings in the former. Facilities for
female observation are thus afforded by the distribution of colour.

**When colours are best seen from one direction, this
corresponds with the position in which the female
would see them**

Again, the magnificent iridescent colours on the
wings of certain butterflies, due to interference of light,

are best seen when the insect is looked at from in front, as it would be by a female when the male is approaching her. Mr. Wallace, however, argues that the male *follows* the female and hovers *over* her, so that she can hardly see the upper side of his wings at all. We know but little of the way in which an insect sees, but the structure of the eye as a large rounded mass made up of radiating elements renders it probable that any object which comes within the area obtained by prolonging the radii will be seen, provided it is at the right distance. Hence the male would be seen approaching the female from behind, in front, or the side, and the only requisite for producing the best impression upon her is that his head shall be towards her, and that the upper side of the wings shall be seen. The courtship of a butterfly usually passes through three stages : in the first, the male sees the female and approaches her ; in the second, they fly together for a variable distance, fluttering around and about each other, although the male is probably the more active and the pursuer ; in the third, the female has been overcome by the attentions of the male, she no longer flies, but settles on the ground or a leaf, while the male flutters over her and finally settles also. In each of these phases the planes of both body and wings are ever shifting, and the upper side of the latter is certainly visible to the female from time to time. It is therefore most significant that the iridescent colours of *Diadema bolina* should be seen from

the front, while they become invisible from the side
or from behind, for the colour is produced in such a
way as to give the female the best chance of seeing it,
a fact which is unexplained by any other theory of
origin except that of Sexual Selection.   At the same
time this observation needs testing by further and
exact observation of the habits of many iridescent
species during courtship.

The evidence for the gradual development of pattern suggests selective breeding

The steps by which some of the most elaborate and
wonderful appearances have arisen, are traced by Mr.
Darwin in the most complete and convincing manner.
When we look at the marvellous eyes upon the train of a
Peacock, or the more beautiful markings on the feathers
of the male Argus Pheasant, it seems impossible that so
wonderful and complete a result can have been produced
by the æsthetic preferences of female birds.   And yet Mr.
Darwin shows the relation between these characters and
much simpler markings on other parts of the surface.
He proves that the one has been derived from the other
by gradual modification, and he points to traces of
the original marking which persist in the complex
appearance to which it has given rise.   Such facts,
while eminently suggestive of the progressive development of simple into complex markings by some
selective agency, seem to be unexplained by any other

theory. It is impossible to understand how any necessities for recognition, any changes in the internal organs, any gradually increasing vitality, could cause the one form of marking to develop into the other, along lines which correspond with the attainment of a gradually increasing æsthetic effect.

CHAPTER XVII

SUMMARY AND CLASSIFICATION

IT now remains to bring together the results arrived at, and to show their relation to one another, in a system of classification.

I have not introduced the terms proposed below into the earlier parts of this book : it appeared better first to illustrate the meaning and use of existing terms by the description of numerous instances. I trust, however, that the new terms may be found to be useful. My friend Mr. Arthur Sidgwick has kindly helped me in choosing the words.

In the following scheme Protective and Aggressive Resemblances are grouped with Mimicry under the first head of Apatetic Colours, because an animal is thus made to resemble some other species or some other object. Protective and Aggressive Resemblances are classed as Cryptic Colours (Procryptic and Anti-cryptic), because their object is to effect conceal-ment ; Mimetic Resemblance and Alluring Colouration are called Pseudosematic Colours, because they usually resemble Sematic or Warning and Signalling

CPSIA information can be obtained at www.ICGtesting.com
Printed in the USA
BVOW07s1516030615

403049BV00022B/222/P